ZARATHUSHTRA AND HIS CONTEMPORARIES IN THE RIGVEDA:

WITH THE DATE OF ZARATHUSHTRIAN CALENDAR

SAPURJI KAVASAJI HODIVALA

Published by

FacsiMile Publisher
12 Pragati Market
Ashok Vihar, Ph-2
Delhi - 110052, India
Phone: 011-47034999
Email: www.facsimilepublishers.com
info@facsimilepublishers.com

Distribution Network
gyanbooks.com
India, USA, Canada, UK, Australia

ISBN: 978-93-3349-815-9 (PB)

First Published, 1913

2nd Impression 2025

Printed at: Gyan Press, Delhi.

ZARATHUSHTRA AND HIS CONTEMPORARIES IN THE RIGVEDA
Author: SAPURJI KAVASAJI HODIVALA

ZARATHUSHTRA AND HIS CONTEMPORARIES IN THE RIGVEDA

Zarathushtra and His Contemporaries in the Rigveda,

WITH

THE DATE OF ZARATHUSHTRA,

AND

THE ZARATHUSHTRIAN CALENDAR.

BY

SHAPURJI KAVASJI HODIVALA, B.A.,

PUBLISHED BY SHAPURJI KAVASJI HODIWALA,
3 E, Sleater Road.

BOMBAY:

Printed by Rustom N. Vatchaghandy at the "Sanj Vartaman"
Press, Nos. 22-24-26, Mint Road, Fort.

1913.

DEDICATED

TO

THE PIOUS MEMORY

OF

MY LATE MASTER,

Jalbhoy Ardeshir Sett Esquire, J. P.

The Eighth Mutawalli of the Maneckji Naoroji Sett's Charity Wakf,

AND

THE AUTHOR OF THE BOOK

"શેઠ ખાનદાનની વંશાવલી તથા ટુંક અહેવાલ."

Born 13th November 1858. Died 12th July 1911.

PREFACE.

It was at first my intention to publish, in the form of a book, my Papers on "Zarathustra," "His Contemporaries in the Rigveda," and "The Date of Zarathushtra," which I had read before the Society for the Promotion of Researches into the Zoroastrian Religion and the Gatha Society of Bombay in several of their meetings. Subsequently I made up my mind to include also my Paper on the "Zarathustrian Calendar," which I had read before the said Research Society in Gujarati.

It has been truly said that "the Veda is a book of seven seals." This remark applies with equal force to the sister of the Vedic language, namely, the Avesta. Prof. Max Muller rightly observes that "the language of the New Testament is child's play compared to the Vedic Sanskrit and Avestic Zand."

Some years' careful study of the Rigveda and the Hindu Scriptures on the one hand and of the Avesta and the allied literatures on the other, brought forth prominently before the mind of the present writer certain conclusions, which have not been so far touched by other writers, and which have been summarised as briefly as possible in the following pages.

There is not the shadow of a doubt that in the distant past the Vedic and the Iranian people were living together as one nation known as the Aryâns. Prof. Max·Muller in his Science of Mythology (p. 180) says: "We may go a step further and prove from such equations as Sanskrit *dâtâ vasunâm*, Zend *dâta vohunâm* and Greek *doter eaon*, 'giver of good gifts' applied to the Devas, that such whole phrases even had been formed by the Aryâns in their undivided state and had been preserved as historical heirlooms from generation to generation......If some critics look incredulous at such equations as *vasunâm* and *eaon*, I am afraid, we cannot help their unbelief. Here, also, if people wish to live, they must learn."

In another place the same writer says: "We know, that there was a time, when the Aryas of India and Persia were not yet separated, and we have historical remains of that period in what the Veda and Avesta share in common, whether in language, in religion, ceremonial or mythology. In that period the old name of God, Asura, must have been the recognised name for Gods, (Ahura—Asura, being the principal element in the name of the supreme deity Ahuro-masdâo), while Deva was not used at all as a name of God or Gods."

"Then again, before that Indo-Iranian period there was that equally real period, which preceded the Aryan Separation, and which has its history in the annals of words, common to the two great divisions of that family the Southern and the Northern."

Then came the Indo-Iranian Separation, which was the result of religious schism. The Vedic and the Avestic people, who were once brothers, became enemies. The latter called the former Devas and Drujas, while the former on their part called the latter Asuras and Dasyus.

For some time, I had fears, that I was the first and possibly quite alone in the field to advance the theory, that the Dasyus mentioned in the Vedas and especially the Rigveda were the Dakhyus—the followers of Zarathushtra. But I have only recently discovered that my fears were groundless. It is a matter of great satisfaction to me, that such an able scholar of Sanskrit, as Prof. Râjârâm Râmkrishna Bhâgawat, has anticipated me, so far as this theory is concerned, although he disposes of the subject in less than a dozen lines. In his book named Mihr Yast (p. 31) he says: "But the Avestic literature is as valuable in fixing the original meaning of *Dasyu*, as is the Vedic in fixing that of the *Deva*. The political organization of the Ahura-worshippers recognised the four divisions of the *nmâna* 'house', the *visa* 'village', the *zantu* 'small district' and the *dahyu* 'large district,' whose 'chiefs' were called the *nmâna-paiti*, the *vis-paiti*, the *zantu-paiti* and the *dahyu-paiti*, respectively. The Deva-worshippers have undoubtedly recognised *vis-pati* in some of the hymns (Rv. I, 7, 26; 12, 27; 11, 31). In the hymn 26, the word *vis-pati* occurs with *hotri*; in the 27th, if the word *daivya* be taken with the *vis-pati* (विस्पतिर्दैव्य :), a suspicion will be raised that equally with the *Vis-patis* of the Devas, the *Vis-patis* of some other people also were known; in the 31st, the Devas are said to have made one Ayu, the Vis-pati of one *Nahusha*. The *Dasyus* with whom the *Devas* often fought were thus in all probability the *Dahyus* or *Dakhyus* of the Avestic literature."

My theory is also supported by Prof. Lassen, who attempts to connect the contrast, *daqyu* : *dasyu* with that of *daeva* : *deva*, and to see in it a result of the religious differences, which had separated the Iranians from the Indians. (See Vedic Index of Names and Subjects by Macdonell and Keith, Vol. I, p. 349).

The name of Zarathushtra is nowhere found in the Rigveda, although the King Vishtâspa, the great supporter of our Prophet, has been clearly mentioned in Rv. I-122-13. I have adduced evidence to show, that Zarathushtra, who, by virtue of his office was called Dakhyuma, was the Dasyu of the Rigveda.

My next effort is to show, that our Prophet was the contemporary of some of the oldest of the Rigvedic Rishis. This naturally led me to the date of Zarathushtra. If Zarathushtra belonged to the Rigvedic times, his date would be identical with that of the Rigveda, which has been determined by several scholars. This, I thought, required independent corroboration from our own books.

The best evidence as to the dates of ancient writings, is, without doubt, that afforded by the astronomical facts recorded in them. This admittedly sound method was adopted by scholars like Bentley, Weber, Jacobi, Pratt, Colebrooke, Tilak and others to determine the dates of the Vedas and the Brahmanas. But, if I am not mistaken, no one has so far worked on the same lines in regard to our own Scriptures. I have, therefore, tried to collect together the required evidence, from which it is concluded, that Zarathushtra lived somewhere near the end of the Taurus age, that is, about 2500 B. C. This seems to revolutionise the traditional date assigned to our Prophet by own kinsmen, the Pahlvi writers of old, and followedby most of the European Scholars of our own days,—according to whom Zarathushtra lived somewhere in the 7th century before Christ. But herein the tradition has blundered, as it has blundered in putting forward the doctrine of Dualism, as I have shown in another place.

The tradition recorded in the 17th Chapter of the Bundehishn about the three fires Frobâ, Gushaspa and Burzin-Meher, and the history recorded in the Zande Vohuman Yashta about the adverse condition, in which our religion had fallen at a certain time, remarkably confirm the conclusion, I have arrived at regarding the date of Zarathushtra, deduced from the astronomical and other proofs.

Although scholars have not so far seen any reference to the great Deluge in the Rigveda, still I am of opinion, that there are a couple of hymns in it, from which we can safely gather, that the Vedic Rishis were the eye-witnesses of the huge calamity. On our side, Jamshed was the hero of the Flood. We find, that in the strophe No. 8 of the Yasna Ha 32, which is a historical chapter of the Gathas, Jamshed appears as one of contemporaries of Zarathushtra. These circumstances have led me to believe that our Prophet, who was a contemporary of the Rigvedic writers, was also a contemporary of Jamshed, or rather, one of the long dynasty of Jamsheds, who had ruled for a thousand years. This theory might seem startling, but it is meant to be startling in order to rouse attention, rather than opposition.

As regards the Zarathushtrian Calendar there has been a keen controversy among the students out here—a microscopic minority taking or rather mistaking Dae for the first month. The theory of Dae being the first month instead of Fravardin was, I think, first started by Roth. The late Mr. K. R. Cama strove hard for nearly half a century to prove, that Dae was the first month, but the fact that our books unanimously mention Fravardin as the first month, and the fact that no one dreamt of of the theory in favour of Dae, before the middle of the last century, have been, up to now, important factors in condemning the theory of Dae being the first month.

So far as I am aware, there is little or no dispute about the commencement of the Parsi year; because we find clear statements in our Scriptures, that our year, (or rather what is called the religious year), commenced on the vernal equinox.

All the Parsis to-day admit, that their calendar is faulty and that is a matter of great regret to the thinking portion of the community. Regarding this important question, the European scholars have so far enlightened us very little. Doctors West, Gray, Geiger and others have dealt with the subject piecemeal and in a fragmentary manner. On our side the literature on this subject has mostly appeared in Gujarati; consequently, the Europeans are, I believe, quite unware of the different controversial points raised here. For this reason, I have thought it fit to write out the matter in English. The subject is abstruse and even students shrink away from it; but any the least assistance and advice, that the Europeans might give, would be greatly appreciated by the Parsis. We also want a few popular leaders to impress upon the community the great necessity of a reform in the Calendar, in the absence of which our costly ceremonies and rituals are getting vitiated every day of the year.

As to the Avesta and Pahlvi quotations, I may say that, as it was not possible to give them in their original characters, I had to give their transliterations, much against my wishes. I have, as far as possible, avoided the introduction of diacritical marks, because they render printing and at times even intelligent reading very difficult. It is enough, if the reader keeps to broader phonetic categories and leaves the proper pronunciation to the student of the language.

A few of the slips and misprints have been noted in the corrigenda; others may be easily condoned by the kind reader.

I must candidly admit, that none is more conscious than myself of the want of systematic arrangement of the different subjects handled in this book. My only excuse is, that this book was at first meant to cover only a small area, but, as it took a long time to go through the press, I went on adding new arguments.

In the end, I may observe that scepticism is very useful in all scientific researches, but it becomes pernicious to the progress of learning, if at the commencement of new inquiries, it demands the degree of certainty, which can only be the result of a long accumulation of evidence. If we only persevere undaunted by gibes and jeers, undismayed by disappointments, the mine must yield sterling gold; for, has not the poet truly said :—

ये नाम केचिदिह नः प्रथयन्त्यवज्ञां
जानंतु ते किमपि तान्प्रति नैष यत्नः ।
उत्पत्स्यतेस्ति मम कोपि समानधर्मः
कालो ह्ययं निरवधिर्विपुला च पृथ्वी ॥

"Let those, who express disapproval against us, know that this is not an attempt for them. There is, or there will be born some one of our opinion; for, the time is boundless and the world is wide."

SHAPURJI KAVASJI HODIVALA.

8 E, Sleater Road,
Bombay, 1*st* *August* 1913.

CONTENTS.

Zarathushtrian Calendar.

CORRIGENDA.

[P.=Page.   C.=Column.   L.=Line.]

On P. 4, C. 1, L. 5, for *preclude* read *prelude*.
On P. 9, C. 2, L. 16, for *dakhundm* read *dakhyunâm*.
On P. 12, C. 2, foot note, for अण read अर्ण.
On P. 13, C. 1, L. 48, after *him* read *Rijrâshva*.
On P. 13, C. 1, last line, for *Sa* read *Sal*.
On P. 14, C. 2, L. 26, for *Ba-y* read *Babylonian*.
On P. 15, C. 2, L. 46, for *sun* read *son*.
On P. 16, C. 1, L. 21, for *accordingly* read *according*.
,,   ,,   L. 26, for *shcrt* read *short*.
,,   ,,   L. 46 for *conceform mauiya* read *cuniform* " *mâniya* ".
On P. 17, C. 1, last line after *10 cl.* read "*to show*".
On. P. 19, C. 1, L. 37, for *kim* read *him*.
On. P. 22, C. 1, L. 44, for *marly* read *early*.
,,   C. 2, L. 29, after *He seems to* read *be*.
Ou P. 24, C. 1, L. 29 for *on* read *one*.
On P. 27, C. 2, L. last but 3, for *way* read *may*.
On P. 29, C. 1, L. 22, for *Rv. VII-27-5* read *Rv. VII-21-5*.
On P. 31, C. 2, L. 5, for *these* read *there*.
,,   ,,   line last but 2, for *bur iu* read *but in*.
On P. 32, C. 1, L. 20, after *which is* omit *the*.
On P. 36, O. 1, L. 39, for नानि read तानि.
On P. 37, C. 1, L. 44, for *possage* read *passage*.
On P. 39, C. 1, L. 11 for त्रिशत्त read त्रिंशत.
On P. 39, O. 1, last line for *hem* read *them*.
On P. 40, C. 2, L. 26 before वर्षे read राम्यहनी.
On P. 41, C. 1, last line, for *adreja* read *dâreja*.
On P. 42, C. 1, L. 23, for *undegnified* read *undignified*.
On P. 43, C. 1 L. 28, for *vegilation* read *vegetation*.
On P. 43, C. 1, L. 49 for *luxurian eorest* read *luxuriant forest*.
,,   ,, L. 51, for *axist* read *exist*.
,,   ,, L. 52, for *temperote* read *temperate*.
,,   ,, L. 54, for *tf* read *of*.
On P. 47, C. 1, L. 17, for *precides* read *precedes*.
,,   C. 2. L. 25 for *puntually* read *punctually*.
On P. 48, C. 1, L. last but 3, for *on* read *an*.
On P. 49, O. 1, L. 35, for *lightenings* read *lightnings*.
,,   ,, L. 41, for *rained* read *round*.
On P. 49, C. 2 L. last but 1, for *Aractic* read *Arctic*.
On P. 52 C. 1, L. 39 1, read " bânumaite would lead us " etc.
On P. 54, O. 2 L. 33, for *genü* read *genii*.
,,   ,, L. 49, for *occurance* read *occurence*.
On P. 55, C. 1, L. last but 1, for *aluriga* read *Auriga*.
,,   C. 2, L. 47, for *astrisms* read *asterisms*.
,,   C. 2, L. 48, for *steller* read *stellar*.
On P. 56, C. 1, L. 11, for *tastes* read *testes*.
On P. 62, C. 2, L. 53, for *fo* read *to*.
On P. 65, C. 2, L. 40, for *b d p* read *Beta, Delta and Pi*.

On P. 67, C. 1, L. 38-39, omit *not*; for *but* read *or rather*.
On P. 67, C. 2, L. 8, for *with* read *we*.
,, ,, L. 45, for *Sagiltarius* read *Sagittarius*.
On P. 69, C. 1, L. 6, for *sun* read *constellation*.
,, ,, L. last but 5, for *cover* read *covers*.
On P. 69, C. 2, L. last but 3, for *thas* read *that*.
,, ,, L. last but 2, for *Suidat* read *Suidas*.
On P. 70, C. 1, L. 42, for *Euslbius* read *Eusebius*.
On P. 71, C. 2, last line for *corresplond* read *correspond*.
On P. 72, C. 1, L. 16, after *which* read *is*.
,, C. 2, L. 24, for *ourage* read *courage*.
,, C. 2, L. 36, for *lighlening* read *lighlning*.
On P. 73, C. 1, L. 42, for *fingurs* read *fingers*.
On P. 73, C. 2, L. 30, for *uacklace* read *necklace*.
On P. 75, C. 2, L. 52, for *ubriugt* read *upright*.
On P. 77, C. 2, last line for *indiclinable* read *indeclinable*.
On P. 80, C. 2, L. last but 6, for *nereby* read *nerebyo*,
On P. 83, C. 2, L. 18, for *barrowed* read *borrowed*.
On P. 84, C. 1, last line, for *rom* read *from*.
On P. 91, C. 2, L. 14, for *Dayankku* read *Dayaukku*.
,, ,, L. last but 1, for *Dakhystân* read *Dakhyustân*.
On P. 92, C. 1, L. last but 3, for *Frobok* read *Frobâk*.
On P. 96, C. 2, L. 16, for *is mâhik* read *mâhik is*.
,, ,, L. 42, for *Dimon* read *Demon*.
On P. 113, C. 1, L. 22, insert inverted comas before *first*.
On P. 115, C. 1, L. 4, for *æibyo* read *aeibyo*.
On P. 128, C. 1, L. 11, for *Nakuhatras* read *Nakshatras*.
On P. 129, C. 1, L. 15, after *Star* read *Lore*.
On P. iv. C. 1, L. 10, omit *as*.
On P. vi. C. 1, L. last but 5, for *Aighar* read *Ajghâr*.
,, ,, L. 7, for *warning* read *warming*.
On P. viii., C. 2, L. 3, for *18th* read *8th*.
,, ,, L. 8, for *Sussanian* read *Sassanian*.
On P. ix, C. 1, L. 33, for *tho* read *the*.
On P. xiv, C, 2 L. 42, for *shanlik* read *shantik*.
On P. xv., C. 1, L. 17, for *Fratvartin* read *Fravartin*.
On P. xvii., C. 2, L. 15, for *possible* read *possibly*.
On P. xxiii., C. 2, L. 43, insert *that* after *appear*.
,, ,, last line for *records* read *record*.
On P. xxvi, C. 1, L. 29, for *some* read *same*.
On P. xxviii, C. 1, L. 16, for *forgotton* read *forgotten*.
,, ,, L, 18, for *calender* read *calendar*.
On P. xxxi, C. 2, L. 39-40, read [998½—(116 × 8)] — 70½.
On P. xxxiii, C. 2, L. 42, put a point before "2422".
On P. xxxv. C. 1, L. 1 for *Dac* read *Dae*.
On P. xxxvi. C. 1, L. 45 for *months* read *days*.
On P. xli, C. 2, L. 24 for *firs* read *first*.

Zarathushtra and his Contemporaries in the Rigveda

AND

The Date of Zarathushtra.

PART I.

Attempts to identify Zarathushtra in the Rigveda.

Several attempts have been made to show that our prophet Zarathushtra was a contemporary of the writers of the Rigveda. The Rigveda consists of the Scriptural writings of the forefathers of our Hindu brethren. It was composed by several seers or *rishis* and was probably the production of several centuries. It consists of ten books each containing several hymns or chapters. As in the case of old religious books, the contents of the Rigveda, are not found arranged in their chronological order.

If Zarathushtra was a man of the Vedic times, naturally our very first attempt should be to find out whether his name occurs in the Rigveda. Attempts have been made to identify *Jarûtha* of the Rigveda with Zarathustra. The following are the references to *Jarûtha* :—

(1) विश्वा अग्ने अप दह अरातीर्येभिस्तपोभिः अदहो जरूथं

"O Agni, burn up all malice with those flames, wherewith of old, thou burntest *Jarûtha*." (Rv. VII—1-7.)

(2) त्वामग्ने समिधानो वसिष्ठो जरूथं हन्यक्षि राये पुरंधिम्

"O Agni, Vasistha, when enkindling thee has slain *Jarutha*. Give us wealth in plently." (Rv. VII—9-6.)

(3) अग्निर्ह त्यं जरतः कर्णमावाग्निः अद्भ्यो निरदहज्जरूथं

"Agni rejoiced the ear of him who praised him and from the waters burnt away *Jarutha*." (Rv. X—80-3.)

From the third passage it is clear that Jarutha must have been some demon who lived in waters.

It was also once tried to show that हिरण्यकशिपु of the Hindu writings was the Zarathushtra of Avesta, because these names are identical in meaning* and because certain incidents in the lives of both these personages were similiar. It is needless to say that such identifications can have but little weight.

Words bearing contrary senses.

It is well known that there are certain words in the Rigveda which are used in quite the contrary senses in different places. The word असुर for instance, is used in the good sense in the earlier parts of the Rigveda, as we find in Rv. I-174-1 "O Indra... protect us, O Asura, preserve us;" on the other hand the same word is used in the later parts of the Rigveda for the enemies of the gods; Cf. Rv. VI-22-4 where Indra is called असुरघ्न "slayer of Asuras."

Similarly the word देव is used in the good sense in numerous places, but there are a few passages in which we find that certain classes of the Devas known as Mura-Devas, Purva-Devas, &c., were wicked Devas. We shall deal with these latter Devas hereafter.

Who were the Asuras and Devas.

The words असुर and देव which were formerly applied to the demon and

* The meaning suggested was "one clothed in yellow garments."

the diety were subsequently used for the people who worshipped. असुर and देव. We shall give here a few examples (1) Rv. X-53-4 येन असुरान् अभि देवा: असाम "Since we the followers of the Deva may oppose the followers of the Asura." (2) Rv. VIII-85 (96)-9 अनायुधासो असुरा: अदेवा: "Weaponless are the followers of Asura, who are not the followers of Devas." (3) In Rv. VII-1-22, IX-62-20 देवा: is used for the followers of Devas.

Similarly in the Avesta, the word *Daeva* is used for the follower of the Daeva religion." For example (*a*) in Vend. VII-56 we have "He is a *daeva*, a worshipper of the *daevas*, one who holds intercourse with the *daevas*, one who adheres to the demons." (*b*) Also in Yasna Ha 9 § 15 we have "O Zarathushtra, you caused all the *daevas* concealed in the earth, who before this time, were running about in the form of *men*." (*c*) In Ha 44 § 20 we find "O Mazda, have the *daevas* been good rulers.......... who fight with these (= faithful men); the Karaps and Ushikhs belonging to whom* have given the earth over to torture." (*d*) In Ha 32-1 the *daevas*, who claim to be the prophets of Ahuramazada, are, wicked persons.

Asuras the followers of Ahuramazda.

When the word *Asura* came to be used in its bad sense in the Rigveda, the word Asuras (plural) was used for the followers of Ahura (=Ahuramazda). This may be seen from the following passages:—

(1) In Rv. X 53-4 we have "since the followers of Devas may oppose the followers of Asura." Here as the word *Devas* is used for men, the word *Asuras* must be used also for men.

(2) In Mâhâbhârata XII-1184 we have इदं तु श्रुयते पार्थ युद्धे देवासुरे पुरा। असुरा भ्रातरो ज्येष्ठा देवाश्चापि यवीयस: ॥

"Oh Prithu's son, this is said (to have been so) in the war between the Devas and Asuras of yore; the Asuras were the elder brothers and the Devas the younger." In this passage we are told that the Asuras and the Devas were brothers and that subsequently they quarrelled with one another.

(3) In Rv. VIII 85 (96)-9 we find that the epithet applied to the Asuras is अदेवा: "opponents of the Deva-followers *or* opponents of the Deva-religion."

Thus the Asuras were अदेवाs; or to use the words of Vendidad 18 § 62 they were *adaeva-yasna* (=non-Deva-worshippers). Now as the author of the Vendidad uses the word *adaeva-yasna* for *Mazda-yasna*, I think that there were at one time only two important religious factions, the *Daeva-yasna* and the *Mazda-yasna*. Thus the word अदेव (=*adaeva-yasna*) in the above passage appears to be used for *Mazda-yasna* only.

War between Asuras and Suras.

We have seen from Mâhâbhârata that a war had taken place between the brothers the Asuras and the Devas. This war is referred to in Rv. I-100-6 and 8 as under: "Humbler of pride, Exciter of the conflict, the Lord of the heroes, God invoked of many, may he *this day* gain with our men the sun-light; may Indra girt by Maruts, be our succour. His help has made him cheerer in the battle." We shall also quote the verses Nos. 17 and 18 of Rv. I-100, as they show that *Rijrâshva*(=Arjâspa of the Avesta as we shall see hereafter) and his followers killed the Dasyus who (as will be seen hereafter) were the followers of Zarathushtra. "O Indra, mighty one, the Varshâgiras sing forth this laud to please thee; Rijrâshva with his fellows Ambarisha, Surâdhas, Sahadeva and Bhayamâna. He much invoked has slain the Dasyus and the

* For *Yaish* see Neriosang.

Shimyus, after his wont and laid them low with arrows. The mighty thunderer with his fair complexioned friends won the land, the sun-light and the waters."

From the above reference to the war between the Asuras and the Devas, it may be presumed that the split between the followers of the Ahuramazdian religion and the followers of the Deva religion took place in the days of the Rigveda. Now as the author of the split on the side of the Ahuramazdians was the great reformer Zarathushtra, "who was the *first* to speak the word against the Devas and in favour of the Ahuramazdian religion" (see Fr. Yt. § 90), we may well expect to come across references to Zarathushtra and his followers in the Rigveda.

Zarathushtra, the Dasyu of the Rigveda.

As we shall see hereafter, the Vedic writers appear to know some of the Iranians by their surnames or professional names rather than by their proper names; for example, Jâmâspa *Baetâs* was known as *Vetasu*, and Peshotan as *Chitraratha*. According to Yasna Ha 19 § 18, Zarathushtra, besides being the spiritual lord in Ragha was also the temporal lord—*Dakhyuma* (=Sk. दस्युम or दस्यु). In Fr. Yt. § 90 Zarathushtra has been called *Dakhyunâm sûro* "the learned of the Dasyus." From these and several other considerations referred to in detail hereafter, I have come to the conclusion that the word *Dasyu*, which is often met with in the Rigveda, is the Vedic name of Zarathushtra, and the plural form *Dasyus* is used for the followers of Zarathushtra. I do not think that (at least so far as the Rigveda is concerned), the Dasyus were the non-Aryan aborigines of India, as the commentators and the translators would have us believe.

Meaning of the word Dasyu.

Several derivations of the name of Zarathushtra have been suggested, one of which is *Zarat-star* "shining star." Now primarily *Dasyu* means the "shining one" (from दस् —shine) though subsequently because of the hatred with which Dasyu was treated by the Vedic writers, the word has come to be used in quite the opposite sense of "robber" (from दंस् to bite). The very fact that the form is not दंस्यु proves that दंस् cannot be its root. In Vendidad 19 §3 Zarathushtra has been called *pouru-kharengho* "full of shining light," which is just the meaning of the word *Dasyu*.

Rv. VII-5-6 may be quoted here in connection with the meaning of the word *Dasyu*. त्वं दस्यूँरोकसो अग्न आज उरुज्योतिर्जनयन् आर्याय. "Thou dravest Dasyus from their home, O Agni and broughtest forth *broad light* to light the Arya." This verse indicates that the *light* (probably *khureh*) once belonged to the Dasyus and was afterwards acquired by the Aryans, that is to say, the Vedic people.

That this *light* was the *Kharenangha* of the Avesta may be gathered from Zamyâdha Yt. § 53. "If any one among men tries to obtain the limitless *Khureh*, he will get the gifts of the Athravans, that is, will get the *light of religious knowledge*."

If Zarathushtra and his followers had the light of religious knowledge, they would be appropriately called *Dasyus** (="shining ones *or* those shining on account of their religious knowledge") in Sanskrit. It appears to me therefore, that originally the word Dasyu must have a good sense but that after the commencement of the hostilities between the Aryans and the Iranians, the word was assigned a bad sense.

Dasyus the followers of Asura.

In Rv. III-29-9 we have अयमग्निः पृतनाषाट् सुवीरो येन देवासो असहन्त दस्यून् "This Agni is the battle-winning hero by whom the Devas have over-

*Similarly Devas also meant the "shining ones."

come the Dasyus." Now in Rv. X-53-4 we have almost the same words put in the mouth of Agni, who says तद्द्य वाचः प्रथमं मसीय येनासुरान् अभि देवा असाम "This preclude of my speech I now will utter, whereby we Devas may kill the Asuras." It will thus be seen that the Dasyus of the former passage are identical with the Asuras of the latter passage; and we have seen that Asuras were the followers of Asura (=Ahura).

(2) This view that the Dasyus were Asuras is further strengthened by Rv. X-170-2 (quoted also in Sàmaveda II-6-3-5-2) where the words Dasyus, Asuras and foes have been used as interchangeable terms.

(3) The most conclusive passage on this point is Atharva-veda X-3-11 where we have राजा देवो वनस्पतिः । सं मे शत्रून् विबाधतां इंद्रो दस्यूनिवासुरान् ॥ "The kingly divine tree shall smite asunder my enemies as Indra (smites) the Dasyus, the Asuras" (S. B. E. Vol. 42 p. 83). Here the Dasyus are identical with the Asuras.

(4) In Manusmriti X-43 we read "In consequence of the omission of the sacred rites.........the following tribes of Khshatriyas have gradually sunk in this world to the condition of Shudras." In § 44 the author mentions the different tribes, among whom we find the name of the *Pahlavâs*. In § 45 the writer says "All those tribes in this world, which are excluded from those born from the mouth, the arms, the thighs and the feet (of Brahman) are called Dasyus whether they speak the language of the Mlechhas or that of the Aryans." No doubt this is an extended sense of the word "Dasyus" in the times of Manu, but the important point to be noted is that the word was also applied to the non-Hindus such as Pahlavâs (=those who spoke the Pahlvi language). The ancestors of the Phalvas, the Avastan people must have also been called the Dasyus in the Rigvedic times.

(5) The Avestan word *Ahura* is used in the plural for the Angelic host waiting on Ahuramazda, and also for the worshippers of Ahuramazda. In Yasna Ha 30-9, and 31-4 *Ahurâonghao* (असुराः) is clearly used for the Angels. In Aban Yt § 85 it is said that the "*Ahurâonghao*, *Danghu-patayo* and the sons of the latter praise the Ardvisura." A Vedic rishi might well have translated *Ahuraonghao* as असुराः or followers of Ahura (=Ahuramazda) and *Danghu-paiti* as the lords of Danghus or दस्युs. In this passage the words असुराः and दस्युs stand in apposition and are meant to explain each other.

Zarathushtra, the Dasyu of the Rigveda and his followers.

We shall now quote a few passage from the Rigveda showing the identification of Dasyu with Zarathushtra and that of the Dasyu people with the followers of Zarathushtra.

(1) Rv. I-103-3 स जातूभर्मा श्रद्दधान ओजः पुरो विभिंदन्नचरद्वि दासीः । विद्वान् वज्रिन् दस्यवे हेतिमस्यार्यं सहो वर्धया द्युम्नं इंद्रः ॥

"Armed with this bolt and trusting in his prowess, he wandered shattering the forts of the *Dasis*; O knowing one, thunderer, *cast thy dart at Dasyu*, increase the Aryan's might and glory O Indra."

From Vendidad XIX-43, we learn that Indra was the arch enemy of Zarathushtra. We also learn from the Zarathushtranâme of Zarathost Beheram that during the invasion of Balkh by Arjaspa, his commander Turbarâtur killed Zarathushtra by throwing a missile at him. Vide also Dinkard, V, Beheram Yashta II-3, Saddar IX-5 and Dadestan LXXII-8. In the last, we read "One was Turibrâdarvakhsha, the Karap, and heterodox sourcerer, by whom the *best of men* was killed." On the other hand, Suidas and others state that Zoroaster was consumed by a supernatural fire.* This latter statement is to some extent borne out by Rv. I-33-7 where we find that Indra burnt Dasyu from heaven.

The above quoted Rigvedic passage raises two important questions, first whether Indra himself threw the dart at Dasyu and second who the *Dasis* were.

As to the first question it must be mentioned that it was the practice of the Vedic rishis to assign any good deed done by the followers of a god to that god, and not to the doers. For instance, in Rv. IV-26-1 Indra is identified with his followers Kakshivân and Ushanâ, two famous Vedic rishis of whom we shall speak in detail hereafter. In Rv. I-169-2 we are distinctly told that "the various doings of all mortal people are done by Indra, in his wisdom.† Similarly we find in the first chapter of the Vendidad that Ahuramazda is represented as having established certain cities, which in plain language would mean that the followers of Ahuramazda (or the followers of the Ahuramazdian religion) established the cities. Accordingly we must understand that in the Rigvedic passage given above, it was not the god Indra who threw the dart at Dasyu, but that some follower of Indra did so.

As to the second question, it may be stated that the Dasis referred to in Rv. I-103-3 appear to be the *Dahis* of the Fr. Yt. § 144 whose Fravashis have been invoked and who followed the Ahurmazdian religion. With reference to the Dâhas Dr. Geiger says:—

"It is probable that the Avesta denotes by this name, the *Daai* of the Greek historians......They extended as far as the Oxus and the Jaxartes, and Herodotus even speaks of the Daai as inhabiting the province of Persis." (C. E. I. Vol. I, pp. 31-48).

(2) Rv. IV-16-9 "Come Maghavan, friend of man, to aid the singer, imploring thee in battle for the sun-light; speed him with help in his inspired invokings; down sink the *sorcerer* (मायावान्), the *prayerless* (अब्रह्मा) Dasyu."

In this verse, Dasyu (=Zarathushtra) is called sorcerer and prayerless. It must be borne in mind that these attributes have been used by the enemy of Zarathushtra, from whom we can often expect statements misrepresenting facts. I think therefore that from the point of view of the Iranians, these attributes bear directly the opposite meanings. The term "sorcerer" may be in reference to the miracles performed by Zarathushtra, as recorded in the Zarathushtra-nâme. I should however think that it refers to the great persuasive power* (माया) which he weilded. The attribute अब्रह्मा means "one devoid of sacred knowledge."

(3) Rv. X-22-8 अकर्मा दस्युः अभि नो
अमंतुः अन्यव्रतो अमानुषः। त्वं तस्यामित्रहन्
वधर्दासस्य दंभय॥

"Near us is Dasyu, *riteless, void of sense, inhuman, keeping alien laws.* Baffle thou slayer of the foe the weapon which this Dâsa weilds." Here the epithets applied to Dasyu deserve special consideration. (*a*) He is called अकर्मा "riteless" or "not performing sacrifices at all." This meaning would support the contention of those who urge that we do not find any reference to rites and rituals in the Gathas. If however we understand the word as bearing the contrary sense, we must presume that sacrificial rites were performed in the Gathic days, though perhaps in a different manner from that of the Vedic people. (*b*) अमंतु literally means "foolish" and is here used

* Civilization of Eastern Iranians Vol. II 216-216.

† Cp. also Rv. III-21-9 "This Agni is the battle-winning hero by whom the Devas (=followers of Devas) have defeated the Dasyus."

* For माया=power cf. Rv. I-88-1 and IX-78-5.

spitefully, as Zarathushtra was a मंतु or "a wise man." This is corroborated by Rv. VI-21-11 where the writer frankly gives out that "Manu was stronger than Dasyu" meaning that Dasyu stood second only to the man *par excellence* known as Manu in point of wisdom. (*c*) अमानुष ordinarily means "inhuman" and also "super-human;" the author uses the word in the former sense, though the suggestion is that he was not an ordinary man. (*d*) अन्यव्रत means "one whose vow is with another god." Professor Apte translates the word thus "one who follows other than Vedic observances, devoted to other gods, infidel."

In this very hymn in verse No. 6 we have a reference to *Ushanâ* or *Kâvya* as follows. अध ग्मन्तोशना पृच्छते वां कदर्था न आ गृहम्. I translate the passage thus: "When you approach, Ushanâ asks you 'why came you two (Indra and Varuna) to our dwelling place.'" And then Ushanâ goes on "why are ye come to mortal man from distant realms of earth and heaven? O Indra, thou shalt speak us fair; our holy prayer is offered up. *We pray to thee for help*......... Around (or near) us is Dasyu riteless, void of sense, inhuman, keeping alien laws; baffle thou, slayer of the foe, the weapon which this Dâsa weilds." The above-said Ushanâ, whose another name is Kâvya, is a special friend of Indra in the Rigveda and is the Kâvya of Yasna Ha 32-14. We shall hereafter speak about him at some length; for the present it is enough to note that it is Ushanâ who prays Indra to baffle Dasyu. In other words a contemproary of Dasyu (— Zarathushtra) prays that the latter may be defeated in his object.

(4) Rv. I-33-4 वधीर्हि दस्युं धनिनं घनेन एकश्चरन्नुपशाकेभिरिन्द्र। धनोरधि विषुणक्ते व्यायन् अयज्वानः सनकाः प्रेतिमीयुः॥

I translate the passage thus:— "Thou slewest with thy bolt the learned (धनिनं) Dasyu, alone yet with thy helpers;......in all directions the *old riteless* ones met with destruction." Here the word अयज्वान: is important; it means that the Dasyus did not perform यज्ञ (sacrificial rites) in the manner of the Vedic people. The word सनका: (old) refers to the fact that the Dasyus were the *elder* brothers of the Vedic people, as is clearly seen in Mâhâbhârata.

(5) Rv. V-29-10 अनासो दस्यूँरमृणः "Thou slewest the Dasyus who spoke indistinctly." Here the attribute applied to the Dasyus is अनास which has two meanings:—(1) अ+नासा = noseless (2) अन् + आसा: = *lit.* mouthless; not-throwing-out-words-properly; speaking indistinctly.

Patanjali, the grammarian has in his introductory lecture preserved a Brahman text, according to which the *Asuras* spoke a language which was a corrupt form of the language of the Devas (see Prof. Bhagvat's Key to interpret the Vedas p. 16). We have seen that the Dasyus were Asuras. The above remark would therefore apply to the Dasyus also.

Now it is not difficult to understand why the Dasyus (—followers of Zarathushtra) have been called indistinctly speaking people." The Avesta is very nearly allied to the Vedic language and it is probable that the Vedic people may not have understood the Avesta language clearly on account of the phonetic changes in the Avesta words.

(6) Rv. IV-28-4 विश्वस्मात् सीमधमाँ इन्द्र दस्यून् विशो दासीरकृणोः अप्रशस्ताः। अबाधेथाम् अमृणतं नि शत्रून् अविन्देथाम् अपचितिं वधत्रैः॥

"Lower than all, thou, O Indra, hast cast down the Dasyus, *abject tribes of the Dasis;* ye drave away, ye put to death the foeman and took great vengeance with your murdering weapons."

This verse is important as showing that it was not with the demons of the air that Indra was fighting, but with men of flesh and blood. We also find that the Dasyus have been called the abject tribes of the Dasis," who, as we have seen, professed the Zarathushtrian religion.

(7) Rv. VI-33-3 त्वं तान् इंद्र उभयान् अमित्रान् दासा वृत्राण्यार्या च शूर वधीः ॥ "Indra both races of opposing foemen, both Arya and Dasa, thou hast struck down."

Also in Rv. X—102-3 we have "O Maghvan, keep away the weapon of the Dasa and Aryan foe."

As a rule the writers of the Rigveda use the word आर्य for the Vedic people" (cf. Rv. X—138-3) but in the above passages, it seems to be used for the Dasyus. If this be correct we have here a proof of the fact that the Iranians were Aryans equally with the Vedic people.

(8) An important incident which took place during the religious fight between the armies of Gushtaspa and Arjaspa has been recorded in the 12th Chapter of the Bundehishna. It is this: When the Iranians were exhausted in their fight with the Turanians and were on the point of being defeated, a portion of the *Komish* mountain, on which the Iranians stood, got separated from the rest and slipped down. The Iranians thus escaped in safety. The mountain was hence called *Mado-faryâd* or *Mad-val-faryâd* (=lit. he came to our help.")

Now in Rv. VIII(70)-59-11 we have a complete corrobation of the above-mentioned incident. अन्यव्रतं अमानुषं अयज्व्यवानं अदेवयुं । अव स्वः सखा दुधुवीत पर्वतः सुघ्नाय दस्युं पर्वतः ॥ "Let his friend the mountain cast to rapid death, let the mountain cast Dasyu down, whose vow is with another god, who is in human, who performs no sacrifice, and who pays no respect to the Devas* (अदेवयुं)."

What the author wants to convey in the above verse may be expressed thus: "It would have been better, if the mountain which came to the help of Dasyu and proved his friend, had in its own fall, cast him down and killed him"; in other words the writer expresses surprise and regret that though the mountain slipped down, the Dasyu standing thereon was not knocked over. Here the word Dasyu is used collectively for Dasyu people or it may refer to Zarathushtra who also took part in the holy wars.

(9) Rv. II-20-8 प्रति यदस्य वज्रं बाह्वोर्धुर्हत्वी दस्यून् पुर आयसीर्नि तारीत् । "When in his arms they (gods) laid the ball, he slaughtered the Dasyus and cast down their *forts of iron*." That there were several forts in the Iranian countries in ancient times is well known. We might mention instances of Kangdez (*Khangha*), Gumbedân, Shyâvakshgarda, for full descriptions of which E. Modi's Dictionary might be referred to.

That there were *forts of iron* in Iran can be gathered from Yasna Ha 11 § 7:—"May not Homa bind thee down, just as the wicked Turanian Afrâsiab was bound down in the middle of the third portion of the earth,—Afrâsiâb *who was confined in a castle of iron* (*pairish-khakhtem* ayanghahe*)."

Darmesteter thinks that the abovesaid passage refers to the place known as *Hankan* (*lit.* "place dug up") where Afrasiâb had built an iron castle underneath the surface of the earth, (see also Bund. ch. 12).

Thus the fact that there were castles of iron belonging to the Iranians is corrobated by the Vedic passage.

(10) In Rv. I—33-4 quoted above we have seen that Dasyus have been called अयज्वानः "not performing sacrificial rites." In this connection, the following question from the

* Cp. *adaeva-yasna* in Vend. XVIII—62.

* *Pairish-khakhta*—परिष्वक्त from ष्वज् to embrace; *lit.* "embraced all round," hence "confined."

"Indian Mythology according to Mahâbhârata by V. Fausboll" (p. 20) is important:—"The *Asuras* were originally just, good and charitable, knew the Dharma and sacrificed and were possessed of many other virtues (XII—8268 to 8361). And therefore Shri, the goddess of prosperity dwelt with them during *Yugâs* from the beginning of the world.

But afterwards as they multiplied in numbers (XII—2396), they became proud, vain and quarrelsome, they infringed the Dharma, they *neglected to sacrifice* (III—8492)......... They said they were as good as he Devas and envied their happiness...... They even challenged the Devas and opposed themselves to the law of Brahmâ (XII—6145); they even succeeded for a time in dethroning Indra.......But as they had thus changed their nature, Shri forsook them."

Dakhyu the Avestan word for Dasyu.

Now let us see whether there is any Avestan word equivalent to Sk. दस्यु. On the analogy of ख्यात् — *khyât* and ख्या: = *khyao*, we should have the well-known Av. word *dakhyu* equivalent to दस्यु.

In the Avesta, the word *dakhyu* has been generally assigned *two* meanings, namely "country" and "people of the country." Whenever the word *dakhyu* occurs with the words *nmâna*, *vis* and *santu*, it must bear the above senses. But if we examine the passages in which the word occurs alone, I think, in a few instance at any rate, it bears the sense of a "tribe."

Dr. Geiger on the word Dakhyu.

In the civilization of the Eastern Iranians (translation by Dastur Darabji P. Sanjana Vol. II p. 5) Dr. Geiger says:—"*Dakhyu* corresponds literally to the Vedic *Dasyu*, which designates the non-Aryan aborigines of the Punjab. The relation of both these terms and their meanings is as follows: the primitive Arian word denoted, as does also its cognate *Dâsa*, hostile tribes. The Indian *Dasyu* retained that signification and served subsequently as a name for the enemies of the gods or demons. But the Iranians understood by the term *Dakhyu*, the land rescued from enemies or country in general." On p. 8 he says "the finer distinction of the Avesta between a tribe and a country, a *Zantu* and a *Dasyu*, besides being of no practical value appears to have been unknown in Western Iran."

With due deference to Dr. Geiger I say that I do not agree with him that the Dasyus were the aborigines of the Punjab; for, I shall show hereafter that the Vedic people knew the Dasyus long before they had moved to the Punjab. Also in Rv. X-49-3 we have "I did not give the Aryan name to the Dasyus;" here the writer suggests that although the Dasyus were Aryans,* they were not called Aryans, probably because of the inimical relations. I also do not agree with Dr. Geiger when he derives the words दास and दस्यु from दा "to cut" (see Vo. I. p. 34); for, the स after the root cannot be explained. I however quite agree with the worthy Doctor, when he observes that the word *Dasyu* originally denoted a *tribe* and that the meaning of a *country* was a later signification.

Meaning of the word Dakhyu.

The passages Nos. 2 to 15 of Vendidad IV refer to different kinds of agreements which are entered into by man with man. From the third agreement onwards, we have a reference to living beings which are given as pledges for keeping the promise, namely, a small animal (*pasu*), a large animal (*staora*), a

* According to ऐ॰ ब्रा॰ most of the Dasyus were sprung from Vishvâmitra.

man (*vira*) and lastly *Danghu* (=*Dakhyu*). It will be seen that the author intends to classify the agreements according to the value to be attached to the living beings which are given as pledges. First a small animal is mentioned, which has a low value Then a large animal is mentioned, which has a higher value. Then comes man whose life has a much higher value. Lastly comes Danghu, whose value must necessarily be still much higher. Could we accept the meaning of *Danghu* to be "a small piece of land" as suggested by Dr. Geiger in C. E. I. Vol. II p. 36 ? I do not think. It cannot also mean "country." Neither of these things is of any value compared with the life of man. Also a country cannot be given as a pledge by an ordinary man to another man. Nor can *Danghu* here mean a "country-man," for, why is a country-man's life more valuable than that of any other man ? It seems to me, therefore, that *Danghu* means the *Dasyu*, the chosen man of God, the faithful follower of Zarathushtra, whose life would be, necessarily, looked upon as more valuable than that of an alien.

The latter part of Vend. IV-2 is a bit awkward in construction but the last two adjuncts of *Danghu* are important; the first being *Khrathwemnahe* "possessed of good intellect," and the second *suyamnahe* "doing good to people" which are applicable only to man.

Farvardin Yashta Sec. 90.

In this passage we are told that Zarathushtra was the first to speak the word against the Devas and in favour of the Ahuramazdian religion. Then follows this important passage :—*Yo sûro vispo hujyâitish paoiryo-tkaesho dakhyunâm*. I translate the passage thus ; "Who (Zarathushtra) was learned (*sûro*) * all-happiness-giver and first leader of the Dakhyus."

In this passage the author clearly points out that Zarathushtra was one of the *Dakhyus*. It does not much matter whether these Dakhyus were the tribe known as the Dasyus or whether they were the inhabitants of the *country*, the Avestan word for which was Dakhyu. It is enough for us that Zarathushtra was *dakhyunâm* (= of the Dakhyus that is, belonged to the Dasyus). I must state here that it is this important word *dakhũnâm* (mas.) used in connection with our prophet, that leads me to think that Zarathushtra has been called Dakhyu (= दस्यु) in the Rig-veda.

It is likely that such Iranian names as Danghu-sruta, and Danghu-fradangha might have been contracted into Danghu (= Dasyu). It is also very likely that Dakhyu (or Dainghu) may have been a contraction of Airya Dainghu (= inhabitant of Iranian country); cf. Yt. 14-50 also Yt. 8-56.

Yasna Ha 19 § 18 & Visp 1 § 9.

In Ys. 19 § 18 we are told that except in Ragha there were five lords (*ratus*) in each territory, namely *nmânya*, *visya*, *zantuma*, *dakhyuma*, and *Zarathushtra*; but in Ragha there were only four lords namely *nmânya*, *visya*, *zantuma* and *Zarathushtra*. In his "Zoroaster" Prof. Jackson gives the reason on p. 203 as under :—"In the papal see of Ragha the temporal power and the spiritual power were united in one person." In the Civilization of the Eastern Iranians Vol. II, p. 151, Dr. Geiger says "It appears that a kind of Zoroastrian papacy existed in Iran. To the high-priest was then assigned a rank high-

* I do not think *sura* is here equivalent to Sk, शूर "brave" it is = सूर "wise or learned man." In Meher Yt. S. 24 the word *sura* is followed by *vispo-vidhvao*, a word bearing the same meaning. In Yasna Ha 81-6 Zarathushtra has been called *vidhvao* "learned man."

er than that of the country princes. In Ragha he evidently possessed temporal as well as spiritual dignity. The high-priest of Ragha was at the same time its prince."

As Ragha is mentioned as having a special connection with Zarathushtra (*Raghà Zarathushtrish*), it is easy to suppose that it must have acquired the important distinction of having four lords only from the time of Zarathushtra. It therefore appears to me that Zarathushtra besides being spiritual lord in Ragha was also its temporal lord, *Dakhyuma* = दस्युम subsequently contracted into दस्यु.

In Vispard I-9 an invocation or invitation is made to an Ahurian (= Ahuramazdian) questioner, Ahurian leader, Ahurian dakhyuma, Ahurian Zarathushtrotema. Here we see that the *Ahurian dakhyumas* (= असुर दस्यु s) bear an intimate relationship with the members of the Ahuramazdian religion. It is these Ahurian dakhyumas who are mentioned as *Asuras* and *Dasyus* in several hymns of the Rigveda.

Before leaving this subject, I shall hazard what is nothing more than a *mere guess* that Zarathushtra, known as *Zaratus* may be the exact equivalent of Dasyu. Diodorus Siculus and Pliny the elder (both of the first century B.C.) speak of Zarathushtra as *Zaratus* (see E. Modi's જરથોસ્તી ધર્મની તવારીખ pp. 55-58). Now the Avesta *z* becomes *d* in other languages; for ex. *zasta*=Pahl. P. *dasta*, *zâmâtar*= Pahl. P. *dâmâda*; *zrayangha*=P. *dariâh*. In sanskrit *z* and *d* are interchangeable, as जंपती = दंपती, ज्योतिस्= द्योतिस्. Also Av. *rta* becomes *shya*, as *maretan*=*mashya*=मर्त्य. Thus *Zaratus* would become *Dasyus*.

Yasna Ha 48 § 10.

Let us now consider Yasna Ha 48-10 where the word Dakhyu occurs. I follow Dr. Mill's/ translation in regard to the first two lines:—"When, Lord, shall come the men of mind's perfection (=of wisdom); when drive they hence this soil of drunkenness?" *

The last two lines may be construed thus:—*Yâ Karapano angrayâ, yâchâ dush-khshathrâ khratû dakhyunâm urûpayeinte.*†

I translate the passage thus:—"Since the Karpans by means of (their) foul zeal, and since the evil rulers by means of (their) plottings harass the Dakhyus." I think that the writer wants to convey in this strophe that the Karpans (=followers of कृप) who were wicked rulers were the enemies of the Dakhyus (= Dasyus).

Yasna Ha 48-12.

We shall consider the 12th verse of Ha 48, where also the word *Dakhyu* occurs. The passage may be translated thus: "Those are the benefactors of the Dakhyus, who, O Mazda, follow thy precepts (*khshnûm*) with good mind, and with truth and deeds of thy monition; indeed, they (=the benefactors of the Dakhyus) have been appointed the opponents of Aeshma‡ (Deva)."

The above verse clearly suggests that the Dakhyus were the opponents of Aeshma Deva. Now although Vendidad Chapter 19-43 refers to the fact that Indra and Aeshma were

---

* Instead of the reading *madahyâ* we have also the reading *magahyâ* which is preferable. The passage would then mean "When drive they hence the impurity of *maga* (= *maghavan*=Indra). In Rv. Indra has been given the epithet मघवन् in several places. Prof. Teile rightly observed that the Av. word *maga* was also used in an unfavourable sense.

† *Angraya* 8/1 of *angra*.
Khratu=8/1 *lit.* "wisdom" here used in bad sense "plottings."
Dakhyunam—gen. used as acc. cf. Fr. Yt. § 106 where we have *ashemaoghanâm avajathnat* (who killed ashmoghs.); see also Ys. I-etc. and Apte's Guide p. 81.
Urupayeinti—from लुप्—plunder, harass—8/8 Causal=they cause pain; see Jackson Gr. p. 190.

‡ I prefer the reading *aeshemahyâ* to *aeshem mahyâ*.

the enemies of Zarathushtra, still I am of opinion that here the Aeshma Deva is no other than Indra himself. For in Rv. I–63-2, I–63-4 and 5, X–83-2 we find that Indra was the god of anger and wilfulness. Hence I conclude that in the abovementioned strophe Indra is said to be the enemy of the Dasyus, a fact which is borne out by a number of passages in the Rigveda. In the above strophe the word *hamaestâro* (opponents) is very appropriate, since its literal meaning shows that the Dasyus *stood against* and fought with the followers of Indra.

Parsis and Parthians in the Rigveda.

Professors Bhagvat and Apte in their "Key to interpret the Veda" have pointed out that there are references to the Persians and Parthians in the Rigveda. In Rv. I 105-8 we have सं मा तपंति अभित: सपत्नीरिव पर्शव: "The Parsus harass me all round like cowives."

Rv. VIII 6-46 शतमहं तिरिन्दिरे सहस्रं पर्शावा ददे राधांसि याद्वानाम् "I wrested from the Yâdva (tribe) one hundred cattle (in the province of) Tirindira and one thousand cattle (in the province of) Parsu."

Rv. VII-83-1 "Looking to (=keeping an eye on) your wealth the Prithus and Parsus (पृथुपर्शवो) marched forward. O Indra Varuna, (these) Dâsa and Aryan enemies were killed by you."

In the Ashi Yt. § 1 we have the word *perethvirâm* which is an adjunct of Ashi, and which might be rendered "brave like a Parthian." In the cuniform inscriptions at Behistan we have the countries *Pârsah* and *Partava* which appear like पर्शु and पृथु of the Rigveda.

PART II.

Contemporaries of Zarathushtra in the Rigveda.

Let us now pass on to the contemporaries of Zarathushtra met with in the Gathas and the Rigveda. In the absence of our arriving at any satisfactory identification of Zarathushtra in the Rigveda, the next attempt should be directed towards making a search for his contemporaries in the Rigveda. If in the Avesta and the Rigveda we can trace names which are almost similar, that is some evidence as showing that they indicate identical persons; but if besides this we can prove corroborative facts connected with those names from both the Avesta and the Rigveda, that is, without doubt, much better evidence. After a careful study of some years, I have arrived at certain results, which I now beg to place before the reader.

King Vishtaspa.

In the Cama Memorial Volume Ervad Sheheriarji Bharucha has quite correctly put forward the suggestion that we have the mention of the well-known King Vishtâspa in Rigveda I-122-13, which passage runs thus:—किमीष्टाश्व इष्टरश्मिरेत ईशानासस्तरुष ऋंजते नृन् Sâyana, supposed that *Ishtâshva and Ishtarashmi* were two Kings. Griffith does not see any reference to any person in this passage, which he translates thus:—"What can he do, whose steeds and rains are choicest? These, the all-potent urge brave men to conquest."

E. Sheheriarji's translation is this:—"What (can) Ishtâshva of the family of Ishtarashma (do)? These overpowering rulers (*i.e.* the Vedic Gods) will subjugate the people."

Dr. Wilson translates thus:—"What can Ishtâsva, (what can) Ishtarashmi, (what can) those who are lords of the earth achieve (with respect) to the leaders of men, the conquerors of their foes." In the foot-note he says :— according to Sâyana " What can the princes who are named or any other princes do against those who enjoy protection of Mitra and Varuna. The construction is obscure and the names which are said to be those of Rajas are new and unusual."

Before translating the above stanza, we shall notice a few of the important points. Some Vedic words beginning with व् and followed by a vowel, drop the व्; for instance, in Rv.-5-41-2 and Rv. I-162-1 the word आयु is said by Sayana and Mahidhar to be used for वायु (= the god of wind). Similarly in Atharva-veda IV-8-88-5 ऋषभ is used for वृषभ (= male). In Persian also we have Andarimân used for Av. Vandarimân, and *ila* for Av. *vira* (=hero). In colloquical Marathi व् is very commonly dropped ; as इष्णु = विष्णु इश्राम = विश्राम. The Greek form Hystaspes for Vishtaspa clearly shows that it must have passed through the stage *Ishtâspa*.

किं is used with nouns in the sense of " wicked," as किंनर = bad man, किंसखा = bad friend, किंपुरुष = despicable man, किंराजन् = bad king. Similarly I think that in the above passage किमिष्टाश्व means " despicable Vishtâspa."

The word ऋंज् = " fry " ; hence " harass."

The conjunction च (" and ") is understood after इष्टरश्मि:

I translate the passage thus :— " The despicable Vishtâspa of the family of Vishtarashma (=Gushtaham), (and) these conquering chiefs harass the people."

The next passage is also important, as it shows that Vistâspa was not an ordinary man. He was a prince adorned with jewels. The passage also contains a prayer by the Vedic rishi that Vishtâspa might be captured a prisoner. The passage runs thus:—हिरण्यकर्णं मणिग्रीवं अर्णः तन्नो विश्वे वरिवस्यन्तु देवाः

Translation :—"May the sea and all the gods give (into our possession as a prisoner) him who has put on ornaments on the ear and jewels round the neck." *

We saw above that according to the Vedic writer, Gushtâspa harassed the Vedic people. This is borne out by Yashta 19-84 :—*Sijdyo daevân apa ashavân*, " He (= Gushtâspa) destroyed the wicked daevas (= followers of the Deva religion)." In Fr. Yt. § 99 we are told :—*Yo dru cha paurvân cha ashâi ravo yaesha* " who with his stunning spear cleared the path of purity."

Finally it may be stated that the writer of the hymn in which the above Rigvedic passage occurs was Kakshivân or Aushij, who as we shall see hereafter was a contemporary of Zarathushtra.

Arjaspa.

In the Cama Memorial Volume E. Sheheriarji quotes Rv. I-100-17 and tries to show that the Avestan name Arejat-aspa was identical with the Vedic name ऋज्राश्व, as both the words are identical in sound and bear the same meaning namely " one who has swift horses." †

E. Sheheriarji further tries to identify the other persons mentioned in the said Rigvedic verse by showing that the names of certain persons known to be connected with Arjâspa in the Avesta, bear the same meanings as the names of the

* Wilson's translation :—"May all the gods favour us with a person (अर्ण = son) decorated with the goldenear-ring and jewel necklace." Griffith's translation :—"The sea and all the deities shall give us him with the golden ear and neck bejewelled.".

† According to Dr. Geiger, the meaning is " having ruddy horses " which, I think, is more accurate (see C.E I. Vol. I p. 174.)

persons in the said verse. Thus he says that अंबरीष was identical with Bidarfsha (= Av. Vidarafshnik) brother of ArjÂspa, since both the names mean "one with beautiful garment;" similarly भयमान = Vandare-maini, father of ArjÂspa, both meaning "the fearless one;" also सुराधस् = Humayaka, brother of ArjÂspa, as both the words mean "one with much wealth."

It would be easily conceded that the identification of persons in two different languages from the meanings of their names, which are quite different in sound, can have but little weight. Hence my opinion is that only the identification of Arejat-aspa with ऋज्राश्व is of some importance.

It might be noted here that the त् in *Arejat* is changed to र् in Sanskrit, exactly as in *Aurvat-aspa*,* which while passing into Pahlvi becomes LohrÂspa.

The Vedic ऋज्राश्व has been referred to in Rv. I-100-16 to 18 thus :—"The red and tawny mare, blaze-marked, ... who, to bring RijrÂshva riches, drew at the pole, the chariot......

"The VÂrshÂgirÂs unto thee, O Indra, the mighty one, sing forth this laud to please thee—RijrÂshva with his fellows Ambarisha, SurÂdhas, Sahadeva, and BhayamÂna.

"He much-invoked has slain Dasyus and Shimyus after his wont and laid them low with arrows."

Rv. I-117-17. "He whom for furnishing a hundred wethers to the she-wolf, his wicked father blinded; to him RigrÂshva, gave ye eyes, O Ashvins."

From the above passages we find, firstly that RijrÂshva had a mare of red colour, secondly that he coveted riches, thirdly that he was, as the commentators supposed, the son of VrishÂgira but was most probably a descendant of VrishÂgira, and fourthly he was blinded for some fault of his. This last fact is to some extent borne out by a passage in the YÂdgare ZarirÂn § 111 where we are told that after the second fight with ArjÂspa, AsfandiÂr caught him and cut out one hand, one foot and one ear and burned one of his eyes with fire.

There is another man to be found in the Rigveda, bearing an almost identical name, which is ऋजिश्वन्. It seems to me that ऋजिश्वन् is but another name for ऋज्राश्व for the following reasons.

(1) The श of अश्व becomes इ; Cf. the Grk. word hippos (=horse). As to the final न् we find that it is added to the end of proper names at the option of the writer; for instance the 18th ancestor of Zarathushtra was called DurÂsruban according to Dinkard and DurÂsruba according to Dadestan. Cf. also Av. Gaya-marethan=Pahll. Gayomard.

(2) Rijishvan also was a warrior who coveted wealth, just like RijrÂshva. Cf. Rv. VI-20-7 "Indra gave to his worshipper Rajishvan imperishable wealth."

(3) Rijishvan killed the Dasyus just as RijrÂshva had done (see Rv. I-51-5 and I-100-18).

(4) SÂyana says in Rv. IV-16-13 that Rijishvan was a King.

(5) The hymn No. 98 of Rv. IX is ascribed to Rijishvan and Ambarisha. The last named person was a follower of RijrÂshva according to Rv. I-100-17. As we know of only one Ambarisha, we might fairly conclude that Rijishvan and RijrÂshva were names of the same person. The name of the father of Arjaspa is the same both in the Avesta and Rigveda. In Rv. IV-16-13 and

*Au is dropped, *r* becomes *l*, *v* becomes *u*, *a* becomes *h* and *t* becomes *r*, Similarly Av. *Spento-data* = Pers. *Spendiar* (*to* = ta becomes *da* and then merges in the following *da*, and *ta* becomes *ra*). Cf. also *Haetumant* = Pers. *Helmand* ; *Saredha* = Pers. *Sad*.

V-29-11 we find that ऋजिश्वन् was the son of विदथिन्. In Aban Yt. § 117 Arejat-aspa has been called *Vandare-mainish*, that is to say, the son of *Vandari-man*. I think that the Sk. विदथिन् and the Av. *Vandare-man* are identical, because the terminations इन् and मन् are practically the same, and the nouns विदथ् (= विदत्) and वंदरे are from the same root विद् (विंद्) "to get" meaning "something got, knowledge." [For comparison we might mention the names of the tenth ancestor of Zarathushtra who has been called *Vidasta* in Bundehishna and *Vandesta* by Masudi (C. E.I. Vol. II p. 198.]

In Rv.I-51-5 we are told that Rijishvan was a bitter enemy of the Dasyus, त्वं......ऋजिश्वानं दस्युहत्येष्वाविथ "You (O Indra) helped Rijishvan when the Dasyus were struck dead." We have seen that the Dasyus were the followers of Zarathushtra. We might compare this with Aban Yt. §§ 116-117 where it is said that Arjâspa fought with Gushtâspa and his Zoroastrian followers.

Baetâs.

Rv. VI-20-8 स वेतसुं दशमायं दशोणिं तूतुजिं इंद्रः स्वभिष्टिसुम्नः । आ तुग्रं शश्वदिभं द्योतनाय मातुर्न सीमुप सृजा इयध्यै ॥

Griffith's translation :—"The crafty Vetasu, the swift Dasoni and Tugra, speedily with all his servants hath Indra, gladdening with strong assistance, forced near as it were to glorify the mother."

My translation :—"Indra, whose good assistance is his joy has, as if to glorify the mother (= earth) forced near it (= has brought down to the ground = defeated) Vetasu who is possessed of ten magics, who has ten (helpers), who is harmful, who is mischievous and who has many servants."

In the passages preceding and following the above verse, Indra is thus addressed "Thou gavest to thy worshipper Rijishvan imperishable wealth." "Resistless with hosts he battles."

As has been already stated, it is not meant that in point of fact Indra made the battle, but his worshipper Rijishvan did so. Thus we conclude from the above verses that by Indra's help Rijishvan defeated Vetasu in battle.

Now who was this Vetasu? I am of opinion that he was Jâmâspa *Baetâs*. Regarding the change of the name *Vetasu* into the Pahlvi or Persian form Baetâs, three points require to be noted :—(1) The change of व् to ब् is very common, *e.g.*, Vishtâspa has been called Bistâspa by Tabri (see Jackson Zoroaster p. 198). (2) The lengthening of अ; for ex., Zarathushtra has been written as Zarâdusht by Masudi (C. E. I. Vol. II-p. 198). (3) The final उ is changed to अ; Cf. Av. Pesho-tanu Pers. Peshotan; also Adam — Baby. Adamu.

Sayana says that "Vetasu was an Asura," which means that he was a follower of the Ahuramazdian religion (see Wilson III-p. 435.)

We shall now try to see how far the description of Baetâs given by the Vedic rishi is justified by our own literature.

In the marriage Ashirwâda, we read "*Din-yâvar bed chun Jâmâspa Baetâs sich*" "May you be helpful to religion like Jamaspa Baeâs the master of astrology." In Yasna Ha 51-18 he is called De-Jâmâspa, the learned Jâmâspa. It is therefore quite in the fitness of things that the Vedic writer should, out of malice, called him दशमाय "possessed of ten magics." In the Yâdgâri-Zarirân we find that when the King Vishtaspa asked Jâmaspa to foretell the result of the war with Arjâspa and when Jâmâspa told him that 23 of his sons and brothers would be killed, the King in wrath called him *Jâdu* (= magician). The Vedic author uses almost a similar word.

The word दशोणि literally means "having ten" that is to say "having ten *helpers*" as Griffith suggests. Now in the Afrine-Zarathushtra, the King Vishtâspa is thus blessed "*jayâonte hacha vo dasa puthra.*" "May ten sons be born to you." It seems from this passage that Vishtâspa had ten sons, all of whom most probably fought in the war with Arjâspa. It is likely that these sons of Vishtâspa might have been the ten helpers of Jamâspa.

Again in the Aban Yt. §§ 68-69 we find that " when Jâmâspa saw the wicked Deva worshippers coming from afar in rows of battle, he prayed that he may get as much victory as the other Iranians have obtained." This shows that Jâmâspa had also taken part in the war against Arjâspa. Thus the statement of the Rigveda is clearly borne out by the Avesta and subsequent literature.

Peshotan.

In Rv. IV-80-18 we have उत त्या सद्य आर्या सरयोरिंद्र पारतः । अर्णाचित्रारथावधीः ॥ "Arna and Chitra-ratha, both Aryans thou Indra, slewest swift on the yonder side of the Sarayu." Now who was this Chitraratha. In Bund. Ch. 29 Peshotan a son of Gushtâspa has been called *Chitro-mino.* According to Dadestan, Peshotan was given this name from the river Chitru-mian-rud where he lived. We give such names even to-day ; Cf. A. B. Tarapore. It seems that the name was subsequently contracted into *Chitra-rud.* The word *rud* at the end of a Pahlvi word becomes *rat* or *rad*; *e.g.*, the river *Torat* of the Bundehishn is nothing but Toor-rud (=swift river). Thus the Vedic writer would easily confound Chitra-rat with Chitraratha.*

We cannot say who Arna was. The name looks like an Avestan name, cf. *Aren vâchi* (*Arn-vâz*). It may be that अर्ण was Vanâra,† the brother of Gushtâspa. Several brothers of Gushtaspa fought with Arjâspa.

Now the points to be noted with regard to अर्ण and चित्ररथ are these:-

(1) Both were Aryans.

(2) Both were killed in a battle.

(3) In the verse No. 19 Indra is thus addressed :—" Thou, Vritraslayer didst conduct these two *forlorn*, the blind one and the lame one." We knew from Shâhnâme that Peshotan was a warrior who fought with Arjâspa. He and his brother Asfandiâr were the sons of Gushtâspa by his wife Ketâyun. After the first holy war with Arjâspa, Gushtâspa heard that his son Asfandiâr wanted to usurp his sovereignty; consequently he *imprisoned* Asfandiâr in the fortress of Gumbidân, where heavy fetters were laid on him. Arjâspa heard this intelligence with delight and ordered his son Kehram (= Grehma of Ha 32-13 as we shall see later on) to invade Balkh, and he himself followed his son (see C. E. I. Vol. II—225).

Asfandiar was subsequently released and was asked to fight with Arjâspa whom he defeated.

When the Vedic writer says that Peshotan was forlorn (= impri-

---

*Similarly the Europeans confound *Khur*-sedji with *Cur*sedji ; Dhunji*bhai* = Dhunji *boy*, as if *Khur* (=sun) and *bhai*(=brother) have any connection with Cur (=dog) and boy (=son) respectively.

† वनार, वनर, भनर, अरन and अर्ण.

soned), he probably confounds the story of Asfandiâr with that of his brother.

Although Peshotan is better known as a high priest, still he seems to have been a warrior also ; for, in Bund. 82·2 it is suggested that he had an army.

(4) According to Rigveda, Arna and Chitra-ratha were killed on the yonder side of the Sarayu. As Griffith and others have observed, this cannot be the modern river Saraju in Oudh Griffith supposes that it was some river in the Punjab. I think, it was the river Haroyu, whereon stood the city of Herât referred to in Vend. I-9. It seems to be the modern river *Hari* which flows near Herât.

Now accordingly to Shahnâme, the scene of the second holy war was somewhere near Nishâpur and Meshed in Khorâssân (see Jackson's Zoroaster pp. 119 and 215). These cities lie within a short distance of Herat on the west of it. It will thus be seen that the scene of the second war with Arjâspa in the Rigveda is practically the same as that given in the Shahnâme.

Humayaka and Hushdiv.

Let us now turn to the Aban Yasht § 113 where Zarir prays that he may conquer *Humayaka*, the worshipper of the Devas. This Humayaka, seems to me to be सोमक* the son of सहदेव referred to in Rv. IV-15·7 to 9, from which we gather that सोमक gave away, as a present, two bay horses to the Vedic writer वामदेव.

As to सहदेव my opinion is that he was identical with the warrior named *Hush-div* who according to Shâhnâme brought up the rear of the troops of Arjâspa in the first holy war (see Jackson's Zoroaster p. 109).* From Rv. I—100-17 we find that सहदेव was a comrade of Rijrâshva, who slew the Dasyus and the Shimyus with the help of सहदेव and others. It seems therefore that according to the Rigveda and Shâhnâma, सहदेव fought on the side of Arjâspa while according to the Avesta, it was Humayaka (= सोमक) the son of सहदेव who did so.

It may be noted here that from the abovenamed Rv. passages, the rishi Vâmdeva seems to be a contemporary of Somaka. Now Vâmdeva was the son of Gotama, who as we shall see hereafter was a contemporary of Zarathushtra. It follows that Somaka was also a contemporary of our Prophet.

Kavis and Grehma.

In the Yasna Ha 32 § 14 we have a reference to the *Kavis* (the Vedic rishi Kavi and his son Kavya or Ushanâ) and Grehma (= Kehram of the Shâhnâme). The strophe may be rendered thus :—" May Grehma of him (= Indra) be in chains. May (our) plan hurl down the Kavis. These are the two mighty frauds (committed by the Kavis) that they went over to the Dregvant (= the abovesaid *wicked* Grehma) for aid ; and that they spoke about killing the cow (to him) who seeks death-destroying assis-

* Cf. *umana* with the cuneiform *maniya* (C. E. I. Vol. II p. 8). In Avesta य is redundantly added (see Kanga Gr. p. 89).

* The word सहदेव would become *Hadha daeva* in Avesta ; then *Hadaeva* which would easily be confounded with *Hu daeva* and become subsequently *Hush daeva*, Or सह *Hasa* = *Hasha* = Husha.

tance (= they preach that he who seeks to keep death at a distance should sacrifice the cow)." *

I may mention here that this passage leads me to suppose that the *Dregvant* of the Gathas was Grehma (= Kehram) the son of Arjâspa. We shall hereafter consider a number of passages from the Gathas which go to show that the Dregvant was a man of power who opposed and even harassed the followers of Zarathushtra. We find however, from the Aban Yt. § 109 and 113 that the most important epithet of Arjâspa was Dravant, a later form of the Gathic word Dregvant. It is therefore probable that the Gathic Dregvant might have been either Arjâspa or his son Grehma (= Kehrem). I am however disposed to think that as Arjâspa is not mentioned in the Gathas, the word Dregvant is the most distinctive epithet of Grehma.

We shall here consider Prof. Harlez's translation of the above strophe Ha 32-14 which is to the following effect :—" The robber belonging to the Kavis has given his intellect a bent towards the path of that (wicked spirit) and he commits these two great mistakes that they (should) appeal to the wicked one for aid and that for him who promises them to keep death at a distance, the cow should be sacrificed."

Prof. Harlez says in the footnote " The Karpans and Kavis were the opponents of the Zoroastrian religion but the Gathas do not show to what religion they belonged. These men and the Usij (of Ha 44-20) correspond with the Vedic names Karpa, Karpanyu, Kavi and Usij but we cannot come to any definite conclusion from mere similarity of names. In this passage the Kavis have been charged with preaching the slaughter of cows and animals. Now this is contrary to the custom of the Indo-Aryan people, who had great regard for the lives of the cattle, which formed their wealth. Also the Vedas show that the enemies of the Aryans were red-skinned or black-skinned and flat-nosed. But none of these remarks apply to the Iranians."

With regard to the above criticism of Prof. Harlez we may observe that similarity of names in books of ancient times affords a proof which should not be hastily discarded. It cannot be gainsaid that the Aryans had great regard for the lives of animals; but the case was quite different when the gods had to be propitiated by sacrifices. We have a clear reference to the sacrifice of cows and oxen in Rv. II—7-5, and of goats and horses in Rv. I—162-3. In Rv. V—29-8 Indra is said to have eaten the flesh of 300 buffaloes.

Some of the enemies of the Vedic people have been represented as black-skinned, but I do not know whether any such adjunct has been applied to the Dasyus. The Dasyus have been called अनासा: but that does not mean that they were flat-nosed. As already seen they were अनासा: (= " indistinctly speaking people "). We thus find that Prof. Harlez's remarks cannot have much weight.

Turning once again to Ha 32-14 we find that the Kavis taught the Vedic people to sacrifice cows with a view to keep death at a distance. This passage is singularly corroborated almost word for word in the case of

---

* I take *mraoi* to be the short form of *Afravaire* 3/3 Perf. At of *mri*. If we take *mraoi* as usual as 3/1 Aor Pass. (= " it might be said ") the third line might be thus translated :—" And that as it is reported, (they were) for killing the cow (for the sake of him) who seeks death-destroying help."

Visentâ 3/3 Imperf., according to Pahl = *padirend* " to go to one to accept."

Duraoshem — used in its literal sense of " keeping death at a distance."

Saochayat — from सुच 10 cl. " to show."

Kâvya by Rv. I—83-5. यज्ञैः अथर्वा प्रथमः पथस्तते ततः सूर्यो व्रतपा वेन आजनि । आ गा आजत् उशना काव्यः सचा यमस्य जातं अमृतं यजामहे ॥

"Atharvan first by sacrifices discovered the path. Then the sun the dear guardian of the Law was born.' *Ushanâ Kâvya Straight-way hither drove the cows, (Saying) let us perform sacrifice in honour of Yama's deathless birth."* *

Ushanâ was the son of Kavi and was hence called Kâvya. In Rv.IV-16-2 he is called Ushanâ, in Rv. I-177-12 he is called Kâvya and in several places he is called by both the names. He was the special friend of Indra. In Rv. I-121-12 he is said to have given Indra his thunder-bolt.

The idea contained in the above-quoted Rigvedic verse and Ha 32-14 is that the god of death was propitiated by sacrifices and that this doctrine was preached far and wide among the Vedic people. A similar idea is contained in Rv. X-14-14 : "Offer to Yama holy gifts enriched with butter and draw near, so that he may grant that we may live long days of life among the followers of Deva religion."

Grehma, the Dregvant of the Gathas.

We have seen that Yasna Ha 32-14 contains a suggestion that the Kavis fraudulently went over to the wicked Grehma for help. It appears that the Kavis were at first on the side of Zarathushtra, for the reason that the word Kavi was an epithet of the king Gushtâspa and other Kayânians but that subsequently they became treacherous and went over to Grehma. This point is borne out by the Pahlvi Zarathushtra-nâme where we are told that the Karaps, Kavis and Usikhs had descended from the ancestors of Zarathushtra and that subsequently they were looked upon as wicked in consequence of the enmity with our Prophet.

As has been observed, Grehma appears to be the Kehram* of Shâh-nâme a son of Arjâspa. Kehram took a leading part in the holy wars with Gushtâspa.

In Ha 32 § 14 Grehma has been called Dregvant (= "the wicked one"). This word Dregvant occurs in several other passages of Gathas, some of which clearly refer to Grehma. I propose to consider here some of the important passages.

(1) Yasna Ha 32-13 shows that Grehma was a man of great powers. I translate the verse thus:—"Whereby Grehma lives in the house of the wicked mind with power. He is the destroyer of this world—who, O Mazda, although his desires are fulfilled, still cries aloud, who prevents the prophet of thy religion (=Zarathushtra) from teaching Asha." †

(2) The last line of Ha 32-12 : "Whereby Grehma prefers the so-

---

* Both Av. and Rv. have *gâush* and गाः आजत् from अज् "to drive cattle for slaughter ; *jaidyâi* from *jan* (= हन्) to slaughter. *Aoshangh* = यम. which here means the god of death; Cf. Shatapatha Brahmana II-8-2-2 ; and Ath. Veda II-8-12-7 अयाः सदनं यमस्य "Go to the house of the god of death."

* For the change of *ga* to *ka* Cf. Av. *Gayamaretan* = P. *Kaiyumars*, Av. *Geush-urvan* = P. *Kaevân;* गंधार = Kandhâra in Rv. I.—126-6.

† *Hishasat*—from the root सस "to sleep." *Marekhtâro* should be sing. not plu. We" might render *Khshathra* as " with the king; if so, the 2nd line would refer to Grehma and Arjâspa ; as the dual form is wanting, the plu. *Marekhtaro* would be allowed ; but there is again the difficulty that *Jigerezat* is Sing. *Ish* is meaning less Cf. Ha 51-14. *Dares* = Sk. दर्शन teaching." The reading *Ydish* is preferable

vereignty of those who love Druj* (=Indra) (that is to say, the Vedic people) to Asha, and also Karapa (prefers &c)." It appears from this passage that Grehma was a very powerful man among the followers of Indra.

(3) In Ha 46 § 7 Zarathushtra who is terribly afraid of Grehma cries out, "Who, O Mazda, will give me protection when the Dregvant has indeed assailed me to do harm." That this Dregvant is a particular wicked man follows from the next verse (which we shall discuss hereafter) where Atri is called *ahyâ Athrish* (= Atri belonging to *him*). The word *didareshtâ* (intens. imperf. At. 3/1 = has "indeed attacked") is very suggestive. It is a historical fact that Kehram attacked Balkh in the second holy war (C. E. I. Vol. II-225).

(4) Ha 46-5 is one of the most difficult strophes. I translate it thus: "May that well-discerning person (*vichirohâns*), who is ruling (*khshayâns*), who is of good knowledge (*hujentush*), who is living with righteousness (*rashnâ javâns*), who is righteous (*ashavâ*), not giving satisfactions (*dritâ adâns*) to the Dregvant,—who is *assailing* (*ayantem*)—by means of vows and promises, speak to his relative, O Ahuramazda (that) 'while he sallies forth, he should crush him (= Dregvant).'" †

* In Ha 48-1 the Pahlvi translator renders *Druj* by the word *Indra*. It may be stated here that though the word Indra has been used for the great Vedic god in numerous passages, still at first it was a common designation of a Vedic king (Cf.Rv. VIII-6-41, VIII-16-7) who was subsequently deified. Prof. Bhagvat in his Key to the Vedas says (p. 18). "The word Indra thus denoted in early times a 'ruler (of the Devas),' each tribe of the Devas, who were undoubtedly a division of mankind."

† Dritâ = *drita* n. plu. Cf. धृति "satisfaction." *Urvâtoish* — better if we had *urvâtâish* as in Ha 31-1; urvâta = व्रत "vows *Ujuithyoi* — Loc. sing. (= in the rising); taking *aetahmi* understood we have loc. absolute construction.

I am of opinion that here we have a reference to the first holy war. Gushtâspa has been called *ashava* here as in Ha 46-14, this being his distinctive epithet. In the Afrin-e-Buzorgân (part of Pâzand Ashirvâda) we have "*Asho bed chun Gushtaspa.*" "Be righteous like Gushtaspa." It will also be seen that Gushtâspa has been called a ruler (*khshayâns*) in this verse. The Dregvant is Grehma.

We are told in the Yâdgâre Zarirân that when Arjâspa heard that Gushtâspa had embraced the Zoroastrian religion, he sent a message to Gushtâspa that should he give up this religion, he would be given homage as a king and also plenty of wealth; otherwise he would be attacked and placed in chains. In the stanza before us, Zarathushtra wishes that Gushtâspa would not please Kehram by making promises of any kind. The relative spoken of in the verse is most probably Zarir, the brother of Gushtâspa, who was ordered to oppose the attack of the enemy in the first holy war.

(5) In Ha 45-1 we have "May not the wicked man of power (*dush-sasti*) kill the people of the world a *second time*. The Dregvant is by his evil religion and tongue turned* (from the right path)."

In this passage the Dregvant has been also called *dush-sasti*. Also we have a reference to the *second* holy war, a short time before which the above passage seems to have been written; for, otherwise we cannot see the force of the word *daibitim* ("second time").

In this Ha No. 45 Zarathushtra preaches his religion but the first important thing that he asks his hearers to do is that steps should be taken to stop the Dregvant from harassing the pious followers a second time.

* For *Avereto* cf. *ashat-varatâ* in Ha 32-12.

(6) Having identified Dush-sasti in the above passage, we can easily see that the same man has been spoken of in the verse No. 9 of Ha 32 which is one of the historical chapters of the Gathas.

Ha 32-9: "The evil man of power (*dush-sasti*) destroys (my) teachings. He (destroys) the strength (*khratu*) of the people by (his) orders. May not (such men) be the obtainers of (their) desire (namely) the mighty destruction* of the good mind. Thus by the word of my spirit, O Mazda, I pray to Asha and to you."

(7) Ha 32-5: "Therefore you beguile (rob) men of their happy life and immortality, because the wicked Mainyu has declared the Dregvant (Grehma) as the ruler to you the Devas (= followers of Deva religion) by means of evil mind, evil words and evil deeds."

I am of opinion that in this passage, there is a reference to the Vedic rishi named मन्यु † of whom we shall speak hereafter. It may be noted that the above passage speaks of the Dregvant as a ruler or a man of power.

(8) Ha 32-11 first line :—"May not those who consult with the chiefs of the Dregvant destroy life." Here also it is clear that the Dregvant was a man of power, since he is said to have chiefs.

(9) Ha 31-18: "May none of you listen to the words and orders of the Dregvant. He has given up the house, village, city and country to distress and death. Therefore kill them (=persons like him) with a weapon."

(10) Ha 46-4: "That tyrannical man (*dus-jobdo hâns*), the Dregvant who troubles the world (*ahemusto*) by his deeds, obstructs those who are the supporters (*vas-dreng*) of Asha and the animals of the town and the country from moving about. O Mazda, he who hurls him down from rule and life, opens those paths (i. e.) of the animals and of wisdom."

(11) Ha 48-2: "O Ahuramazda, tell me as you are omniscient, before that war which is mine (=of which I am the cause) comes on to me, will the pious man (= Vishtâspa) defeat the Dregvant ? That surely will be known as a good deed of the world."

The third line is thus translated "Will the pious defeat the wicked." It is a mere truism to say that the pious men in general will defeat the wicked. Where is the good of putting such a trite question to Ahuramazda? It is clear that we must have a reference here to a particular pious man and a particular wicked man. The Dregvant is such a troublesome man that his destruction would be looked upon as a great performance.

Before closing this subject of the Dregvant it may be observed that in his Sk. translation of Ha 31-18, Nerioshang well nigh suggests that the Dregvant was some particular individual. The translation of Nerioshang's Sanskrit is under :—"May none of you present thus listen to the word and precept of the wicked man, because that *Ashmog* (heretic) causes (lit. gives) evil deeds and death and injustice to the house, province or village. Therefore strike him a blow with the hand." So far Nerioshang is quite near the mark, but he diverges from it when following the Pahlvi translator, he adds the gloss "for purifying the words of the *Ashmogs*, make ready the weapons for *them*."

Dr. Mills in his Gathas (p. 480) says "*Dregvato* is obviously the *hvo* of verse 10, the dush-sasti of v. 9, *dregvatem* of v. 5 and v. 14 and *dregvato* of v. 16."

Agastya or Mana.

At one time I was inclined to think with Ervad Sheheriarji that in

---

* *Hâiti* = साति "destruction."

† *Aka mainyu* may mean "evil spirit."

Yasna Ha 32 § 10 there was a reference to the Vedic rishi Mâna (*hvo mâ nâ*)* better known as Agastya. But the difficulty of grammar about *mâ nâ* not being nom. sing. is unavoidable. Also the word *hvo* (*that*) shows that the author is talking of the person whom he has already mentioned. *Hvo* points out that the man referred to is *Dush-sasti* whom we have identified with the Dregvant (=Grehma).

If any one is tempted to identify *mânâ* with Mâna, he would do well to consider Rv. VII-33-13, I-173-4, I-171-4, I-174-2, I-178-5, I-182-3, I-175-3.

Mainyu.

Mainyu, a Vedic writer seems to be a contemporary of Zarathuhsta. He was the writer of the Hymns Nos. 83 and 84 of the 10th Book of Rigveda. He is mentioned in Ha 32-5 which we have already translated in connection with the Dregvant. The fact that the whole of the Ha No. 32 is historical, and the meanings of the words *aka-manangha, aka-mainyu* and *dregvant* suggest the probability of Mainyu being the name of a person.

Vasishtha, Puru and Angiras.

The 15th stanza of the Ha No. 43 of the Yasna seems to refer to the Vedic rishis,—Vasistha, Puru and Angiras. It may be stated that the translation that I propose to give has been suggested by the following pregnant remarks of Dr. Haug : " Zoroaster exhorts his party to respect and revere Angra (Yasna 43 § 15) *i. e.*, Angirases of the Vedic hymns who formed one of the most ancient and celebrated priestly families of ancient Aryans......These Angirases are often mentioned together with the Atharvans 'fire priests' and both are regarded as the authors of the Atharva Veda. This work was for a long time not acknowledged as proper Veda by Brahmins because its contents were mostly foreign to the Vedas.......We find great similarity between it and passages in the Yashts and Vendidad."

* *Hvo mâ nâ* = Verily that man.

I do not think that the Angirases were inclined towards the Zoroastrian religion, because nowhere in the Rigveda (so far as I can see) have they been spoken of with contempt; they were not the friends of the Zoroastrians, at least in the Rigvedic times. Hence my opinion is that Zarathushtra rightly hated the Angirases, as we find in Ha 43-15 and 44-12.

Ha 43-15—The third and fourth lines are construed thus : (*Noit*) *tushnâ-maitish vahishtâ, noit dregvato paourush nâ chikhshnusho khyât.*

Translation :—"O Ahuramazda, then indeed I regarded thee as bountiful when (that angel) came to me with good mind and informed me with wisdom that *neither the harmful-intellected† Vasishtha‡, nor Puru¶ belonging to the Dregvant (=Grehma) is dear to us; indeed they§ have regarded all the Angras$ (=Angirases) as righteous."

If Paouru (=Puru) was an enemy of the Zoroastrian religion, we should expect to find his name in the historical chapter of the Gathas, *viz.*, Ha

* As to Syntax with *noit* see Kanga Gr. p. 295.

† *Tushnâ*—just as from तिज् "to sharpen", we have तीक्ष्ण "sharpened," so from तुज् " to hurt " we would have तूक्ष्ण (=Av *tushna*).

‡ *Vahishta*=Sk. वासिष्ठ name of a man originally signifying "the best." Ervad Modi in his "King Solomon's temple, etc." says at p. 52 that Xerxes, the son of Darius had a wife named *Vashti*, which name he derives from *Vahishtâ* "the best."

¶ *Paouru*—Cf. *vouru*= उरु.

§ *Toi*—In Av. when the dual form is not available, the plural is used as here. See Mills Gathas p. 468.

$ Sâyana says अंगारेभ्यो जातो महर्षिः अंगिराः "Angiras was a great sage born from Angârs. In ऐ० ब्रा० 8-34 we have ये अंगाराः आसन् ते अंगिरसो अभवन् "Those who were Angârs became Angirases. (See ऋ० वेद IV-29-6-3).

32; and as a matter of fact we find his name in the 6th verse * as under: "The sin of Puru shall be punished by such means as are reported."

We shall consider Ha 44-12 where also we have a reference to Angra (=Angiras). I translate the verse thus :—

"O Ahurmazda tell me truly that which I ask thee. Who are righteous and who wicked (among the persons) with whom I am debating? Towards which of the two (=the righteous and the wicked) is Angra (=Angiras); or is he Angra (=Angro-mino) himself? As he the wicked one opposes me and thy gifts, why is he not regarded Angra (=Angro-mino)"? †

Let us now turn our attention to Rigveda VII-6-3 where Vasishtha shows his contempt for the Dasyus (=Zarathushtrians) thus :—

न्यक्रतून् ग्रथिनः मृध्रवाचः पणीः ॥
अश्रद्धान् अवृधान् अयज्ञान् ॥
प्र प्र तान् दस्यूः अग्निः विवाय पूर्वः
चकार अपरान् अयज्यून् ॥

"Far far away has Agni chased those *Dasyus*, the foolish, faithless, rudely-speaking niggards, without belief, or worship or sacrifice and in the east has turned the godless westward."

Vasishtha was a friend of Puru who was probably a prince and whom he mentions in Rv. VII-19-3. In Rv. VII-96-2 we are told that the Purus (followers of Puru) lived on the grassy banks of the Sarasvati (=Harakhaiti).

The rishi Angiras was one of the mightiest followers of Indra. This rishi was a relative of Kakshivan (=Aushij).

Vasishtha mentions the Angirases in two or three places in Rv. VII.

Kakshivan or Aushij.

The rishi Kakshivan was the writer of the Hymns Nos. 116 to 126 of the 1st Mandal of the Rigveda. He was also called Aushij (=son of Ushij). He seems to the Usij of Yasna Ha 44 § 20 which runs as follows :—"O Mazda, I ask this; have the Devas (= followers of Deva religion) ever indeed been good rulers —(they) who have fought with these (= my followers); of whom* Karapa and Usij have given over the earth to the god Aeshma † (= Indra); of whom Kavi has increased in foul strength. They do not cherish her according to Law for the increase of agriculture."

In Rv. I-112-11 Kakshivân says "O you heroes (=Ashvins)...... you freed the rishi Atri, whom the five tribes honoured, from the fiery pit, baffling the guiles of the malignant Dasyu (people) repelling them in succession." Atri was the priest

---

* Dr. Mills in his Gathas at p. 474 observes "Just at this strophe (Ha 32-6) may begin the allusion to individuals." I think that the allusion begins at strophe No. 5.

† As to the spelling of the word *Angra* a close study of the Mss. is necessary. In Vendidad and Yt. 19 § 43 the spelling is uniformly the same namely with ङ् as the second letter (hereinafter briefly called A). In the Gathas the spelling varies, though Geldner adopts न् as the second letter (hereinafter briefly called B) everywhere. I think that A is correct for Angro-mino and B for the name of a person. In Ha 43-15 A is rightly found in a majority of Mss. In the strophe before us, the word occurs in three places. As to the first Angro, eleven Mss. correctly give the spelling B, it being the name of a person; one Ms. reads *Angero* (with न्) which very nearly approaches अंगिरस् (cf. Av. *yim*, *dim*, *chim*. Gathic *yem*, *dem*, *kem*); six Mss. give the spelling A; and five Mss. read *Angaro* (with न्). As to the second and the third Angro, Geldner seems to be guided by the majority of Mss. the spelling B being found in 12 and 8 Mss. respectively, as against 7 and 3 Mss. where we have the spelling A.

The Ms. C 1 (belonging to Cambridge written in 1700) gives the spelling of the three Angros thus :—Spelling B, A and A. This writer has correctly seen the difference between the two spellings. In Ha 45-2 once again the Ms. C1, gives the correct spelling. In Ha 57-17 Geldner rightly adopts the spelling A.

* *Lit.* through whom.

† *Aeshma*—god of anger known in the Vedas as मन्यु (= Indra.)

of Kakshivân and is referred to in Yasna Ha 46 § 8 which we shall discuss hereafter.

One point may be here noted in connection with Kakshivân. In Rv. 1-118-11 he says "I invoke you Ashvins at the *first break of the everlasting* morning." This seems to show that the writer lived somewhere in the north polar regions. The same rishi, however praises the munificence of a King named Svanaya-bhâva who lived on the western banks of the Indus (*vide* Rv. I-126). May it be that the rishi, leaving his northern colony, had returned to his mother country? We shall see hereafter that some of the Vedic people had migrated from their home in central Asia to colonise the north pole, which they abandoned at the advent of the great flood.

Gotama.

Gotama, the son of Raghugana was the writer of the Hymns Nos. 74 to 93 of Rv. I., and was a well-known rishi. He was a friend of Kâvya and Atri (as is seen in Rv. 1-83-5 and I-183-5) who were the contemporaries of Zarathushtra.

Fravardin Yt. § 16 mentions this Gotama as under: "By virtue of the lustre and glory of these (Farohars), the *renowned one (vyâkhano)* was born —who preached his religion in the assemblies, who preferred wisdom, and who came* out successful in the controversy with the contemptible Gotama."

Although the Avestan writer does not name the renowned man it is clear that he has the famous Zarathushtra in mind; for, we find that in Ha 9 § 14 and other places Zarathushtra is called "the renowned in the Airyana—vaiza; similarly in the Dadestan 72-8 the writer speaks of Zarathushtra thus: "One was Turibrâdarvaksha by whom the *best of men* was killed."

In Yasna Ha 31 § 5 Zarathushtra mentions a certain rishi who was most probably the rishi Gotama. I translate the verse thus. "Tell me to know that blessing (*vahyo*) which you have given me through purity. (Tell me) to know with my good mind, O Ahuramazda that which will not happen and which will happen—of which (knowledge) the *rishi* may not partake."

The later Revayats represent Byasa (व्यास) as having gone to Zarathushtra for discussing religious questions with him and as having ultimately succumbed to his arguments. Vyâsa was a personage of more recent times. He edited the Vedas and is said to have put them in their present form. It seems to me that the Revayats have confounded the writer with the editor of the Vedas, and that it was Gotama and not Vyâsa who carried on discussions with Zarathushtra.

Turning to the writings of Gotama we find that there is only one place in which the Dasyus are expressly referred to, namely in Rv. I-78-4, where we read "Thou (Agni) who shakest off our Dasyu foes."

According to our learned Dastur Darabji P. Sanjana, the above passage of the Faravardin Yt. refers to Nodhas, son of Gotama. The rishi Nodhas wrote Rv. I-58 to 64; but I am of opinion that in the Fravardin Yashta, Gotama is alluded to for the following reasons:

(*a*) The Av. form of नोधस् would be something like *Naodangh*. Assuming however that it would be *Nâidyâongh*, we find (as Max Muller points out in Rv. 1-62-13) that Nodhas was also another name for Gotama. It is also very likely that here the word नोधस् means "a poet," as in Rv. I-124-4.

(*b*) The word *naidyâongh* is elsewhere used in the sense of "treating with contempt." It may be an adj. comp. degree (=" weaker, more needy.")

*Here the present tense shows that the action has already taken place; see Kanga Gr. p. 804.

One of the sons of Gotama was Vâmadeva who was also a well-known Vedic writer. In Rv. IV-16-9 the author says "Down sink the sorcerer, the prayerless Dasyu." Here the son of Gotama speaks of Zarathushtra with contempt.

Prof. Darmesteter thought that the above passage of the Fravardin Yashta referred to the controversies victoriously carried on by the Zoroastrians against the impostor Gaotema who also bore the name Budha. We cannot agree with this opinion.

Budha.

Prof. Darmesteter observes "The Daeva Buiti who, by the order of Angra-mainyu, tries to kill Zarathushtra is......the *demon who resides in the idols* and is the same as ButÂspa worshipped in India. ButÂspa the founder of the Budhist sect is no less a personage than Bodhisattva, from which it follows that Buiti is nothing but the object of the Budhist worship, the Budha or better the Bodhi....... In the Yashtas again it is striking to find Zoroastrians engaged in religious warfare with an enemy who bears one of the names of Budha, Gotama."

The Daeva Buiti is thus mentioned in Vendidad 19 §§ 1-2 ' "Thus spake the evil doer Angra Mainyu, the deadly one, 'Druj, rush down and kill him.' The Druj the demon Buiti came rushing along......Zarathushtra chanted aloud Ahunavairya ......The Druj the demon Buiti being dismayed, rushed away."

In Vend. XI-9 Zarathushtra says '*Perena Buidhi, perena Buidhija*' "I fight against Buidhi, I fight against the son of Buidhi."

The Pahlvi translator has rendered *Buiti daevo* by *Bût-shedâ* (—the demon Bût). But this does not necessarily signify Budha, the founder of the well known religion known after him. It seems very probable that the Buiti is the Vedic rishi Budha who was not however so well known in the Rigveda as his son Pururavas. In Rv. X-95 we find a dialogue between Pururavas and his wife Urvashi, a heavenly nymph who consents to live with him on certain conditions. After 4 years the conditions are broken and in consequence the nymph vanishes. Pururavas manages to meet her again and implores her to return. In the course of this dialogue Urvashi thus praises her husband महे यत् त्वा पुरूरवो रणाय अव-र्धयन् दस्युहत्याय देवाः "O Pururavas, the gods increased thee for mighty work to kill Dasyu." It will be seen that this writing practically corroborates the passages of Vendidad already quoted.

In Rv. X-95-14 Pururavas threatens to commit suicide in these words "Thy lover shall fly away this day to go to the farthest distance for ever without return. Then let him be placed on the lap of destruction and there let fierce wolves devour him." In other words Pururavas means to say that if Urvashi does not return, he will commit suicide, ordering that his corpse shall be exposed in a place where after the manner of the Zoroastrians, wolves would devour him. At this Urvashi cries out "Pururavas, do not die, do not fly away, let not the *ill-omened* (अशिवासः) wolves devour thee." The epithet "ill-omened" applied to the wolves by Urvashi shows that this method of the disposal of the dead bodies was repugnant to the feelings of the Vedic people, who were accustomed to अग्निसंस्कार (cremation). In Rv. X-16-4 the burning fire is called *auspicious* (शिव) whereas the wolves have been called *inauspicious* (अशिव) above.

Turviti and Dabhiti.

From Vendidad 19 § 43 we find that Tauru and Daivi were the enemies of Zarathushtra. Tauru has been represented as a Deva, the friend of the Deva Zairi and the opponent of Haurvatat, who presides over water, prosperity and health. The demon Tauru brings about the scarcity of water and produces illness. In one Ms. we have the word *Taurvi* instead of Tauru.

I think that these demons Tauru (= Taurvi) and Daivi are the personages तुर्वीति and दभीति mentioned in the Rigveda. The termination ति in Sk. is redundant; cf. देवताति used for देवता in Rv. I-55-3. Turviti was a prince highly favoured by the god Indra; for we read in Rv. II-13-12 "Thou (Indra) for Turviti heldest still the flowing floods for Vayyâ* easily to pass." Also in Rv. IV-19-6 we read "Thou, O Indra, for the sake of Turviti and Vayyâ didst stop the great stream, flowing, *all-sustaining*; at their prayer didst check the rushing river and made the floods easy to pass."

Although in the above passages, Indra is said to have stopped the all-sustaining rivers, still for reasons already stated it appears that it was Taurviti (a follower of Indra) who stopped the waters for some benefit of his; he is therefore rightly called the opponent of Haurvatat, the angel presiding over water and prosperity.

Daivi was the demon of deceit and roguery. His Vedic name seems to be Dabhiti. We have the following references to him in the Rigveda:—Rv. II-13-9 "Thou (O Indra) for Dabhiti boundest the *Dasyus* not with cords (= in a prison without cords = in the grave)." Rv. II-15-9 "Thou Indra slewest *Dasyu* and keepest safe Dabhiti."

It seems therefore that Turviti and Dabhiti were Aryan princes who were the enemies of the Zarathushtrian religion.

Bandhu.

Bandhu and his three brothers Su-Bandhu, Shruta-Bandhu, and Vipra-Bandhu were the seers of the Hymns Nos. 57 to 60 of Rv. X. They were the sons of the sister of Agastya who was a great enemy of the Dasyus.

Just as the Yâdavs were the descendants or followers of Yadu, Kaurava of Kuru and Paurava of Puru, so Bendva (= Gathic form of Bandva) was the descendant or follower of Bendu (= Bandhu). Bandhu like his maternal uncle Agastya, seems to be an enemy of Zarathushtra; for, we read in Yasna 49 § 1:—

"O Ahuramazda, the young mighty Bendva fights with me who am desirous of propitiating those who move on evil paths with Asha; come to me with good gifts for (= to remove) my difficulties, through good mind; I seek his (= Bendva's) death."

Kripa.

Kripa (= Av. Karpan) was also one of the enemies of our Prophet. There are several references to Karpan and his followers in the Avesta. We have already considered Ys. 44 § 20.

We shall now translate Ha 32 § 12; the last line whereof may be construed thus: *Yâish Grehmâ ashât drujem-eshânâm khshathrem varatâ; Karapâ cha.*

Translation:—" Ahuramazda calls those wicked who by their words keep back men from holiest action, who speaking jestingly take the lives of cows; and whereby Grehma* (= Kehram) prefers the sovereignty of those who love† Druj to (*lit.* going away from) Asha; and also Karapa (prefers etc., etc.)"

In the above passage, the author seems to bring about a contrast between Asha and Druj. Now Ashavahishta is the enemy of Indra. It seems therefore that the word Druj is used for Indra ‡. Thus the expression "those who love Druj" would mean "those who love Indra" that is to say "the Vedic people."

* Vayyâ—father or friend of Turviti.

* *Grehmâ*—occurs only once, *viz.*, in the above passage; *Grehmo* occurs in §§ 18 and 14 of the same Hâ. The crude form seems to be here *Grehman*.

† *Drujem* is governed by the root contained in the noun *ishanâm*.

‡ In Ha 48-1 the Pahl. translator renders Druj by Indra.

From the strophe before us we find that Karapa was a king or a prince of the Vedic Aryans. The references to Kripa in the Rigveda are very meagre. He was a prince favoured by Indra, since in Rv. VIII-3-12 we read "O Indra, help (us) as thou gavest help to Rusham, Shyâvaka, Śvarnara and *Kripa*." Cf. also Rv. VIII-4-2.

Atri.

In the passage No. 8 of Ha 46 (which is also a historical chapter like Ha 32) we have a reference to the well known Rigvedic rishi Atri. The Sk. equivalent of *Âthrish** is आत्रिः just as *Âthravan* = अथर्वन्

I translate the strophe thus:—"May not Atri belonging to him (*ahyâ, i.e.*, the wicked Grehma) who gives up to harm the settlements which are mine, injure me with (his) deeds. Retribution will come to him with hatred—every kind of hatred—O Mazda, in such manner † that it would verily deprive his body ‡ of (*lit.* keep his body from) happiness of life but not of misery."

Two points attract our notice in the above stanza (1) that Atri gave trouble to the provinces under the jurisdiction of Zarathushtra and (2) that some bodily punishment was inflicted on him. Now this Atri was a Vedic rishi and the writer of the hymns Nos. 37 to 43 of the 5th book of the Rigveda. According to Sayana he was the priest of Kakshivân or Aushij (see Rv. V-41-5). Also in Rv. I-183-5 the Vedic writer Agastya or Mâna mentions Atri along with Gotama. We have already seen that Gotama and Aushij were the contemporaries of Zarathushtra.

* On the analogy of आश्वमेध the son of अश्वमेध and आस्त्रबुध्न the son of अस्त्रबुध्न, *Athrish* would be the son of *Athrish*. In Rigveda the initial अ is often lengthened, as आग्ने used for अग्ने in Rv. X-16-10. Hence my opinion is that in the above passage there is a reference to आत्रि.

† *Yâ—tâ lit.* by that means by which

‡ *Lit.* keep his body from

As regards the second point mentioned above, it appears from several passages in the Rigveda that Atri was thrown into a fiery pit by the Asuras, from which he was saved by the Ashvins.* We thus see that the Gathic strophe is clearly corroborated with regard to the corporal punishment which the rishi Atri had to suffer.

A few Vedic names.

It would not be out of place to give here some Vedic names which are similar to those met with in the Avesta.

(1) *Keresa*—in Sraosha Yt. § 6 looks like कश the author of the hymn No. 7 of the Valkhilya hymns—the eleven hymns which are usually inserted after Rv. VIII-48 but which are not noticed by Sayana and which are probably later interpolations.

(2) *Kunda* in Vend. 19 § 41 = कुण्डपाय्य in Rv. VIII-17-13.

(3) Drujaska in Vend. 19 § 41 = द्रुह्यु (= name of a Vedic tribe) in Rv. VII-18-6 and 14.

(4) *Erezi*—Zamyâdha Yt. § 67, a river in Afghanistan = आर्जिक (Rv. IX-113-2) which according to Sâyana was the country of the ऋजिक s. named probably after the river Erezi. It would appear that the Vedic writer lived in Afghanistan.

(5) *Râma* in Ys. 49 § 4 = Râma of Rv. X-93-14. The Avestan form *Râmem* is very peculiar and occurs nowhere else.

* Cf. Rv. I-112-7 "Wherewith you made the fiery pit friendly for Atri's sake." Rv. I-117 8 "O you heroes,......you freed the rishi Atri whom the five tribes honoured from the fiery pit, baffling the guiles of the malignant Dasyu people."

PART III.

Relationship between Aryans and Iranians.

I have observed above that the Ha No. 32 of the Yasna is a historical chapter. I have tried to show that in several strophes of this Ha, we have references to different Vedic rishis and other personages, namely to Manyu, Puru, Yima, Kâvya and Kripa in the strophes Nos. 5, 6, 8, 14 and 15. Also the arch-Daeva Kehram has been mentioned as Grehma in the verses Nos. 12, 13 and 14, as Dregvant in verses Nos. 5 and 11, and as Dush-sasti in the verses Nos. 9 and 10.

I now propose to consider the first four stanzas of this Ha,—the first stanza being the most important for our purpose. Prof. Geldner rightly observes that "The first strophe sometimes states the subject, *e. g.*, Ha 30 § 1; and the concluding strophe is frequently an *oratio pro domo* of the prophet considered as a speaker, *e. g.*, Ha 33-14, 43-16, 45-11, 50-11" (see Dastur Peshotan Memorial Vol. p. 42).

I think that the first four strophes of Ha 32 indicate the subject. They contain a dialogue between the Devas and Ahuramazda, in which the Devas, claiming relationship with Him, request Him to accept them as His prophets and the promoters of His gospel. Ahuramazda declines to allow their request for the reasons mentioned in the strophes Nos. 2, 3 and 4.

The strophe may be construed thus:—*Airyamnâ mat, daevâ akhyâ khaetush châ ahyâ veresenem yâsat. Ahurahyâ Mazdâo manoi mahmi urvâsemâ, &c., &c.*

Translation:—"The Devas claimed (*lit.* sought) His* (= Ahuramazda's) relationship, His colleagueship with a request to Him (saying) 'the mind of Ahuramazda being great, we rejoice. Shall we be Thy prophets, shall we drive away those who hate Thee?'"

The translation I have given will appear clear by converting the Gathic passage into Sanskrit; thus: अस्य स्वतुः याचत् (?) अस्य वृहणं स्मद् अर्यमणा। अस्य देवाः महति मने (मनसि) असुरस्य भ्राजामः (or राजामः) (सु) मेधसः । ते दूतासः असाम तान् दारया (म) ये वः द्वेषन्ति ॥

The Pahlvi translator has correctly grasped the meaning which runs

---

* *Akhyâ* refers to Ahuramazda mentioned later on. Cf. Sk. and Pahl. translation of *ahyâ yâsâ*.

Khaetush—acc. plu. (= relationships); Cf. *gâtush* (Kanga Gr. p. 86). The plural shows that sevral kinds of relationships were claimed, some claiming to be brothers, some cousins and so on.

Yâsat—3rd prs. sing. and has for its subject *Daevas* in the plu. This is a kind of poetical license; Cf. Ha 34–9 *Yoi......... avazazat...... aeibyo* (= to those who lead a life); Ha 32–13 *Marekhtâro jigarezat* (= destroyers bewail). See Dr. Mills Gathas p. 504.

Veresenem—translated in Sk. as स्वपंक्तिता "own-class-ness, tribe-brotherhood." This word is very appropriate; it shows that the ancient Indo-Iranians were working together (*varez*) probably as tillers of soil (*varez* = to till).

Airyamnâ—In Ha 54-2 *airyaman* is a prayer which gives victory and righteousness. The word literally means "that which pleases, hence request." Nerioshang renders it by सद्यादेशता "obedience." Pahlvi does not help us.

Mahmi—is a peculiar form. In Sk. पूर्व, अवर, अपर, अंतर, दक्षिण &c., form their loc. by the suffix ई or स्मिन् (= Av. *hmi*) *maz + hmi = mah + hmi = mahmi*.

Mahmi manoi—Loc. absolute construction, "mind being great." The Devas are confident that Ahuramazda, if he is called of libral mind, would grant their request. They as it were try to cajole and coax Ahuramazda in order that he may appoint them the prophets of his religion. *Mahmi manoi* might also mean "egoistically" (*lit.* "in my mind").

thus: "The demon sought that reward* of His (*i.e.*, Ahuramazd's own) on account of relationship; that (reward) of His on account of tribe-brotherhood † with friendliness, saying 'we are thy tribe-brethren.' The demons sought that (reward) of His with this egoistic thought, that is, they said 'our thought is as righteous as Zarathushtra's.' They sought that joyfulness of Ahuramazda. They said 'shall we be thy spokesmen, shall we be thy promoters.'"

Translation of Nerioshang's Sk.:—"Through His, the Lord's prayer, they are among those who are desirous (of seeing their request fulfilled) on account of the dependence, that is to say, (they say to the Lord) 'we are thy dependents, tribe-brethren and order-bearers.' Through favour of Him, those among the demons (are desirous) of the pleasure of the Lord and mercy of the Omniscient one, (saying) 'shall we become thy praisers? that is, shall we bring about thy glory, shall we tear asunder those who torment thee?'"

It will thus be seen that from the above Avestan passage we deduce two important facts, first that the followers of the Deva religion were closely related to the followers of the Ahuramazdian religion—a fact which, as we have already seen, is corroborated by Mâhâbhârata; and secondly that among the Deva-worshippers there were several learned rishis who claimed to be the prophets or promoters of the true religion.

We shall now cast a hasty glance over the next three stanzas. They are important as showing that the followers of the Ahuramazdian religion did not entertain the claim of the Daeva worshippers to be their prophets. It deserves to be noted that no answer whatever is given to Ahuramazda as regards the claim put forward by the Devas on the score of relationship. If silence means consent, evidently that claim was admitted.

The strophe No. 2 is an answer by Ahuramazda with reference to the cajoling words in which the request was made by the Devas. Ahuramazda says that the flattering tone in which the application is made will have no influence upon Him. He says "my principal is Armaiti, *i. e.*, frankness or candidness. I do not want flattery."

The strophes No. 3 and 4 state why the Devas are unfit to become the prophets of the Ahuramazdian religion. The reasons given in the strophe No. 3 are that they have descended from the evil-minded one; that their followers belong to the Druj (=Indra) and the perverse mind; and that they spread deceipt and roguery in the world. The 4th verse states that the Devas excite men to do wrong acts.

From the 5th strophe onwards the Gathic writer gives detailed description of the leading Deva-followers, who were a source of great trouble and anxiety to Zarathushtra and his disciples.

Iranians the Devas of yore.

In connection with the relationship between the Deva followers and the Ahura followers we shall consider Rv. VI-59-1 a strophe which, though very simple, has been considered obscure. The second line of the strophe is हतासो वां पितरो देवशत्रव: इंद्राग्नी जीवथो युवं ।

"O Indra and Agni, *your fathers the enemies of the Devas* were killed (and) you survived." The commentators were at a loss to understand this passage as to how the Pitris of the Devas could be the enemies of the Devas. In the Research and Review Vol. I, Part I, (p. 4)

* Dr. West adopts the reading *Jân* for *yân* (= life); the second translation gives the meaning as *mezda* (= reward), which is the grant of their request made below.

† Nerioshang renders *vârunih* by स्वपंक्तिता, Dr. Mills by *productiveness* and Dr. West by *serfdom*.

Mr. A. C. Sen, M.A., rightly suggests that "These enemies of gods were the Iranian rishis, the ancestors of our kinsmen the Parsis, who on account of the excesses in connection with the worship of Indra, lost faith at first in that comparatively recent god and ultimately in all the gods."

Classes of Devas.

The Devas were divided into 4 classes.

(1) The Devas proper who are described as being engaged in incessant warfare with the Devas of the other classes.

(2) The Mûra-Devas about whom in Rv. VII-104-24 we read "Let the Mura-Devas die, let them not see the rising sun."

(3) Shishna-Devas* who are detested in Rv. X-99-3.

In Rv. VII-27-5 we have "may not the Shishna Devas approach our holy worship."

(4) Pûrva† Devas who were the Ahura-followers. Sâyana, a strict follower of the Vedic tradition has rendered Purva Deva by *Asura* (see Wilson Vol. IV, p. 68). Also in Amarkosh Purva Deva is a synonym for Asura.

Also in Rv. VII-27-7 we have this important statement. देवाश्चित् ते असुर्याय पूर्वेऽनु क्षत्राय ममिरे सहांसि Griffith translates the passage thus:

"Even the earlier Deities submitted their powers to (thy) supreme dominion."

Considering however the two preceding verses in which the enemies of Indra and the wicked Sishna-Devas are mentioned, I would translate the passage thus:—"The Purva-Devas have assigned thy (Indra's) powers to the Ahurian (= Ahuramazdian) Lord." Two points are brought out here, (1) that the Ahuras (= followers of Ahura) were formerly Devas, and (2) that they looked upon Ahura as the Lord instead of Indra (see Prof. Bhagvat's Key to interpret Vedas p. 15).

* "Lewd savages" according to Griffith.

† *Purva*=elder in point of time.

Did the religious split between Aryans and Iranians take place before or after their separation.

Dr. Haug thus speaks about the subject in his Essays, "The causes that led to the schism ...... were of social and political as well as of a religious nature. The Aryan tribes after they had left their natural home, which was in all likelihood a cold country (see Vend. Ch. I, II) led mainly a pastoral life and cultivated only occasionally some patches of land for their support ...... Some of these tribes whom we may style the Iranians proper, became soon weary of these constant wanderings and after having reached such places as between the Oxus and Jaxartes rivers and the high land of Bactria, as were deemed fit for permanent settlements, they forsook the pastoral life of their ancestors and their brother-tribes and became agriculturists. In consequence of this change, the Iranians estranged themselves from the other Aryan tribes which......regarded those settlements as the most suitable objects for their incursions and skirmishes......The success of the attacking Deva-worshippers was mainly ascribed to spells (mantras) and sacrificial skill. Their religion therefore must have been an object of hatred in the eyes of Iranians, although the latter were well aware that it was closely related to their own and even to a certain extent identical with it. Their own religion had therefore to be totally changed in order to break up all communication with the devastators of their settlements. The Deva religion was branded as the source of all mischief and wickedness, and instead of it the Ahura religion of agriculture was installed, which separated them thenceforth for ever from their Brahmanical brethren."

We shall now give a long quotation from the remarks of Prof. Tiele with regard to the above subject in his brochure named "The religion of the Iranian people" translated by Mr. G. K. Nariman. He says "If the Zoroastrian religion is called forth by a reformation, this religious upheaval could not have taken place prior to the separation of the Indo-Iranians. It was initiated at a later date. The contrary is at all events advanced in the well known theory of Martin Haug, which makes the disruption of the East Aryans into Iranians and Indians the result of a religious schism. This view to which now but few scholars adhere, derives its plausibility from the striking circumstance among the two races that while both have so many religious concepts and practices in common, the gods of the one are the wicked spirits of the other, and conversely the intelligences which are *here* abominated and warred against are *there* the recipients of adoration. Devas and Asuras were both names applied to divine beings from times immemorial......It is true that Asura has gradually acquired with the Indian, partly in the Vedic era, a derogatory sense, in that the spirits so styled were hostile to the Devas......Again while the Indian kept on calling these gods Devas, *Daeva* came to be synonymous with the Iranian Drukhsh, the spirit of falsehood...... There is no denying these facts but the conclusions sought to be educed therefrom do not hold water. More penetrating examination shows that they must be elucidated in another way.

"In the first place long after the Iranians had settled on the banks of the Sarasvati and the Ganges, the word Asura retained its elavated sense. In the hymns of the Rigveda, the word with most of its derivatives is still an honoured epithet of the gods Varuna, Agni, Indra, Soma and Rudra. Only occasionally and for the most part in the later books of the Rigveda, it is that we have to suspect a reference to wizard spirits inimical to the celestials; and not till we come down to the Atharva Veda and the Brahmans that this sense is found to preponderate.

"On the other hand the Iranians have more than one god to whom the Indians pray to as Devas, to wit, Mitra, Aryaman, Soma. The Iranian comprehends them under the general appellations Yazata and Bagha without belying his Zarathushtrian creed. Only in Vendidad X-9 and XIX-43 we come across a few Indian deities which are hostile to Zarathushtrian Yazatas—passages which are very late.

"In fine, throughout the Veda there is no trace of a conflict with the dogma of Zoroaster and not the faintest testimony that the minstrels and Brahmans were cognisant of the worship of Mazda, which would have been the case to a certainty, had hostility to the reform movement led the Indians to secede from their union with the cognate sept and to wander far a field in search of a separate habitat of their own.

"Accordingly the Vedic and Zarathushtrian religions did not spring when both the tribes were flourishing together. The birth of the Vedic and the Zarathushtrian religion was posterior by far to their separation."

The first important point to consider is what were the rivers Sarasvati and Ganges referred to by Prof. Teile. As has been shown by several scholars, the Ganges has been mentioned only twice in the Rigveda, *viz.*, in Rv. VI-45-31 and X-75-5. In the former of these two passages, however, the word *Gangâ* is stated by some to be used for a woman of that name. The latter passage clearly refers to the river at present known as the Ganges. But in neither of these passages nor in the hymns where these passages are found, have we any reference to the word Asura, nor have the traditional writers of the said hymns, used the word Asura anywhere else in its elevated sense. On the other hand the river Sarasvati has been mentioned in several places. In Rv. VII-2 where the river has been mentioned the writer uses the word Asura in its elevated sense. But it is material to consider what this river was. In Rv. VIII-36-6 she has been called "the mother of the floods......with fair streams, strongly flowing, and fully swelling with the volume of their water." In Rv. VII-95-1 and 2 she is said to be "the sure defence, surpassing in majesty and might all other waters, pure in her course from mountains to the ocean." It is clear that this description can hardly apply to the small stream in India, at present known as the Sarasvati.

In Rigveda Samhita Vol. I (1869 pp. 44-46) Prof. Max Muller says "It is possible that as early as the composition of the laws of the Mânavâs... the river Sarasvati had changed her course and that the place where that river disappeared under ground was called *Vinashana* 'the loss'.........It is very curious that while in the later Sk. literature, the disappearance of the Sarasvati in the desert is a fact familiar to every writer,* no mention of it should occur during the whole of the Vedic period, and it is still more curious that in one of the hymns of the Rigveda we should have a distinct statement that the Sarasvati fell into the sea......Thus the loss of the Sarasvati is later than the Vedic age. ......At present the Sarasvati is so small a river that the epithets applied to the Sarasvati in the Veda have been quite inapplicable to it. The Vedic rishis, though acquainted with numerous rivers .... called the Sarasvati the mother of the rivers."

I am of opinion that the Sarasvati was the Harakhaiti of the Avesta, situated in Kandhar. The Iranians and the Aryans were living together harmoniously on the banks of this river in ancient times; and therefore it is but natural that the word Asura should have been used in its elevated sense in those days.

* See Raghu-vamsha III-9.

Prof. Teile further observes that the Zoroastrians continued to worship the Yazatas such as Mitra Soma, &c., just like the Indians and that there is no mention of the hatred of the Indian deities such as Indra, &c., upto the time of the Vendidad.

We cannot agree with this conclusion. That Zoroaster was living with the followers of the Deva religion, is proved from Yasna Ha 32 where there is a clear history of the Deva-people. There are numerous passages in the Gathas which clearly show that Zarathushtra hated the followers of the Deva religion. Consequently the religious schism must have certainly taken place during the time that the Zarathushtrians and the Deva worshippers were living together.

We also cannot agree with the last observation of Prof. Teile that in the Rigveda there is no trace of a conflict with the dogmas of Zarathushtra. If Dasyu was Zarathustra, we have numerous references to the conflict. Moreover several enemies of the Deva religion, who were the followes of Zarathushtra have been mentioned in the Rigveda.

It is true that the Vedic rishis have nowhere detested the worship of Ahuramazda, but that they knew of the existence of some other god than their own, is proved from such epithets as अन्यव्रत ("whose faith is with another god") applied to the Dasyus.

Iranian influence on Vedic religion.

It must be noted that in the later Rigvedic times, some of the writers seem to have been influenced by certain dogmas of the Iranian faith. The Zoroastrians or rather the Mazdayasnians originated the doctrine of monotheism, which most of the old Vedic rishis at first discarded; but in course of time some of the writers seem to have admitted the suitability of the doctrine.

In Rv. III-54-3 we read एकत् ध्रुवं पत्यते विश्वमेकं चरत् पतत्रि विषुणं विजातं । "One All is Lord of what is fixed and moving, that walks, that flies this multiform creation."

In Rv. I-164-46 we have "They call him, Indra, Mitra, Varuna, Agni ......to what is One, sages give many a title."

The above two Rigvedic passages' (in as much as they belong to the earlier portions of the Rigveda), seem to have been written before the religious split between the Aryans and the Iranians, and may have afforded to the Zarathushtrians a key to their doctrine of monotheism, which they brought forth into prominent relief. On the other hand, the hymn No. 82 of Rv. X (which is ~~the~~ quoted below) clearly belonged to much later times, when the word Asura had already acquired a bad sense and must therefore have been written after the religious schism. I am of opinion that this writer was influenced by the monotheistic teachings of the Zarathushtrians, as can be gathered from the language used by him. The abovementioned hymn is dedicated to विश्वकर्मन् the All-doer Almighty. I shall give here a few of the passages. "The father of the eye, the wise in mind, created both these worlds...... Mighty in mind and power is Visvakarman (the All-doer), maker, disposer and most lofty presence. Their (= Rishis') offerings rejoice in rich juice where they value the Only One, who is beyond the constellation of the Seven Rishis. Father, who made us, disposer, who knows all races and all things existing......He who is earlier than this earth and heaven, before the Asuras and Devas came into existence."

Doctrine of the Classes.

Similarly the later Vedic rishis appear to have picked up the Iranian doctrine of the "Four Classes," while the people of the two religions were living together. Prof. Darmesteter suggested (and herein Prof. Teile follows him) that in Yasna Ha 48 § 5 we have a glimpse of the doctrine of the Three Classes, the prince, the priest and the peasant. The strophe is very simple, but unless we see in it a reference to the above doctrine, it is difficult to see the connection between the different lines of the stanza. The doctrine of the Three Classes existed up to the time when Yasna Ha 11 § 6 was written, since in that passage, only the Three Classes have been mentioned. This doctrine was in course of time, further developed into Four Classes, priest, warrior, peasant and workman, as we find in Ys. 19 § 17. Now this doctrine of the 4 classes is found only in two places in the Regveda, *viz.*, in Rv. I-113-6 and X-90-12. The first of these passages has been rightly regarded as a later interpolation. The second runs thus ब्राह्मणोस्य मुखमासीत् । बाहू राजन्यः कृतः । ऊरू तदस्य यद् वैश्यः । पद्भ्यां शूद्रो अजायत ॥

"The Brahman was his (Purusha's) mouth; of both his arms the Rājanya (=Khshatriya) made; his thighs became Vaishya ; from his feet the Sudra was produced." This stanza also belongs to a later age (*vide* stanza No. 9). The doctrine of the 4 classes was working in full swing in the days of the Bhagvatgitā (B. C. 3rd century) and the Manusmriti (B.C. 2nd century), and has been handed down in tact to our own times. Similarly on the Zoroastrian side, the doctrine has continued to remain in full force ever since it was established though with some modification. The priestly classes both Indian and Iranian, who were the repositories of knowledge and who monopolised all learning to themselves were so fascinated with this doctrine of the classes that they have always done their utmost to keep it in tact with a view to maintain their supremacy.* As there is no mention whatever of the Three Classes in the Rigveda, and the doctrine of the Four Classes is met with only in the latest book of the Rigveda, it is safe to assume with some scholars that the Indians were indebted to the Zoroastrians for this most attractive institution.

Considering the above facts I am inclined to believe that Prof. Teile's contention is erroneous and that Dr. Haug's theory that the separation of the Aryans and the Iranians took place after the religious schism and was the direct result of the latter, must be accepted.

Home of the Vedic people.

Let us now say a few words about the home of the Vedic people. The ancient home of the Aryans was not situated in the Panjab as is often wrongly supposed ; it was situated in Central Asia, in the country washed by the Sarasvati and the Rasâ.

When Rv. VI-61 was written, the Vedic Aryans were living on the banks of the Sarasvati ; for, the author says in verse No. 9 सा नो विश्वा अतिद्विषः स्वसॄः अन्याः ऋतावरी । अतन् अहेव सूर्यः ॥ "She has spread us beyond all foes, beyond her sisters, holy one, as the sun spreads out the days."

Also in the verse No. 14 we read :—"May we not go from thee (Sarasvati) to distant countries." In Rv. VII-96-2 we are told that a Vedic tribe named Purus dwelt on the grassy banks of the Sarasvati. For reasons already stated the Sarasvati was the river on the banks of which, was situated the country known as Harakhaiti in the Avesta, which was near the modern Kandhar. It was near this country that the Vedic people once lived.

It also appears from Rv. I-112-12 that the Vedic Aryans lived on the banks of another river named रसा which was the *Ranghâ** of the Avesta.

After stating that the Ashvins helped, in different ways, the Vedic rishis Atri, Aushija, (Kakshivân) and others, the writer says that the river Rasâ was "made to swell full with water floods." Evidently it was on the banks of this river that the said Vedic rishis lived. It is to be noted that here and in a few other passages in the Rigveda, the Rasâ is an actual river on the surface of this earth, although in Rv. IX 41-6 and other places, it makes its appearance as a mythical river ; the reason being that when the people living on its banks had moved away from it they only remembered it by name. Prof. Max Muller thus observes (in his Vedic Hymns I-323) : "The Rasâ known to the Zoroastrians as the Ranghâ, was originally the name of a river, but when the Aryans moved away from it into the Panjab, it assumed a mythical character and became a kind of Okeanos, surrounding the extreme limits of the earth."

That the Deva followers lived on the banks of the Rasâ is corroborated from Vendidad I-20 : "Ahuramazda created the 16th city near the waters of the Ranghâ ; and in opposition to Him, the Angro-mino, full of plague created the oppression (*zyâm*)† produced (*lit.* given) by the Devas and the spread (*aiveshtâra*)‡ of attacks (*taojyâ*¶) on the country."

* A curious example of this may be given from the last chapter of the Saddar, wherein the writer enjoins that Pahlvi should be taught only to a priest. Similarly in Gautama's Institutes of Sacred Law XII-4 to 6 we read "If a Sudra listens intentionally to (a recitation of) the Veda" his ears should be filled with (molten) tin or lac. If he recites (Vedic texts) his tongue should be cut out. If he remembers them, his body shall be cut in twain."

* Oxus or Jaxartes (see Modi's Dic.)

† *Zyâm*—from ज्या "to do harm," from which we have also *zyâna* (=ज्यान) oppression." The root *zyâ* is used as a nominal base ; cf. *dâ* =" wisdom " from the root *dâ*.

‡ Cf. Sk. प्रसार.

¶ From *tuj* (तुज्) "to injure;" Cf. Vedic तुज् ="to attack." (See C. E. I. Vol. I p. 26.

From this passage we gather that the Ahuramazdians established their 16th city on the banks of the river Ranghâ, which was often attacked by the followers of the Deva religion.

Were the Dasyus the non-Aryans of the Panjab?

Here we shall once again revert to the Dasyus, about whom Dr. Geiger thus remarks (in C. E. I. Vol. I p.35): "That by the latter name (=Dasyu) the non-Aryans of the Panjab are meant, probably no scholars will deny." I do not agree with the worthy Doctor for the following reasons:

(1) We have seen that the river Rasâ (or Ranghâ) was well known to the writer of Rv. I-112-12 who lived on its banks, and also that in later times when the Aryans had moved away from it to settle into the Panjab, the river assumed a mythical character. Now the same Vedic writer in the very next stanza mentions a prince named *Trasadasyu*—a name which carries with it the sense of a "terror to the Dasyus." It is clear that the Vedic Aryans who possessed such a name must have already come into contact with the Dasyus before they went to the Panjab. Evidently therefore the Dasyus must have belonged to some place between the Ranghâ and the Panjab.

(2) The rishi Bharadvâja wrote the Hymns Nos. 1 to 30, 37 to 43 and 53 to 74 of Rv. VI. As we have seen above the author states in the Hymn No. 61 that the Vedic people who were then living on the banks of the Sarasvati(=Harakhaiti) were driven there "beyond all their foes" (see verse No. 9); and in the verse No. 14 he prays that the Vedic people "may not go to distant countries from the Sarasvati." Now this author mentions the Dasyus in several places in his writings; *e.g.*, in Rv. VI-17-8 we find "Indra, thou alone hast tamed the Dasyus." As the Vedic Aryans had not proceeded to the Panjab, as they had been driven by their foes from their habitations only as far as the Sarasvati near Kandhar, the Dasyus do not appear to be the aborigines of the Panjab, as Dr. Geiger would have us believe.

(3) In Rv. X-123-4 we have the mention of the rishis first going to India and settling on the banks of the Sindhu. The passage is ऋतेन यंतो अधिसिंधुमस्थुः Mr. Sen thus translates the same: "Going in the right (=straight) direction they (the rishis) settled on the banks of the Sindhu" (see Research and Review Vol. I Part I p. 32). Mr. Sen observes "The 4th Rik is of very great importance. It speaks of the coming of the Pitris to India and of their settling on the banks of the Sindhu." This would show that the Aryans had not moved to settle into the Panjab up to the time of the 10th Book of the Rigveda, which admittedly belonged to a comparatively recent age.

PART IV.

Date of Zarathushtra.

We now come to the most important part of our subject, namely the date of Zarathushtra, which we shall try to determine from different standpoints.

If Zarathushtra belonged to the times of the Rigveda, its date would be the date of our Prophet.

Prof. Griffith on the date of the Rigveda.

The following are the remarks of Prof. Griffith about the date of the Rigveda: "Independently of the evidence afforded by Iranian tradition, there can be no reasonable doubt of the great antiquity of the Rigveda Samhitâ, which with the exception of the Egyptian monumental records and papyrus rolls and the recently discovered Assyrian literature is probably the oldest literary document in existence. But it seems impossible to fix with anything approaching to certainty any date for the composition of the hymns. In the first hymn of Book I ancient and recent or modern rishis or seers are spoken of and there is other internal evidence that some hymns are nuch older than others. Colebrooke came to the conclusion, from astronomical calculations, that a certain Vedic calendar was composed in the 14th century before the Christian era, from which it would follow that as this calendar must have been prepared after the arrangement fo the Rigveda and the inclusion of the most modern hymns, the date of the earliest hymn might be carried back, perhaps, some thousand years. The correctness of Colebrooke's conclusions, however has been questioned and some recent scholars consider that his calculations are of a very vague character and do not yield any definite date. In the absence of any direct evidence, the opinions of scholars vary and must continue to vary with regard to the age of the hymns of the Rigveda. The reasons, however (to quote Prof. Weber) by which we are fully justified in regarding the literature of India as the most ancient literature of which written records on an extensive scale have been handed down to us are these:—In the more ancient parts of the Rigveda Samhita, we find the Indian race settled on the north-western borders of India in the Panjab and *even beyond the Panjab*, on the Kubhâ (the Kophen or Kabul river) in Kabul. The gradual spread of the race from these seats towards the east, beyond the Sarasvati and over Hindustan as far as the Ganges can be traced in the later portions of the Vedic writings almost step by step. The writings of the following period, that of the epic consist of accounts of the internal conflicts...as for instance the Mahabharata or of the spread of Brahmanism towards the south, as for instance, the Ramayana........What a series of years, of centuries must necessarily have elapsed before this boundless tract of country inhabited by wild and vigorous tribes, could have been brought over to Brahmanism?' "

Was the North Pole the first Home of the Vedic Aryans?

From certain passages in the Rigveda, etc., Mr. B. G. Tilak in his "Arctic Home in the Vedas" has concluded that the Vedic Aryans lived on the north pole in olden times, that up to the advent of the great ice age, the climate of the north polar regions was not so chill as at present and that after the great deluge on account of the extremely cold climatic conditions our Vedic ancestors came down and settled in Central Asia.

Judged by the internal evidence of the Rigveda itself, Mr. Tilak's theory is found to be slightly inaccurate,

The more probable theory seems to be that our Vedic fore-fathers lived in the Aryavarta on the banks of the rivers Sarasvati and Rasâ, that a few adventurers left their native place and colonised the distant lands in Asia, Europe, &c., and went even as far as the circumpolar regious and there established a colony at the time when the climate was genial and fit for human habitation and that the great flood compelled them to return to their mother country.

Sarasvati the Home of the Aryans.

The river Sarasvati is wrongly indentified by some with the Indus, which latter was the Hapta—Hindu of the Vendidad. As already stated Sarasvati was a river, whereon stood the country known as Harakhaiti in the Vendidad and which was situated somewhere near the modern Kandhar. It was on the banks of the Sarasvati that the ancient Aryans first lived, as appears from Rv. II 41-17 त्वे विश्वा सरस्वति श्रितायूंषि देव्यां । "On thee divine Sarasvati, all the generations have their stay." Also in Rv VI-61-14 the poet thus prays. "O Sarasvati......let us not go from thee to distant countries." It appears that the Vedic people had not till then moved away from it to settle into distant countries.

Circum-polar Dawn.

Let us now turn to Rv. VII—76-3 and see what the rishi Vasishtha says therein तानि इत् अहानि बहुलानि आसन् या प्राचीनं उदिता सूर्यस्य । यतः परि जार इव आचरन्ती उषः ददृक्षे न पुनः यतीव ॥

"Many days* have verily passed since the rising of the sun aforetime; † and about which, O Dawn, you are seen moving on, as towards a lover and not like one (= woman) who forsakes." The author wants to say that a period of several days has elapsed between the first appearance of the dawn and the actual rising of the sun which followed it. It is clear that the writer was acquainted with what is ordinarily called a *day* (since he uses that word) and that he must have been residing in the polar regions where the dawn is of much greater length than our dawns. It follows that the writer must have once lived in Central Asia and must have subsequently gone to the polar or circum-polar regions. This conclusion is corroborated by the Hymns Nos. 88 and 89 of Rv. VII, some passages whereof we propose to consider here.

Vasishtha going to the Polar regions.

In Rv. VII-88-3 we read "When Varuna and I embark together and urge our boat into the midst of ocean, when we ride over the ridges of waters, we will swing within that swing and be happy." Here we are told that the rishi and the god Varuna started together on a voyance or in other words, the rishi started on a voyage by the favour of the god.

The next verse I translate thus:— "Varuna placed the rishi Vasishtha the singer in a boat and made him a good worker (at his oars) through his might, when on a fine day of days *the heavens broadened and the dawns (lengthened).*" Here we find that Vasistha moved on until he reached the circumpolar regions, where the dawns are of considerably greater length.

Then we come to the most important passage Rv. VII-88-7.

ध्रुवासु त्वासु क्षितिषु क्षियन्तो व्यस्मत्पाशं वरुणो मुमोचत् । अवो वन्वाना अदितेः उपस्थाद् यूयं पात स्वस्तिभिः सदा नः ॥

I translate the verse as under:—

"While we live in *these polar regions* and win favour from the lap

* The commentators are not right when they take अहन् (= day) to mean "splendour." In Rv. VI-9-1 अहन् is applied to dark as well as bright period of time. In Rv. I—165-4 Sayana says that अहः includes night.

† Lit. "Verily many were those days which were aforetime at the uprising of the sun."

of Aditi (= earth), may Varuna untie the bond that binds us. Protect us, O you (gods) with blessings ever more." The writer is so pleased with this new colony that he prays that so long as he is alive on this earth, he may not again come into contact with his fellows in the mother country.

It may be mentioned here that the words ध्रुवासु क्षितिषु have been translated "fixed habitations;" the words are so simple that it is a matter of surprise that the commentators have not seen any reference to the Poles in them.

We gather from the above passage that some Vedic Aryans had in olden times left their mother country to establish a colony in the polar countries.

Deluge story in the Rigveda.

But the story of Vasishtha does not end here; for, in the very next Hymn (No. 89)—which, however seems to be a much later production—there is an allusion to the Great Deluge. Before we consider that Hymn, let us for a moment turn to Rv. VII-87-1 which I think shoulp form part of the Hymn No. 89. The verse runs thus: "Varuna cut out a path for the sun and led the ocean floods of rivers onwards. Like a horse let loose among the mares (*i.e.*, with great speed) he made mighty floods for days together." Here there is a clear reference to the Great flood and yet the translators do not say a word about it.

Vedic Noah's Arc.

Rv. VII-89-1 says: मोषु वरुण मृन्मयं गृहं राजन् अहं गमं । मृळा सुक्षत्र मुळय ॥
I translate the passage thus:—

"O King Varuna, let me quickly enter into the house of clay. Good Lord, have mercy, have pity." All the translators taking मो षु as two separate words give the translation as "Let me *not* enter into the house of clay, that is to say, let me not be buried in the earth." I am of opinion that here at any rate मोषु is used in the Avestan sense. If we are to study Avesta by the light of Sanskrit, why should we not study Sanskrit by the light of Avesta? The meaning I have given above becomes clearer if we remember that among the Vedic people, cremation (and not burial) was the general method of the disposal of the dead. Moreover as we shall presently see, the author was in the midst of floods and so it would be absurd to talk of his being buried in the earth. It appears that the house of clay referred to in the above passage was something like the Vara of Jamshed mentioned in the Vendidad. Both the Avesta and the Rigveda agree that the Vara was not a mere ship—exactly like the ship of the Jewish Noah or Babylonian Xisuthros or Greek Deukalion or post-Vedic Manu—but that it was an earthen structure built on a ship.

Then follow the verses Nos. 2 to 5: "O Thunderer, when I move along tremulous like a windblown leather bag, have mercy, have kindness, good Lord. O powerful God, through want of strength I went astray. Thirst found thy worshipper, though he stood in the midst of flood-waters. O Varuna, whatever the offence may be, which we men committed against the heavenly host, when through want of thought we violated thy laws, punish us not for iniquity, O God." Here we find that the rishi had started to go back to his mother country; he therefore prays Varuna to be merciful.

Slightly deviating from our subject we shall note here the Babylonian description of the great flood which closely resembles that of the Rigveda. Parnapishtim speaks to Gilgamesh "The city of Shurippak, a city which as thou knowest lies on the Euphrates was corrupt; so that the gods thereof decided to bring a rain storm upon it. All of the great gods, Anu their father, Bel the warrior, their counsellor, Ninib the bearer of destruction......were with them to proclaim their resolve to the reed-huts (the ordinary houses of Babylonia).

Ea sends a special message to Parnapishtim, an inhabitant of Shurippak thus: O man of Shurippak, son of Kidem-Marduk *erect a house, build a ship*; abandon your goods and look after the souls; throw aside your possessions and save your life. Load the ship with all kinds of living things. Over you a rain storm will come; men, birds and beasts will all perish.......

Thus I built six stories, so that the whole consisted of seven apartments. The interior I divided into 9 parts......All that I had, I loaded on the ship......With living creature of all kind I loaded it.......Upon the first appearance of the dawn there arose from the horizon dark clouds, within which Rammon caused his thunder to resound......Rammon's whirl-wind sweeps the heavens and all light is changed to darkness...... Brother looks not after brother, man cares not for another. In the heavens even the gods are terrified at the storm......The gods including Anunnaki wept with Istar. The gods in their depression sat down to weep, pressed their lips together and were overwhelmed with grief. The storm could no longer be quieted. For six days and nights, wind, rain, storm, hurricane swept along. When the seventh day arrived the storm began to moderate.

Parnapishtim says: Bitterly weeping I looked at the sea; for, all mankind had been turned to clay...... I opened a hole......and dumbfounded I sat down and wept. Tears flowed down my face. I looked in all directions—naught but sea. After 12 double hours an island appeared. We approached the mountain Nisir (—protection)."

I have shown above that the Vedic people had at one time colonised the north polar regions. That the Vedic men did actually inhabit the polar regions has been proved beyond any doubt; still in order to satisfy the sceptics, I think it right to adduce a few proofs from Rigveda, &c., showing that our forefathers did once colonise the polar countries.

Long Dawns.

(1) Rv. I-113-13 शश्वत् पुरा उषा व्युवास देवी अथो अद्य इदं व्यावो मघोनी । अथो व्युच्छात् उत्तरान् अनु द्यून् अजरा अमृता चरति स्वधाभिः ॥

"Previously the goddess dawn shone *continuously* and shows this light to-day richly. So will she shine *for days to come, young, immortal* she moves with pleasure." Mr. Tilak says that पुरा refers to the by-gone age (युग) but I think it can be taken to refer to the past.

(2) In ऐ० ब्रा० IV-7 it is said that before commencing the Gavâm-ayana sacrifice, a long recitation of 1000 verses is to be made by the priest. The time for the recitation is after *midnight* when the darkness of the night is about to be relieved by the light of the dawn" (see Rv. VII 67-2 & 3). In तै० सं० II-1-10-3 we are told that sometimes the recitation, though commenced at the proper time, ended long before sunrise and in that case the Samhita requires that a certain animal sacrifice should be performed. Apastamba (XIV-1-2) after mentioning the above sacrifice adds that even all the ten mandals of the Rigveda may be recited if necessary. This shows that in those days the period abovementioned must have been exceedingly long.

(3) In तै० सं० IV-3-11 we find that the dawns were 30 in number, that they went round and round in 5 groups reaching the same appointed place and having the same banner for all. We shall summarize some of the verses. Verse (1)—"This verily is she that dawned first......" Verse (2): "Moving together in a common abode, the two dawns, the two wives of the sun.....move about.".

Verse (3): "The three maidens move along the path of Rita—one protects the projeny, one the vigour and one the ordinance of the pious." Verse (4): "That which was the fourth acting as rishis, on the two wings of the sacrifice, has become the four-fold *stoma.*" Verse (5): "The creator created five and five sisters of them." Verse (6): त्रिंशत स्वसार उपयंति निष्कृतं समानं केतुं प्रतिमुंचमानाः । ऋतून् तन्वन्ते कवयः प्रजानतीः मध्ये छंदसः परियंति भास्वतीः ॥

"The thirty sisters bearing the *same banner* move on to the appointed place. They the wise create the seasons; refulgent, knowing, they go round amid songs."

तै० सं० V-3-4-7 explains the above verses thus: न वा इदं दिवा न नक्तं आसीत् । अव्यावृतं ते देवा: एता: व्युष्टी: अपश्यन् । ता उपादत् ततो वा इदं व्यौच्छत् ॥

"It was *undistinguishable*; neither was it day nor night. The gods perceived these dawn-bricks; they laid them. Then it (= sun) shone forth." These verses conclusively show that the Vedic rishi had actually seen the polar dawn, which extended over a period of 30 consecutive days.

Long Day.

We shall once again consider Rv. VII-76-3 which we have already quoted "Verily many were those days which were aforetime at the uprising of the sun; and about which, O Dawn, thou art seen moving on as towards a lover but not like one (= woman) who forsakes."*

Sayana is puzzled as to how the word "*days*" (अहानि) could be applied to a period of time anterior to sun-rise; for, he says "the word अह: is used only to denote such a period of time, as is invested with the light of the dawn;" he therefore goes back to the root-meaning and renders the word as "splendour." This meaning however is not tenable, as it is quite unusual. We do not know of a single passage where the word carries that sense. In Rv. VI-9-1 it is said that अहश्च कृष्णं अह: अर्जुनं च. There is a *dark day* and a bright day." Here if we render अह कृष्ण as dark splendour," there is a contradiction in terms. Mr. Tilak finds fault with Sâyana but is himself driven into a corner; for, a man who is a resident of the north pole and has never seen the equatorial regions is not likely to have any idea of an ordinary *day* (अह:). This verse therefore leads us to suppose that the Vedic people must have been at first the residents of Central Asia and must have subsequently gone to the polar regions.

But Mr. Tilak tries to meet the above inference thus: "In such passages the word *day* or *month* simply denotes a measure of time equivalent to 24 hours or 30 days... ...It is quite possible to mark the periods of 24 hours by the rotations of the celestial sphere or the circumpolar stars and these could be or *rather must have been termed days* (the italics are mine) by the inhabitants of the place." On p. 48 he says "To the observer at the north pole, the completion of horizontal circuit of the sun or of the stars will serve as a measure of ordinary days or period of 24 hours."

* Mr. Tilak explains the stanza thus: "There are three clauses one principal and two adjectival. The principal clause asserts that those days were many. The first relative clause states that 'the days were those which were aforetime at the uprising of the sun,' that is 'which preceded the uprising of the sun.' But if the days preceded the rising of the sun, one might think that they were pervaded with darkness. The second relative clause therefore states that though those days were anterior to the rising of the sun, still they were such that 'the Dawn was seen to move after or about them as after a lover and not like a woman who forsakes.' In short the verse states (1) that many days passed between the appearance of the first morning beams and sun-rise and (2) that these days were faithfully attended by the Dawn, meaning that the whole period was one of continuous dawn, which never vanished during the time."

Mr. Tilak does not sppear to have been satisfied wtth his own explanation, given above; for he proceeds "In the first Chapter of the old Testament it is said 'God created heaven on the first day......while the sun was created on the fourth'. Here the word day is used before the sun was created.'" Mr. Tilak forgets that the Vedic verse was written by a man who had actually seen the phenomena; whereas the statement in the Bible was the utterance of God.

But says Mr. Tilak "We need not affect a hyper-critical spirit in examining the Vedic expression in question." Such a kind of argument requires no answer.*

Long Darkness.

In Rv. X-124-1 Agni is said to have "stayed too long in long darkness." (ज्योग एव दीर्घं तम आशयिष्ठाः)

In Atharva Veda XIX-47-2 the poet cries out that the night's yonder boundary is not seen (न यस्याः पारं ददृशे) and therefore he thus addresses her "O specious dark night, may we uninjured, safely reach thy end; O dear one, may we safely reach thy end."

In तै० सं० we are told that अव्युष्ट्यै वा एतस्यै पुरा ब्राह्मणाः अभैपुः

"Formerly the Brahmans were afraid that it would not dawn." This cannot refer to long winter nights, as Sayana suggests; for, the word "formerly" is very suggestive.*

The Brahmans were so much afraid of long darkness, that they thought it fit to perform penance; for, in तै० सं० II-1-2-4 we are told that "as the sun did not rise, the Deva-followers performed penance." (असौ आदित्यो न व्यरोचत तस्मै देवाः प्रायश्चित्तिं ऐच्छन्)

Exactly at the north pole the long night would continue for 6 months and similarly the long day would last for 6 months and in circum-polar regions the year would consist of one long night and day. This fact is referred to in several places. (1) in तै० सं० III-9-22-1 it is stated एकं वा एतत् देवानां अहः यत् संवत्सर : "That which is a year is but a single day of the gods." (2) Mahabhartha III-164 रात्रिर्दिवसश्च तेषां संवत्सरेणैव समानरूपः "night and day is equal to their year." (3) Manusmriti I-67 दैवे राज्यहनी वर्षे "Among the demons, night and day form a year." (4) Vendidad II-41 *Taechit ayare manyante* yat yâre. "They consider one year as a day." It is important to note that this statement is made in connection with the Vara of Jamshed. In the immediately preceding passage we are told that "the stars, moon and sun appear to rise and set *once*," which must mean *once a year* in the case of the fixed stars and the sun, and *once a month* in the case of the moon; for, there is no propriety in saying that they rise once a day.

All the above passages prove that at one time, the Aryans lived in the polar country, which however was simply a colony.

---

* Rv. X-138-3 where we find that "the sun unyoked his car in the midst of heaven" does not, I think, help us to prove the Arctic theory. In support of this theory Mr. Tilak places great reliance upon Fravardin Yasht § 57 where we are told that "the sun, moon and stars remained stationary for a long time through the oppression of the Devas, before the Fravashis showed them the path of Asha." I am inclined to think that this passage refers to the state of the world at its commencement t has nothing to do with the polar regions.

* Mr. Tilak also relies upon Vend. VIII-4 to 10 where it is stated that in heavy rains, snow, storm or darkness the lifeless body may be kept at home in a Kata for 2 nights, 3 nights or a month long. This refers clearly to the northern Persia. We should not rely upon such passages to prove the Arctic theory.

Deluge story in Shatapatha Brahmana.

After the great deluge caused by the heavy ice-floods, Manu the ancestor of the Hindus thought of sail ing back to his mother country. This deluge story has heen also narrated in Shatapatha Brahmana I-8-1-4 to 6. A large fish * informed Manu † that in such and such a year the flood will come when he should prepare a ship and enter it. Manu did accordingly. The fish then swam up to him and to its horn he tied the rope of the ship and by that means he passed swiftly up to the yonder *northern*‡ mountain (एतं उत्तरंगिरिं).

Now if we suppose that Manu was unacquainted with Central Asia, and that his mother land was in the north pole, then since he had gone down towards the south, he should have called the mountain where he landed the *southern* mountain, and not the northern one. But the important argument that Arya-Varta in Central Asia was the mother country is firstly as seen above the direct evidence in Rv. VII—88 to the polar regions and secondly the fact that the rishis who talked of long and eternal dawns, days and nights knew also of the ordinary dawns, days and nights (Cf. Rv. VII —71-1, VII—42-5).

As to the position of Arya-Varta we find from Manusmriti II—20-17 that सरस्वतीदृषद्वत्योः देवनद्योर्यदन्तरं । तं देवनिर्मितं देशं ब्रह्मावर्तं प्रचक्षते ॥ "The region between the divine rivers Sarasvati and Drishadvati is called Brahmavarta (=¶Aryavarta). Sarasvati was the river Harakhaiti near Kandhar. Drishadvati was probably the river Dârej in Iranvej (see Bund., Ch. 20). Thus Aryavarta or Iranvej seems to have been situated in the Central Asia, which was the mother land of the Aryans.

From the arguments advanced above we arrive at certain important results: (1) that the primitive home of the Aryan people was Central Asia, (2) that some of the Aryans thence migrated to the North Polar regions, (3) that owing to the great deluge these emigrants had to return to their mother country, (4) that the deluge happened in the days of the Rigveda, (5) and that if Zarathushtra was a contemporary of the Rigvedic rishis, the date of the Rigveda, as also that of the great flood would be the date of Zarathushtra.

Yima Vivanghan.

If Zarathushtra belonged to the times of the deluge, we establish (what might at first sight appear) a startling proposition, namely that Zarathushtra was a contemporary of Yima (= Jamshed). This may seem to violate all traditions but on a careful consideration it will be found that that is not so.

In Yasna Ha 32 § 8 Zarathushtra refers to Yima thus: "Of (or among) *these* sinners Yima Vivanghan has been heard—who in order to please us men reviled the Lord of the world." The demonstrative adjective "these" shows that the writer actually points out the sinners, one of whom is Yima. As already seen the Ha No. 32 is a historical chapter of the Gathas, in which Zarathushtra mentions some of his most wicked contemporaries. Thus there is a strong reason to believe that the above Yima who was probably a great ruler was also a contemporary of our Prophet.

The expression "in order to please *us* men" shows that Zarathushtra might have been one of the subjects of the King.

* Vishnu in the form of fish.

† The seventh Manu, a king called वैवस्वत मनु.

‡ This northern mountain is supposed to be the Hindukush mountain but my opinion is that it was the Haraberezaiti mountain which was on the north of Iranvej.

¶ आर्य = Airyana वर्त = *vasha*, *vesha*, then *Veja*. ष् is changed to ज्. Similariy *Drishad*=*dereshad*=*deresha*=*dereja*=*dâreja*.

The Yima of the Vendidad and the Shahnâme seems to have been a pious and God-fearing man at first* ; but subsequently he became so very proud that he even went to the length of reviling Ahuramazda and proclaiming himself the creator of the world. (Cf. Vend. II-6 and Shahname). This brought about his fall and he was thenceforth looked upon as a wicked sinner. This unhappy incident of his life is alluded to in Ha 32 § 8 and is corroborated by the following vivid description in the Shahnâme :

"He suddenly turned his eyes towards his great throne, he did not find his equal on the earth. That God-knowing king became proud, turned away from God and became ungrateful. He called *great men*†.from the army and spoke these undignified words 'I do not know any one in this world except myself. Art is become known in this world through me. No famous king has seen the kingly throne as I have seen. I have decorated this world with beauty. This earth has become whatever I wished her to be. Your appetite, sleep and rest are owing to me. All that you wear and all your desires are owing to me. Greatness and kingdom are mine. Who says that there is any Lord besides myself? The world regained health through the medicine (I prescribed), so much so that sickness and death did not destroy any one. Although several kings may have flourished in this world, still who has kept back death as I have done. Know that you have life and vitality through me. He is a demon who will not turn towards me. When you know that I have done all this, you should look upon me as the creator of the world.' "

From the second chapter of the Vendidad we find that Jamshed, while he was pious, had been given a warning by Ahuramazda about the advent of the great ice-flood and had been asked to build a *vara* which was most probably a ship with buildings built thereon. The story of the deluge stops short abruptly in the Vendidad, but two important points attract our notice ; first that in those regions the year consisted of but one day and night—they being the polar regions, and secondly that the *ahu** (temporal lord) and *ratu*† (spiritual lord) in the *vara* were respectively, Urvatannar (the third) son of Zarathushtra) and Zarathushtra himself. It seems to me that the writer wants to convey by the latter statement that Zarathusntra was appointed *ratu* or high priest soon after the *vara* had landed on the soil of Central Asia,—in other words soon after the subsidence of the deluge. This is not a mere guess but has the historical testimony of Clemens as we shall presently see. Thus Jamshed, the hero of the flood would be a contemporary of Zarathushtra and would be rightly allotted some space in the historical chapter of the Gaths after his fall.

Was the Vara of Jamshed originally a country.

It is true that in the 29th Chapter of the Bundehishn we are told that the Vara-e-Jamkard was a country and that it was identical with Iranvej ; and hence it might be said that Zarathushtra became the spiritual head in this country established by Jamshed, long after the time of the latter. This line of argument can be met on the following grounds :—

(1) In the first Chapter of the Vendidad, we find the names of the sixteen countries established by the

* In Shâhnâme Jamshed is represented as saying "by favour of God I am a king and a priest. I shall keep back the hands of the wicked from doing evil deeds. I shall make the soul go the path of light."

† Cf. "in order to please *us* men" in Ys. 32-8.

* A chief, not necessarily a king.

† High priest.

Iranians ; but do not find therein the Avestan equivalent of the name Vara-e-Jamkard. If it was the same as Iranvej, why the original name was changed, we do not know.

(2) The deluge story is found in many nations and in almost all of them we have the mention of a ship or something like it.

(3) In Vend. II-22 we read: *Snaotho-vafra snaejâi barejishtaeibyo gairibyo bâmshnubyo Areduyâo.* "Falling snow would fall (so as to cover the space) from the depth of the Ardvisura to the highest mountains." Also the para. 24th runs thus: *Paro zimo aetanghâo dakhyeush anghat vâstrem. Iem âfsh paurva vazaidyâi. Pascha vitakhti vafrahe, abdacha idha Yima anguhe astvaite sadaydi.** "Before the winter there would be plenty of vegetation (*vâstra*) in (*lit.* of) this country. That the waters would push away first. Afterwards the melting of the ice and the clouds, O Yima, would bring destruction† in this corporeal world."

It is clear from the above that what Jamshed was asked to guard against was not mere cold winter, but a great flood attended with cold winter. The seventh chapter of the Bundehishn is clear beyond any doubt on this point that the flood was the result of heavy rains. It is therefore difficult to believe that the *Vara* was a sort of enclosure, much less a country which could afford any protection against the flood which covered the high mountains.

(4) Even if we admit that the Vara of Jamshed was a country established by him, still one point is clear that the last passage of the second Chapter in the Vendidad in which it is stated that Zarathushtra was the ratu of the Vara is intimately connected with Jamshed and the history of his time, because there is no reason to suppose that any extraneous matter would be incorporated into this chapter.

* *Sadaydi* from शाध् "to destroy."

† It is conclusively proved that before the advent of the Glacial epoch, a luxuriant forest vegetation, which can only grow and exist at present in the tropical and temperate climate, flourished in the high latitudes of Spitzbergen where the sun goes below the horizon from November till March See Arctic Home in the Vedas p. 22.)

Facts which prove that Jamshed was a contemporary of Zarathushtra.

(1) In the commencement of the second Chapter of the Vendidad Ahuramazda is asked "To whom among men did you *first* teach the Mazdayasni Zarathushtri religion excepting Zarathushtra," and the answer is "to Yima" The Mazdayasni Zarathushtri religion presupposes the existence of his founder, and if Jamshed learnt this religion after Zarathushtra, he must have been a follower of Zarathshtra.*

(2) The fact that Yima is mentioned in the historical Ha of the Gathas (namely Ha 32) wherein half a dozen contemporaries of Zarathushtra have been spoken of, shows that Yima also belonged to the time of Zarathushtra. It is also to be noted that in the above passage the writer points out a particular class of sinners (*aeteshâm aenanghâm*) one of whom was Yima.

(3) In the Homilis, of Clemens,† after wrongly identifying Zarathushtra with Nimrod, the writer says "Him the Greeks call Zoroaster. *After the great deluge*, he longed for empire and being a great magus, he forced by magical arts, the horoscopic star to give him the empire." This is practically what we find in Vendidad II-43, where we are told that Zarathushtra was the ratu in Jamshed's Vara. It is very likely that the empire referred to was the papal supremacy at Rae of which Zarathushtra was a *Dakhyuma* (=priestly governor) subsequently

* Scholars may not agree with me here, but it is a link in the argument which deserves to be seriously considered.

† See Zarathushtra in the Gathas p. 188.

contracted into Dakhyu or Dasyu by the Vedic writers. In the above quoted passage, Zarathushtra is represented as belonging to the times of the great flood to which Jamshed certainly belonged.

(4) We have seen that according to the Shatapatha-Brahmana, the seventh Manu was saved from the great flood. This Manu was the son of Vivasvat. The name of Yima's father was also Vivasvat (=Vivanghân) so that here we have some ground for the presumption that the Avestan Yima was identical with the Vedic Manu. Dr. Wilson sees an allusion to the great flood in Rv. II-33-13 where Manu is stated to have selected medicinal plants. Now we have seen that the writer of Rv. VI-21-11 suggests that Dasyu (Zarathushtra) stood only next to Manu.*

It is not wrong to suppose that the author wants to speak of Dasyu as if he was a contemporary of Manu (identical with Yima.)

(5) On this point the history of ancient Persia is also of great importance to us. We shall consider some of the facts in detail.

From the chronology given in the Bundehishn Ch. 34 we find that Jamshed ruled for 616½ years and subsequently went into exile for 100 years. After him came Zohak who ruled for 1000 years. Then came Faredun who ruled for 500 years. Then followed Minocheher who ruled for 120 years. Shahname agrees in all these particulars except as regards the reign of Jamshed which according to it lasted for 700 years. We however learn from Vendidad II that Jamshed ruled for more than 900 years and from Gosh Yt.§ 10 Ashi yt. § 30 and Vend. II-20 it seems clear that he ruled for 1000 years.

According to Shahname, Faredun married the two daughters of Jamshed named Erenvâch and Savanghvâch. This is somewhat corroborated by Gosh Yt.§ § 13-14 and other passages in the Avesta where Faredun prays that he may release from the hands of Zohak the two abovenamed ladies whom Zohak had forcibly married. It is inconceivable that Faredun a young man could have married the ladies after they were more than 2000 years old.

We learn from the Bundehishn Chap. 31 that from Gayomard, Yima was the 8th descendant, Zohak also was the 8th descendant, Faredun the 17th one, Minocheher the 29th one and Zarathushtra the 43rd one. Now since Zohak ruled for 1000 years after Jamshed—who was Zohak's contemporary—it would follow that he lived for 2000 years an idea which is quite ridiculous.

Science proves that the longevity of man cannot possibly extend beyond 125 to 150 years. In several places in the Rigveda we find that all that the rishis wish for is a life of 100 years. Cf. Rv. VII-66-16 "a hundred winters may we live;" also Rv. VII-101-6 "may this rite save me till my 100th year*."

Bundehishn has assigned a period of 283 years from Gayomard to Jamshed, and as 9 persons flourished dnring the period, each generation would consist of 30 years.

Also Gayomard has been assigned a period of 30 years. Mashyo appeared 40 years thereafter. If we omit these two periods, we have to distribute a period of 213 years among 7 persons. This gives a duration of 30 years to a generation

Vishtaspa was the 13th man and Zarathushtra the 14th man from Minocheher. It would follow that these two personages must have been the contemporaries which was actually the case. We know that Gusetâspa was 30 years of age when Zarathushtra was born. Now after

*.The same writer refers to Baetâs, Ushanâ and Rijishvan in the hymn immediately preceding.

* Berosus considered on astrological grounds that man might attain the age of, 116th year (Pliny Hist. Nat. VII-50).

the reign of Minocheher, Jube Tuhmaspân came to the throne and ruled for 5 years. According to Firdusi, he was 80 years old when he came to the throne. Thus between him and Zarathushtra there was a period of $80+5+15+150+60+120=430$ years and as 14 generations lived during the period, the duration of a generation would consist of 30 years.

In modern times also we find that a generation consists of 25 to 30 years.

But on the other hand we find that between Gayomard and Faredun (17 persons in all) a period of 2000 years expired. Thus each generation would be of 118 years. If we go up to Minocheher, a generation would be of $\frac{2500}{29}=86$ years; and if we go as far as Zarathushtra it would be of $\frac{2970}{43}=69$ years. It will be seen that the duration varies considerably at different stages and cannot be relied upon.

We have seen that Bundehishn assigns 500 years to the rule of Feredun. Firdusi however says that he ruled only for 50 years and then divided his kingdom among his three sons Selam, Tur and Iraj. It cannot be that either Bundehishn or Firdusi has committed a mistake. Both are probably right but the proper explanation has to be sought for from different standpoints.

We heve seen that in Yasna 32 § 8 Yima has been classed among the sinners. Now from Fr. Yt. we find that the Fravashis of wicked persons such as Zohak, Afrasiab and even Nodar have not been praised. How is it then that the Fravashi of Yima is remembered in Fr. Yt. § 130? * It appears that this latter Yima must have been a pious man, so that we find that even according to Avesta there were at least two Jamsheds, one pious and the other wicked.

In Fr. Yt. § 87 we are told that Gayomard was the first man who listened to the Commandments of Ahuramazda. He was thus the first prophet. Now according to the Bundehishn, Jamshed was the 4th king and 8th descendant from Gayomard. How is it then that Mirkhond mentions Jamshed as the 30th prophet? The most probable answer seems to be that there must have been several Jamsheds.

From the above circumstances it appears that Jamshed, Zohak and Faredun were most probably the names of dynasties* of kings ruling in different parts of Iran simultaneously. As the dynasty of Jamshed ruled for 1000 years we conclude that there were about 33 Jamsheds, taking the period of a generation at 30 years. Most of these were probably good rulers but the last was a wicked one. Now according to the Bundehishn, Zarathushtra was the 35th man from Jamshed. If this Jamshed was the *first* Jamshed, it would appear that Zararhushtra was a contemporary of the *last* Jamshed who had seen the great flood.

Date of Zarathushtra from the date of the deluge.

We have seen that Zarathushtra was a contemporary of the writers of the Rigveda, and also that the great flood broke out in the days of the Rigveda and was witnessed by the Vedic rishis. We have also tried to prove, independently of the Rigveda that Zarathushtra belonged to the times of the deluge. Thus either the date of the deluge or the date of the Rigveda would be the date of our prophet. Now according to the Bible chronology 2348 B. C. was *about* the date of the de-

* It may be urged that Av. writers praise good characteristics of even the most wicked persons; as in Afrin-e-Zarathustra "*Hazanghro bardhi Yatha Azoish Dahakai.*" This is not correct. In the above passage *Yaokhshti* is used both in good as well as bad sense. "May you be of 1000 clevernesses as Zohak was possessed of 1000 tricks."

* See Tarikhe Shahne Iran by Pallonji B. Desai pp. 280-281.

luge.* This would also be the date of Zarathushtra. This date is practically corroborated by not less than 9 ancient writers including Ctesias and Diodorus Siculus (both of the first century B C.) who place Zarathushtra 2200 years before Christ.† We shall see hereafter that 2500 B.C. would be the most probable date of Zarathushtra.

Date of the Rigveda according to Colebrooke.

Prof. Griffith in his introduction to the translation of the Rigveda says :—Colebrooke came to the conclusion from astronomical calculations that a certain Vedic calendar was composed in the 14th century B. C. from which it would follow that as this calendar must have been prepared after the rearrangement of the Rigveda and the inclusion of the most modern hymn, the date of the earliest hymn must be carried back some *thousand* years‡."

A Vedic calendar is given in the Atharva Veda XIX-7-2 to 4 and also in the Taittiriya Samhita, which mentions all the Nakshatras placing कृत्तिका first. Now from the Surya Siddhant of Burgess we find that "अश्विनी नक्षत्र coincided with the vernal equinox in 570 B. C., and since then it has been the first. Two thousand years before that date कृत्तिका was the first asterism." Thus कृत्तिका would be the first asterism in (2000-570=) 1430 B. C. which would also be the date of the Atharva Veda.

We however note that in the starry chart given by Burgess on page 468 of his book, the equator of the earth in the year 2350 B. C. meets the ecliptic very near the कृत्तिका नक्षत्र belonging to the constellation Taurus.

The above inconsistency is probably due to the following fact. Each asterism occupies about 13⅓ degrees, and every point in it moves 1 degree in about 71 6 years. Thus 13⅓ degrees would be traversed in about 950 years. Thus 1430 B. C. was the date when the last point of Krittika coincided with the sun on the vernal equinox ; and 1430+950=2380 B.C. was about the date when the first point coincided with the sun.

It should be noted that the initial point of the Hindu zodiac is 10 degrees west of the constellation Aries (see Plunket's Anc. Calendars and Constellations pp. 26 and 92). Thus the sun entered the last point of Aries 71 6 × 10 = 716 years before 570 A. D., *i. e.*, in 144 B. C. which was very nearly the calculation

* This seems to be approximately correct; for in Bund. VII where we have been given the description of the deluge we find that it broke out in the month of Tir belonging to the constellation Cancer which was the fourth from the Aries. Evindently therefore the Aries was the 1st constellation in those days; and the age of Aries commenced somewhere about 2500 B. C. Also from Shahname we find that when Jamshed came to the throne, the sun was in conjunction with the Aries on the day of the vernal equinox. If this happened at the beginning of the Aries age, the date would be 2500 B. C. In the Old Testament in the light of the Ancient East Vol. I p 56 it is said "Yao (a mythological emperor) restored the earth from the results of a flood like the Deluge about the year 2850 B. C." According to Abulhasan Kuschiar however the date of the deluge was 8102 B. C. (see Times Calendar). This does not seem to be quite accurate.

† See Ervad Modi's History of the Zoroastrian Religion in Gujerati p. 71.

‡ In Encyc. of India p. 1181 Colebrooke's calculation is given as under "According to Colebrooke, at the epoch of the Vedas the summer solstice was in the middle of Ashleshâ the 9th lunar mansion. Therefore Regulus was half a lunar mansion + 9°, that is 16°-40' east of the summer solstice at that time On the 1st January 1859 the longitude of Regulus was 147°-52'-80". Hence Regulus was at that date 57°-52'-80" east of the summer solstice. The summer solstice had therefore retrograded through 42 -12'-80" = 42.208 degrees since the epoch of the Vedas. And as the equinoxes and the solstices move backward on the ecliptic at the rate of 1° in 72 years, it must have occupied 70 × 42.208 = 8039 years to effect the change. Hence the age of the Vedas was 8089 on 1st Jan. 1869 or their date is 1181 B. C."

The 1st point of the Hindu zodiac is 10° west of Aries ; thus we should take the date back by 10 × 71.8 = 716 years.

of the Greek astronomer Hipparchus (who lived from 200 to 125 B. C.). Hipparchus found that in his time (150 B. C.) the sun entered the Aries at the vernal equinox. Now according to the Hindu system Aries occupies a space of 31 degrees in the Zodiac. Therefore the sun entered the first point of Aries in $(71 \cdot 6 \times 31) + 150 = 2269$ B. C.

Turning to Albiruni's India (translation by Sachau II-84 to 86) we find that "the two stars of Ashvini stand in our time (A. D. 1030) in two-thirds of the Aries (*i. e.*, between 10° to 20° Aries) and the time of Varâhamihir precedes our time by about 526 years. Therefore by whatever theory you may compute the motion of the fixed stars (or precession of the equinoxes) the Ashvini did in his time certainly stand in less than one-third Aries (*i e.*, they had not come in the precession of the equinoxes further than 1° to 10° Aries.)"

From the above it appears that the Ashvini became first 500 years before Varâhamihir (A. D. 504), that is in A. D. 4; and that 2000 years (that being the period which the two constellations Bharani and Ashvini would take to pass through $13\frac{1}{3} + 13\frac{1}{3}$ degrees, requiring $26\frac{2}{3} \times 71 \cdot 6 = 1933$ or approximately 2000 years). Thus according to Albiruni 2000 B C. would be the date when Krittika was the first asterism. (See also Plunket p. 94).

In his "Myths and Marvells of Astronomy" Proctor says at p. 340 "The sun and the Pleiades opened the year with the commencing spring in 2170 B.C."

Mr. Tilak gives 2500 B.C. as the date for the age of the Pleiades. In the Transactions of the Society of Biblical Archæology (p. 237) Professor Sayce says "The sun entered the first point of Aries at the vernal equinox in the time of Hipparchus and it would have done so since 2540 B.C. From that epoch backwards to 4698 B.C. Taurus ...would have introduced the spring."

I think (as we shall see hereafter) that it would not be wrong if we assign to the Rigveda and especially the earliest portions of it the date 2500 B.C.

Date of the Rigveda according to Plunket.

In the excellent book named "Ancient Calendars and Constellations" pp. 115-130 E. M. Plunket tries to prove the date of the Rigveda from some of the Vedic hymns. I shall briefly give here some of the arguments.

(1) Indra-Vritra Myth: Indra is primarily and essentially a personification of summer solstice, which is an important agricultural epoch in India. It brings with it the rainy season. Before this season all the land is parched and arid ... Indra as a personification of the season which so punctually brings the rain in India is an atmospheric god, the enemy of the demon of draught......But Indra is much more than this. According to the Rigveda "Indra is the highest of all," "Indra placed the sun high in the sky." "Indra tore off one wheel of the sun's chariot." "Indra stopped the tawny courses of the sun." All these phrases are at once to be clearly inrerpreted, if we think of Indra as the personification of summer solstice...... The demon of the solstitial Indra personified is not a snake-like cloud (*ahivritra*), it is the snake-like constellation known as Hydra ...... At about 4200 B.C. Hydra extended its enormous length for more than 90° along the invisible line known as the heavenly equator and was also bisected by the line known as the colure of the summer solstice...For an observer in the temperate zone, all through the nights of midwinter the whole length of the dreadful Hydra was at the above date visible above the hosizon. The dark midwinter season was therefore the time of the Hydra's greatest glory. At every season of the year except at

that of mid-summer, some portion of the monster's form was visible during the night. But at the summer solstice no star in the constellation might show itself for ever so short a time. This is true however of the latitude 40° N., a latitute considerably to the north of any part of India.

Note :—From the above remarks, it would follow that the Vedic people lived somewhere in the north. Could it be that they lived near Merv the latitude of which was 38°.? Plunket is somewhat inconsistent, as at one time she talks of India and at another time of the north. As we we shall presently see, Plunket assigns the date 3000 B. C. to the composition of the Vedas.

(2) INDRA-SOMA MYTH—Macdonell in his Vedic mythology says "in the Soma hymns there may occasionally lurk a veiled identification of ambrosia and the moon......though on the whole with a few exceptions .....the Soma god is a personification of the terrestrial plant and juice." The German writer Hillebrandt very strongly upholds the view that Soma in the Rigveda often signifies the moon and specially in Mandal IX. If we consider that Indra's conquest over Vritra represents the god of the summer solstice with his bright weapons conquering and driving from heaven and earth the constellation Hydra, we can easily understand how in this contest Indra might be strengthened by copious draughts of Soma, *i. e.*, by the bright light of the full moon flooding the heavens......At about 3000 B. C. the full moon of the mid-summer or solstitial season was always to be observed in the constellation Aquarius. With this thought in our mind, if we read Mandal IX. in which Soma is so often described as rushing impetuously to the pitcher and as surrounded by celestial waters, we can easily recognize an allusion to the *mid-summer full moon in the constellation Aquarius* ; and further when we read the legend so often repeated that the eagle brought the Soma to Indra, we have only to look at the celestial globe to see the eagle (Aquila) directing its flight at the pitcher of Aquarius......In Rv. IV-27 devoted to the Soma-bearing eagle, an allusion to the small but well-marked out constellation Sagitta (the arrow) may be detected.*

(3) APAM-NAPAT MYTH—Apâm-napât or " Agni in the waters " has been explained as suggesting "lightening" or "latent heat existing in water " or the "emission of flame from the surface of waters either in the shape of inflammable air or as the result of submarine volcanic action." Plunket explains the myth as "the fire of the sun in the celestial waters of Aquarius." At about 3000 B. C. the sun was in conjunction with Aquarius at the time of winter solstice. Those hymns therefore which dwell upon the myths of Agni hiding himself in, being born in and rising out of the waters may be considered as referring to the sun at the winter solstice in conjunction with Aquarius.

Date of the Rigveda according to Mr. Tilak.

Mr. Tilak says "in my Orion...I have shown that while the Taittriya Samhita and the Brahmans begin the Nakshatras with the Krittikas or Pleiades, showing that the vernal equinox then coincided with the aforesaid asterism (2500 B. C.) the Vedic literature contains traces of Mriga or Orion being the first of the Nakshatras and the hymns of the Rigveda or at least many of them which are undoubtedly older than the Taittiriya Samhita contain references to this period, that is, about 4500 B. C. approximately " (Arctic Home p. 420).

* Rv. IV-27-3 runs thus " when the hawk screamed (with exultation) on his descent from heaven and (the guardians of the Soma) perceived that the Soma was (carried away) by it, then the archer *Krishanu* pursuing with the speed of thought and stringing his bow, let fly an arrow against it."

It may be mentioned that Mr. Tilak takes the extreme limit into consideration. In order to determine the other end of the Orion age we should deduct 2100 years from the last date.

Age of the Rigveda.

I shall now give a few of the direct proofs about the date of the Rigveda—which are the results of my own investigations.

(1) In Rv. V-54-13 we have "O Maruts, let that wealth in thousands dwell with us, *which never vanishes like Tishya from the sky*." It is here stated in plain words that in the days of the writer the asterism Tishya appeared all night above the horizon. Tishya is the 8th asterism at present and is in the constellation Cancer. It is easy to see that the Cancer would appear *all* night when the sun is in *opposition* to it; or in other words when the earth is exactly between the sun and the Cancer. It follows that at that time the sun was in conjunction with the sixth constellation from Cancer, that is with Capricornus.

Now from the same hymn No. 54 of Rv. V. it appears that the author speaks about the rainy season or rather the middle of the rainy season. Compare the following · "Lightenings aglow with flame are flashing in your hands, O Maruts." "The Maruts inundate the earth with floods of pleasant meath." "with Maruts laden with their water casks, let the spring flow." "The waters sweeping rained are thundering on their way."

That the rainy season had at the time considerably advanced appears much clearer from the preceding hymn written by the same author. In Rv. V-53-6 and 7 we read "Munificent heroes, they (= the Maruts) have cast the heaven's treasury down for the worshipper's behoof (सुदानवो ददाशुषे दिवः कोषं अचुच्यवुः) ...The bursting streams have spread abroad in flood."

The rains commence in India in the middle of June, but the home of the Rigvedic people was in the north-west, somewhere near Kandhar and even beyond. We know that the commencement of the rains in Central Asia takes place in September-October. Consequently the author seems to write about the rains of November. At that time the sun was in the Capricornus. Thus the sun was in the Taurus at the spring equinox We shall see hereafter that the ancient Vedic year commenced in spring. As has been pointed out by Dr. Sayce the Taurus was the first sign between 4698 B.C. and 2540 B.C., when the above Rigvedic passage appears to have been written.

(2) In Rv. II-12-11 we have the exact date of the commencement of Indra's fight with Vritra: यं शंबरं पर्वतेषु क्षियन्तं चत्वारिंश्यां शरद्यन्वविन्दत्. As Mr. Tilak has shown in the Arctic Home pp. 279-282 this passage means that "Indra found Shambara dwelling on the mountains on the 40th day of autumn."

Now Vasanta or the spring commenced the year in the olden times; for in तै० सं० II-1-2-5 we find "There are three lustres of the sun, (one) in spring or in the morning, (one) in Grishma or the midday and (one) in winter or the evening." Here the three seasons have been compared with the three parts of the day, and as spring is compared with the morning, the first part of the day, it follows that it was the first season of the year.

Mr. Tilak says "Sharad is the fourth season of the year and the 40th day of Sharad would mean 7 months and 10 days or 220 days after the first day of Vasanta......In short the passage means that Indra's fight with Shambara or the annual conflict between light and darkness commenced on the 10th of October, if we take the year to have commenced with March." (See Arctic Home, p. 282.)

We have seen that the above passage of the Taittiriya Samhita mentions only three seasons and that seems also to be the case in Rv. I-164-48. Mr. Tilak, however, assigns six seasons to the year. If we assume the existence of three seasons, the day of Indra's fight would fall 8 months and 40 days after the commencement of the spring (=21st March) or about the 1st of January.

Now the story of the Shambara is mentioned in many places in the Rigveda, and everywhere it represents Indra's fight with Vritra (see Arctic Home, p. 281).

Indra's fight with Vritra would be marked by the appearance of the constellation Hydra in the skies and Indra's conquest over Vritra would be mythologically represented by the disappearance of the Hydra at night. Now on a reference to the Astronomical chart (plate No. X) given by Plunket (p. 121) we see that at about 3000 B. C. in Lat. 23 degrees N. the constellation Hydra would be visible throughout the night at winter solstice and invisible at summer solstice. It would follow that the earliest portions of the Rigveda were written about 3000 B. C.

(3) We have the most conclusive proof of the age of the Rigveda in Mandal III-56-2 to 4.

Verse No. 3—"The three—breasted and the three uddered Bull (= Taurus) who wears all forms, with a brood (प्रजा) in many places rules (पत्यते) majestic (माह्निनावान्) with his triple aspect, that Bull the father of the eternal ones."

Verse No. 2—"One immutable supports six burdens; the cows proceed to him the true, the highest. Near stand the three mighty ones, the coursers (अत्याः). Two are unconcealed (=are visible आगुहाः) one is invisible *(अदर्शि)."

Verse No. 4—"The bold one has known the ranks (पदवीः) of the Adityas."

Here the constellation वृषभ (= Taurus) is expressly mentioned.

He rules majestic, because he is the first constellation. The Adityas are the twelve months and we are told that the Taurus who is the supreme ruler, knows the successive order of the different months of the year. The verse No. 2 refers to a cluster of 7 stars whereof one is immovable and six are movable. Of these six stars three are big ones, two are visible and one invisible.

Evidently we have here a reference to the कृत्तिका नक्षत्र (=the asterism Pleiades) which forms a portion of the Taurus and consists of 7 stars. The three breasts and the three udders are probably the six stars of the Hyades. Their number is usually given as 5 but varies from 2 to 7. Hyades literally mean the rainy ones", and "the three udders" would also convey the idea of rain. "The brood in the many places" are the smaller stars in the Taurus.

That in the above passage, the constellation वृषभ (Taurus) is represented as the first one of the year appears from the following : (a) that he has been stated as ruling majestically; (b) that the cows or the rays of the sun proceed to him, in other words that the sun is in conjunction with him ; (c) that he has been called the true, the highest and the bold one ; (d) that he knows the order in which the months are named; (e) and that he is the father of the eternal ones, that is to say the stars or the constellations.

It would not be out of place to give here short descriptions of the Taurus, Pleiades and Hyades for comparison with the Vedic passages. *Taurus*, the bull is a constellation of

* The translators supposed the words to be गुहाः "concealed" and दर्शि "visible". I take the words to be आगुहाः unconcealed and अदर्शि=invisible. Just as आगाध is the same as अगाध so आगुहाः would be the same as अगुहाः

very great antiquity containing the Pleiades and the Hyades, two star clusters. Ptolemy catalogued 44 stars in the Taurus, Tycho Brahe 43 and Heveleus 51.

Pleiades were the seven daughters of Atlas and Pleione and sisters of the Hyades. Owing to grief at the death of their sisters, they were changed into stars by way of consolation. This group is particularly rich in bright stars and is full of *nebulosity.* The central star Alcyone and also the Pleione and the Atlas are of the third magnitude.

Hyades "the rainy ones" were in the Greek mythology, the daughters of Atlas and Aethra. Their number varies between 2 and 7. Their brother Hyas was killed by a snake. They lamented him so bitterly that Zeus out of compassion changed them into stars.

G. C. Lewis in the Astronomy of the Ancients (pp. 65-66) says "The constellation of the Pleiads consists according to Ideler of one star of the third magnitude, three of the fifth magnitude and two of the sixth magnitude and many smaller stars. It is therefore scarcely possible for the best naked eye to discern more than six. Hipparchus affirms that seven stars can be really perceived in a clear moonless night. The ancients designated the Pleiads as a constellation of seven stars and gave a fictitious reason for the fact that only six were visible. Some said that the seventh had been struck by lightening, others that it had been removed to the tail of the Great Bear. Ovid said that the seventh concealed herself out of shame for having bestowed her love upon a mere mortal, Sisyphus.

Alcyone the brightest of the Pleiads is considered to occupy the position of the central point, round which our universe of the fixed stars is revolving.

We thus see that the Taurus was was the first constellation when the Rigvedic passage in question was written ; and he was the first between 4698 B.C. and 2540 B.C. It was about the latter date that much of the Rigveda was written. Consequently the latter date would be the date of Zarathushtra.

PART V.

Date of Naotarians from Ashi Yasht.

Ashi Vanghuhi has been usually represented as the angel presiding over righteousness, good fortune and wealth. But I think that an important characteristic belonging to it has been lost sight of. The point that is first aimed at is to prove that Ashi is also the angel of the vernal equinox, which was a day of rejoicing among the Persians and was known as the Jamshedi Naoroz. We shall also prove that Mithra too was an angel who presided over the vernal equinox.* The propositions sought to be established being quite novel deserve our most careful attention. We shall therefore approach the subject from different standpoints.

We shall first consider a few of the passages of the Ashi Yashta. In para. No. 2 we are told that "He who praises Ashi with offerings praises Mithra with offerings." Here Ashi has been identified with Mithra (= the light of the sun)†. In Meher Yashta §66 Ashi is represented as "accompanying Mithra," and in §68 she is said to hold the chariot of Mithra."

In para. No. 3 of the Ashi Yt. she is represented as having *raya* "lustre" and *Kharenangha* "glory."

In para No. 6 she is addressed as *bânumaite*‡ (= with the sun). In Sanskrit भानु means the 'sun", hence the epithet *bânumaite* would lead us to suppose that the sun forms part of her paraphernalia.

* Similarly among the Hindus, Fâlgun-otsava or Holika is the festival of the spring equinox, held in honour of the god Krishna.

† Mithra is the angel of the sun's light; cf. Meher Yt. 13, 145, Vend. XIX-28. In Dâdestân 31-14 Mithra is said to be in the Taurus. As Dr. West says Mithra is used for the sun in this passage of the Dadestan.

‡ Bânu=भानु means the sun, and also the ray.

Ashi is also called *shâite bânubyo vyâite* "shining with rays and rejoicing."

In paras Nos. 17 to 22 there is a lively description of the birth of Zarathushtra. Ashi asks "who are you who are calling (or remembering) me, whose voice I heard, being the best of those who much call me? Then he who was Spitama Zarathushtra said thus (it is I)......At whose birth and prosperity the waters and the trees rejoiced, at whose birth and prosperity the waters and the trees began to grow. Then Ashi Vanghuhi of great dignity said thus 'O righteous Zarathushtra Spitama stand near me, ascend my chariot.' Thus speaking she gently patted him from right to left and left to right."

It appears from the above passages that Zarathushtra was born about the time of the vernal equinox when the waters begin to flow and the trees to grow, that the angel presiding over that day was pleased to hear the voice of Zarathushtra at his birth and that his voice was much sweeter than that of any other man.

FAROHARS CONNECTED WITH THE SPRING.—In Fr. Yt. § 49 we are told that the Fravashis come towards the village at the time of *Hamaspathmaedaya** (=*lit.* "that in which sacrifice is performed at the end of the year"), which is the last day of the year. We thus find that the Faro-

* The word *hamas* in Hamaspathmaedaya is = Sk. समा f. सम n. "year"; Cf. पापषम (= bad year), सुषम (= good year). The exact equivalent of *hamas* is समस् which is not found alone but is found in ऐषमस् (= happening in the year). *Path* is equivalent to Sk. पत् m. f. n. and पत m. (= flying away, ending). *Maedaya* is=Sk. मेध्य (= sacrificial thing). *Hamaspath* is the same as Sk. समांत (=end of the year). *Hamaspathmaedava* is a Bahuvrihi Comp. and an adjunct of *ratu* and means "that in which there is (performed) sacrifice at the end of the year." The expression *aretho-kerethana* which is usually found in connection with Hamaspathmaedaya, is equivalent to Sk. ऋतकतन "cutting of sacrifice or ऋतकृतं "performance of sacrifice."

hars come into this world at the end of the year.

From Yasna Ha 1st we see that Maidyozaremaya (= midspring) is the first gâhânbâra ; therefore Hamaspathmaedaya is the last gâhânbâra. Thus according to the Avesta the year began with spring. The same is found from Pahlvi writings. Now since the coming of the Farohars is placed at the end of Hamaspathmaedaya the last day of the year, it follows that this coming takes place very nearly at the commencement of spring.*

Again from Fr. Yt. § 93 we find that the trees and the waters rejoiced at the birth of Zarathushtra and began to flow. It is evident that Zarathushtra was born at the commencement of spring. Now from tradition and later Pahlvi literature we find that Zarathushtra was born in the commencement of the month Farvardin, the month of the Farohars. Here also we see the close connection of the Farohars with the beginning of spring. For this reason the month Farvardin would be most appropriately the month of the spring.

Now we arrive at the most important passage No. 66 in the Meher Yashta where we are told that "Mithra is accompained by Ashi, Pârendi, Kyâni Khureh, Dami Upaman and the Farohars." Mithra is the supreme lord over these divinities, he being mentioned first. We have seen that the Farohars presided over spring; therefore all their companions, such as Mithra, Ashi, &c., also presided over the spring time.

As to Ashi we have seen that in Ashi Yt. § 2 she has been identified with Mithra and in § 16 she has been called the sister of Mithra. She is thus closely connected with Mithra.

It is well worth noting here that both the Fravardin and Ashi Yashtas give the same description of the birth of Zarathushtra which took place at the beginning of spring. Could this be because the Farohars and Ashi presided over the spring time?

As to Pârendi, she has been invariably mentioned as the companion of Ashi. In Vispard VII-2 she has been praised along with Mithra.

The Kyâni Khureh is the royal glory of the Kyâni kings, and as they were crowned on the Jamshedi Naoroz day, which fell near the spring equinox, the Khureh seems to be closely connected with spring.

Now we come to Dami Upaman, the angel of wisdom, which has been praised in Vispard II-9. In that Chapter the five epagomenæ or gatha days have been revered. Mithra has been praised along with the fourth gatha and Dami Upaman with the fifth. From the Afrin-e-gahanbara we see that the last gatha day belonged to the Hamaspathmaedaya or the spring equinox. Thus Dami Upaman, the companion of Mithra would also appear to be connected with spring.

We have thus strong reasons to say that Mithra, Ashi, Dami and Farohars were the presiding angels of the spring equinox and that Mithra was the chief of these.

Let us now turn to Rigveda to see whether we can adduce any further proof in support of our proposition that Mithra presided over spring. In Rv. X-61-17 we read "Vaitânara (= fire) shall milk the cow who has never calved, when I encompass

---

* In the Avesta times the length of a day was measured in two different ways. The period from dawn to dawn was called *ayare*, and that from evening to evening was called *khshpara*. Thus if by the one method the year ended at the dawn on 21st March, by the other method it ended in the evening. Now if we assume that the coming of the Farohars takes place in the noon on 21st March, it is easy to see that by one method the Farohars come during the last day of the year and by the other method during the first day of the year. It is, I believe, for a similar reason that Siroz (first monthly) and Sâl (first yearly) ceremonies of the dead are performed on the 30th and 31st days, and 365th and 366th days respectively. Similarly fire is kept burning in the night on the 8th day of Adar Mâh instead of the 9th.

Varuna and Mitra with lauds." According to Prof. Ludwig "the cow that has never calved" is the *New Year* which has not yet distributed its treasures. It will thus be seen that in Rigveda also Mitra is mentioned in connection with the new year which as we have already seen, commenced with spring.

Porphyry (233 A. D.) informs us that a particular position in the Zodiac had been assigned to Mithra, that of the equinox; and in this position he had the north to his right and the south to his left. Mithra was hence celebrated not merely as the light which daily vanquishes the night but even as the one, which at each *spring* time triumphed over the long winter nights and restored the rejoicing beneficent summer brightness. (See Dr. Rapp. Cama's trans. p. III.)

Plunket says (p. 61)—" The great festivities in honour of Mithra were as a rule celebrated at the spring equinox and were celebrated even among the Roman festivals. In many sculptures we find that the Scorpion (the constellation Scorpio of the Zodiac opposed to Taurus) joins Mithras in his attack upon the Bull and always the genii of the spring and autumn equinoxes are present in joyous and mournful attitudes......The conviction is clearly forced upon our minds that the Bull slain by Mithras in these Roman representations, is the Zodical Bull overcome and banished from heaven in the day time by the sun-god and at night by Scorpio, the constellation in opposition. With almost equal conviction we arrive at the conclusion that this triumph of Mithras was associated traditionally——*in Roman days it could only have been tradionally*——with the occurance at a remote date of the spring equinox, during the time that the sun was in conjunction with the constellation Taurus."

In Mr. K. R. Cama's "Mithric worship" we find the following :—

"Dupius in his Origin de tous les Cutts Vol. IV says, 'In former ages Taurus which Mithra mounts was the first of the zodiacal signs ; thus Porphyry, speaking of Mithra, assigns to him his place in the zodiac near the vernal equinox in the signs of Aries and Taurus. For Mithra like the bull is the generator of all creation ; the generating faculty requires to be placed in the sign of the vernal equinox......The connection of Mithra with Taurus is illustrated by a bull, which the conqueror fixes himself upon and subjugates. This is an ingenious emblem of his passage in the zodiacal sign of Taurus...... In all the monuments a scorpion or the sign opposed to Taurus attaches itself to the testicles of the bull to devour them. This astrological emblem expresses in the most sensible manner the cessation of the productive force of Taurus at the moment, the sun attains the sign of Scorpion or that of the autumnal equinox which is opposed to it.'"

Mr. Cama observes "we have a tradition of the primeval Gavyodad being killed and the creation of the animal and vegetable kingdoms having sprung from his dead body. To the would-be initiated it is possible that the cosmogony as current then was perhaps meant to be explained by the representation. But it passes my comprehension why just Mithra of all other Yazads should have been entrusted with the deed. The more probable solution is that the young man is the priest entrusted with sacrifices whose business it is to personally attend to the various ceremonies connected with animal sacrifices, which on occasions are required to be presented to Mithra. The same thing is done at the present day. On the Jashne Mehergan and on similar other occasions, our Iranian coreligionists sacrifice an animal thus : They cut it by the neck and removing the head and the liver destined to be placed in the Homa ceremony, the animal is roasted entire.

Those present at the festival consider it religious duty to partake of at least one morsel therefrom."

I may say that I do not agree with the explanation of Mr. Cama. We have several representations of Mithra riding the Taurus, but as Mr. Cama says, we find nothing of the kind in Avesta. We however do find that in the Meher Yashta, Mithra is represented as riding in a chariot.

MITHRA'S CHARIOT. This chariot is made of heavenly sub-stance (§ 67) It is a beautiful carriage (§ 124) and has only *one* wheel (§ 136) and one pole (§ 125). It is drawn by four white horses, which are brilliant, beautiful, *not casting shadows* (*asâya*) and moving in the celestial space. The food of these horses is celestial (§ 136), Mithra drives in this chariot and is accompanied by the bounteous Rashna on his right and the pure Chisti on his left. Dami Upaman is his third companion, who has for his *kehrpa* (= conveyance) the grunting Boar with sharp teeth (§ 127.)

Now all this vivid description shows that the chariot of Mithra is none other than the constellation known as the Charioteer, or Chariot or Auriga, which is the northern paranatellon (=companion constellation) of the Zodiacal constellation Taurus. The Chariot is immediately on the north of the Taurus and some of its stars actually form part of the Taurus. (See Primitive Constellations by R. Brown II-18 and I-119 map.) * In the Chapter on Constellations and Coin-types, R. Brown says about the Charioteer and its 4 horses "The type of the divine personage seated in the four-horse carriage is thoroughly Euphratean............Another object found in the Phoenician cemeteries is a terra-cotta chariot drawn by 2 or 4 horses and occupied by one or more persons" (idem I-168).

The four horses are, I think, the 4 big stars of the constellation—one of the first magnitude, one of the second and two of the third.

We thus find that although in the Avesta, Mithra is not represented as riding the Bull, still he is depicted as driving in the Chariot, a constellation in its immediate vicinity. He is followed by his comrade Dami Upaman who rides on the grunting sharp-teethed Boar (=the Sea-monster), a constellation which is situated on the south of the Taurus.

Now why is it that of all the other constellations, the Chariot and the Boar are ridden by Mithra and his accomplice Dami? The reason is not far to seek. As has been stated the Taurus and his companion constellations the Chariot and the Boar were at one time the leaders at the vernal equinox.*

It is true that in the Ashi Yashta, the vehicle of Ashi is not the Boar but the Chariot. As, however, Ashi is the sister of Mithra, the writer of the Ashi Yashta makes the northern paranatellon of the Taurus (= the Chariot) the conveyance of Ashi, while the author of the Meher Yashta represents the southern paranatellon of the Taurus (= the Boar) as her conveyance. Thus there is no inconsistency here.

The analogy of the picture of Mithra as found in the Avesta with the Mithric representations and figures is clear beyond doubt but does not end here. "The twentieth Persian lunar mansion is Vanant (=o, i, k, Scorpionis) the *Stinger* (fr. Av. *van* = to strike)......Vanant is one of the four chief asterisms in the Persian stellar scheme, an illus-

* In the Babylonian sphere the Chariot or Auriga adjoined the Bull (Prim Constellations I-180, 359).

* Aiz (Gr. Aix, Lat. Capella) the brighest star of the Chariot marked the new year at a time prior to B. C. 2540 when the Pleiad was connected with the vernal equinox (Prim Const. II-244).

tration of the original great importance of the Scorpion. Now we come to a most interesting piece of ritual, the meaning of which its votaries have lost for ages. 'When a sheep is slaughtered......the *testes* are for the star Vanant' (Shayast la Shayashta XI—4). Thus is the Scorpion-star Vanant linked and identified with the Scorpion which seizes the tastes of the Mithraic Bull" (Prim. Constellations Vol. I, p. 75).*

We thus see that Mithra, Ashi and the Farohars are all intimately connected with the beginning of spring.

It would appear that when Ashi asks Zarathush ra to ascend her chariot (§21) it is meant that she would protect the infant Zarathushtra against his enemies ; also that the birth of Zararhushtra was connected with the constellation of the Chariot the northern companion of the Taurus.

NAOTARIONS—We now come to the passages in the Ashi Yashta which contain important historical legends. In para. No. 55 we have "when the Turanians and the Naotarians who had swift horses displeased (*pazdayanta lit.* trampled) me, then I (= Ashi) concealed my body *under the foot of the male Bull*, the bearer of burden. But young boys and unmarried maidens found me out." The Avesta passage is extremely simple and bears no other sense. In para. No. 56 the above passage is repeated, except that here we are told that Ashi concealed herself "*under the neck of the male Ram*, possessing a hundred-fold strength.

The Bull and the Ram in the above passages are easily recognized as the constellations Taurus and Aries.

Naotar was according to Shahname a king of Persia who ruled for 7 years after Minocheher. The Naotarians were his sons Tus and Gushtehem and his chiefs Kobad, Kârun, Sâma and others. A great war took place between these Iranians on the one side and the Turanians headed by Afrasiab, Bârmân and others on the other side. The result was that the Iranians were completely routed and Afrasiab became the ruler of Iran. Several pitched battles were fought during the war and it is very likely that one of them took place on the day of the vernal equinox. Instead of being a day of joy, it must have been a day of great disappointment for the Persians ; consequently it is not difficult to understand why Ashi was displeased. With a view to show her sorrow, as it were, the Yazata of the vernal equinox with the sun by her side (*bânumaiti*) concealed herself under the foot of the Taurus; or to put the matter in simpler words, the above historical event took place on the day of the spring equinox, when the sun entered the foot of the Taurus.

We also know from history that the Iranians under Gushtaspa had to fight wars with the Turanians undar Arjaspa. According to Aban Yt. § 98 Gushtaspa belonged to the

---

* We have seen that Mithra and the Farohars presided over the commencement of spring. It is therefore quite in the fitness of things that the month belonging to spring should be named after the Farohars, the presiding divinities of the spring equinox. But it might well be asked why the month was not named after Mithra. The reason appears to me to be this. Excluding the 8th, 15th, and 23rd days, we have 27 days in a month corresponding with the 27th lunar asterisms. The day named after Mithra rightly occupies the *middlemost* position, in confirmity with its name which signifies "union," it being the uniting bond of the first half of the month with the second half. For a similar reason and for the reason that the Farohars had been already assigned the first position, it is that Mithra has been assigned a position in the *middle* of the year when the union of the equal day and night takes place on the autumnal equinox. It may be noted that the 17th and 19th Hindu asterism (અનુરાધા and મૂલ) which are portions of the Scorpio are according to Surya Siddhant presided over by Mithra and Pitris respectively.

Naotar family.* This war may be therefore said to have taken place between the Naotarians and the Turanians. We know that in the first religious war, the Iranians suffered a heavy loss. This defeat at the hands of the Turanians is most probably referred to in tho para. No. 56 and it would appear that the event occured in the commencement of spring when the sun entered the neck of the Aries.

In the Primitive Constellations by R. Brown (Vol. I, p. 337) it is said that "the head of Aries was reverted and looked back towards Taurus," so that we see that the foot of Taurus is within a very short distance of the neck of Aries. This shows that the two Avesta passages refer to historical events which must have happened within a comparatively short inverval of time. The latter event must have occured about 2500 B.C. when at the spring equinox the sun entered the first point of Aries, most appropriately termed the neck of the Ram. A few years before that date at the spring time, the sun entered the last point of Taurus, termed in the Yashta, the foot of the Bull. The date of Zarathushtra will have thus to be placed in about 2500 B. C.

It is somewhat difficult to understand the statement that young boys and girls found out Ashi who was concealed. I think that the author wants to convey that on the particular day in question, the boys and girls of those days took special delight in watching the heliacal rising of the constellation, much in the same manner as the children of our time take great interest in watching an eclipse. Plunket rightly observes "It is probable that the *heliacal rising* of certain bright stars in the constellations at some special season of the year, rather than their culmination at noon or at midnight, may have been the occasion for the interest taken in them" (p. 248.)

* As proved by the late Ervad Tehemuraspa Ankleseria, Zarathushtra also belonged to the family of Nodar, the great grandson of Faredun. (See Report of Kholkarnari Mandli 1890 to 1898 p. 21.)

Date of Zarathushtra from the Gathas.

Apart from the evidence of the Avesta and the Rigveda, we have the authority of the Gathas themselves for determining the date of Zarathushtra.

The whole of the Ha No. 50 of the Yasna seems to be clearly a continuation of the cow legend in Ha No. 29 which contains a colloquy between Geush Urvan and the divine powers. I shall give here a summary of Ha 29 giving the order in which in my opinion the different strophes should occur.

Ha 29-1. The soul of the cow cried out "why did you create me, who has created me? I have been oppressed by *aeshma*, hajas, *rema*, &c.

Ha 29-2. Then Geush Tashna asked Asha "who is the lord of thy cow......Who is his beneficent lord who will drive away *aeshma* along with the wicked things (—*hajas*, *rema*, &c.)"

Ha 29-3. To him Asha replied "he is not an oppressor but a non-tormentor for the cow. Among these (persons) I do not know him who will promote the respectable rishis.* He is the most powerful among living men whose speech his supporters follow."

Ha 29-4. An ethical stanza but irrelevant.

Ha 29-6. Then Ahuramazda said "......not one Ahu is known nor Ratu with righteousness. The creator created thee (Cow) for *prosperity* and *blessings*".

Ha 29-7. Irrelevant but ethical.

Ha 29-9. Then the soul of the Cow wept (saying) "I have got an undesired lord in my calamity. It is

* Ereshvâonghao—acc. plu.

the voice* of a weak man. I wish to have a puissant lord."

Ha 29-8. He who has heard my monitions is Spitama Zarathushtra.

Ha 29-5. Then with hands uplifted towards Ahura my soul (and that) which is of the Cow Azi—we two †—praised Mazda with different questions. Is there no oppression ‡ on the straight-conquering one? (is there) no (oppression) for the bearer of prosperity who is surrounded with wickednesses (—*aeshma*, *hajas* &c.)

The expressions Azi Cow, straight-conquering one and bearer of prosperity will be explained hereafter.

Ha No. 29-9 has reference to the birth of Zarathushtra, as we shall see hereafter. Ha No. 50 is a continuation of Ha No. 29. Therein Zarathushtra makes his appearance as a grown up man and a prophet. He wants to show that he is not such a weak man as the Cow supposed him to be at his birth. The first thing, therefore, that he does is to propitiate the Cow¶ by praying to Ahuramazda that He, Asha and Vohuman might protect the Cow against *aeshma*, *hajas*, &c.

While praying to Ahuramazda, Zarathushtra naturally turns his eyes towards the sky where his notice is attracted by the luminaries and specially by the conjunction of the sun with Taurus. Zarathushtra then expresses a desire that the Cow, the bearer of prosperity, might not be deprived of her lustre by the bright rays of the sun.

We shall translate the first three stanzas of Ha 50 and give a summary of the rest.

Ha 50-1. "Does my soul desire what and assistance from whom? Who is, who is indeed the protector of my animal, O worshipful Ahuramazda, tell me (*ajdâ*), other than Asha, Thyself, and the Best Mind?"

We now come to the most important verse Ha 50-2 in which we have a reference to the conjunction of the sun with the constellation Taurus. I translate the verse as under:

"O Mazda, how can (that man) see (*ishasoit*)* the fight making (*rânyoskeretim*)† Cow (=Taurus) — who always wishes her to be the bearer of prosperity (*vâstravaitim*) for himself. O Asha do not seat (or place, *nishânshyâ*) (her) straight conquering ‡ rays (*âkâsteng*)¶ in the fierce$ splendours (*pishyasu*) of the Sun. Grant this bequest."

The Cow in the above strophe is the constellation Taurus. In the starry atlases, the Bull is represented as rushing with great fury to make a fight and I think that the idea has been appropriately conveyed by the word "fight making." As the brilliant lustre of the Taurus has been overpowered by the bright rays of the sun, the author cannot see that auspicious constellation, which is the bearer of prosperity in this world; he therefore desires that its lustre may not be deprived by the light of the sun. Just as in modern times we are anxious to see the moon on the new moon day, so is the author anxious to see the constellation, it being the precusor of spring, the season of prosperity. If the above line of argument is correct, the sun

---

* Here *vâk* is used in the sense of "inarticulate sound". Cf. Rv. VIII-89-11. "The deities generated *vâk* the goddess and animals of every figure speak it."

† Ahvâ — आस्व.

‡ Frajyaiti—Cf. ज्यानें.

¶ Cf. *Khshnevishâ geushchâ urvânem*, "May I please the soul of the Cow."

* *Ranyoskerete*—रणकृति "doing fight" In Beheram Yt. § 26, an adjunct of Bûza (=Capricornus) is *rena* "fighting, which is practically the same as *rânya*. This word might also mean "the producer of delight," as Taurus ushered in the spring, the season of joy.

† *Ishasoit*— incho. 8/1 *isha* = इष् to see.

‡ Erezajish—2/8 fr. *ereza* + *ji* (to conquer.)

¶ *Akâsteng* 2/8 of *âkâsta*, "lustres, rays."

$ *Pouru* पुरु *lit.* excessive, abundant.

was at that time in conjunction with the constellation Taurus.

The expression "straight-conquering" (=conquering completely) is important. The ancient people marked the stars by their heliacal rising; consequently the constellation rising immediatly before the sun at the commencement of the year at the spring equinox would be justly said to conquer the other zodiacal constellations completely.

From the names of the days of the month we see that Atar (Mars), Apo (Venus), Hvare-Khshathra (Sun), Mâongha (Moon) and Tishtar (Mercury) are all heavenly objects; we might therefore with great reason conclude that Geush Urvan (Gosh) is also a luminary of the skies.

From the Fr. Yt. § 22 and other places it appears that *gao* is not the same thing as *zem* (=earth). No doubt in many Av. passages, *gao* bears the sense of the "earth," but that is not its primary meaning. At one time the Cow (=Taurus) introduced spring and was the supreme ruler of the earth. In course of time, the ruler came to be used for the ruled.

In several passages in the Gathas the Cow is called *Azi*. I agree with the Pahlvi translators and Neriosbang that Azi was the name of the Cow. This Azi Cow seems to be identical with the Apis Bull of the Egyptians, which was regarded as a symbol and incarnation of Osiris, the husband of Isis, the great divinity of Egypt. From a drawing in Eber's Egypt Vol. I, p. 121 it appears that the Apis Bull was marked by equal areas of black and white colours. Such equal areas would fitly symbolize the equal day and night of the equinoctial season. (See Plunket p. 233).

In the book named "Osiris and the Egyptian Resurrection" by Wallis Budge we are told that "there was a bull, to whom the title 'Bull of Heaven' was given and he was the master of all the fields of heaven and of all the cattle therein. With this bull, Osiris was identified" (see Vol. I, p. 399). We also read that Osiris has been called *Ahi* in some places (Vol. II, p. 60). Could this Ahi be the same as the Azi of Avesta?

Osiris was the lord of the year lord of the cattle, lord of the truth, and the beater of the sinners. (Idem Vol. II, pp. 51, 347).

In the Book of the Dead, it is said that "in a shrine sits Osiris the ruler and judge of the dead accompanied by 42 assessors and before him stands the balance on which the heart of the deceased man is to be weighed against truth. Thoth stands behind and registers the result. (Encyc. Bri. Ed. II, Vol. 9, p. 56).

Osiris thus resembled Mithra in several respects. He was like Mithra the judge of the actions of the dead. Just as Mithra presided over the light of the sun, so was Osiris the divinity of the sun. The original name of Osiris was Hysiris, which meant "the many-eyed one," a peculiar epithet of Mithra (see Report of Kholkarnari Mandli, 1890-98, p. 184).

We have already seen that Mithra had an intimate connection with spring; there is threfore a good reason to believe that Osiris also was connected with spring; and no doubt that was so, for, we are told that one of the most characteristic celebrations of the Egyptians was that which took place at the date of the supposed entrance of Osiris into the moon at the beginning of spring.

Thus it would appear that the Cow Azi had also an intimate relationship with the season of spring.

The verse No. 9 of Ha 29 speaks of *vâchem neresh asûrahyâ* "the voice of a weak man" which means the cry of the then-born Zarathushtra. In that Ha, the reference to the birth of Zarathushtra is not brought out so clearly as in the Bundehishna. In the 4th Chapter of the Bundehishna we have the same Cow legend wherein the birth of our prophet is clearly referred to beyond any doubt; for, we find that the spirit of the Cow thus cried out before Ahuramazda. "Whom have you given the chieftainship of the creation? When there is calamity in this world, when the trees become withered up, when the waters are dried up, where is that man about whom you said 'I will *create* that man who will preach prohibition from wickedness.'"

Now turning to Fr. Yt. § 93 and Ashi Yt. § 18 we find that Zarathushtra was born at the commencement of spring. Thus it appears that the constellation Taurus was in conjunction with the sun at the vernal equinox in the time of Zarathushtra.

In Ha 29-9 the Cow complains that she has obtained *anaeshem khshânmene râdem* "an undesired chieftain in (her) *calamity*." The *khshânman* (क्षीणता) seems to me to be the approaching end of the supremacy of Taurus.* As already seen, the Taurus was the leader before 2500 B. C. which would therefore be the date of Zarathushtra.

I shall now translate Ha 50-3 which, as all the translators are agreed and as the relative pronoun *yâm* indicates, bears a close connection with the preceding stanza.

"O Mazda and Asha, may (she) verily be for him who with the strength of purity prospers the nearest settlement which the Dregvant destroys*—(she) whom he cherishes (*choista*) with his devotion (khshathra) and good mind."

The rest of the Ha 50 is devoted to the prayers of Ahuramazda beseeching his help.

Ha 50-4—"O Ahuramazda, may I praising worship thee always with holiness and best mind and might, by which the prayerful (*isho*) reach (*lit.* stand going as far as) the path (of his desires)—(saying) may I hear clearly the praise in Heaven."

Ha 50-5—"O Holy Ahuramazda do much please the reciter of the Mânthra (= prophet) with strong and visible help, so that with strength he may place us† in happiness."

Ha 50-7 "I have devoted myself to thee . . . May you be for my aid."

Ha 50-8 "May I, O Mazda, encircle thee with well-known songs."

Ha 50-9 "By these worships, may I praising reach thee."

Ha 50-10 "That which pleases (lit. deserves) the eyes (when attended) with pious deeds (*vareshâ*),‡ that which (pleases the eyes) with completely good actions§ (together) with these (prayers), and that which (pleases the eyes) with good mind—(namely that) *the stars* (of Taurus) *and the sun the enlighter of the day move* (*together*)—is for thy praise, O Holy Ahuramazda."

I think in the above strophe also the author refers to the conjunction of the sun with Taurus. It also appears that on the particular day in question, pious and meritorious acts were performed, it being the new year's day.

---

* In the 4th Chapter of Bundehishna it is said that when the first-created Bull (Gavyodâda) died, out came from his body Gosh Urvan and cried "whom have you given the chieftainship of the creation, &c., &c." This Gavyodâda is stated to be the cosmic cow; but I cannot understand why this cow should have died just at the birth of Zarathushtra. Could it be that this first created cow was Taurus who died, that is, whose sovereignty came to an end at the birth of Zarathushtra?

* *Bakshaiti* fr. भक्ष् to devour, to destroy. *Choista*—cf. *chishmahi* in Ha 35-5.

Anghaiti—3/1 subj. pre. used in the sense benedictive.

† Probably Zarathushtra and his followers,

‡ *Vareshâ* cf. वृष: "meritorious act."

§ *Pairi-shyothanâ* cf. परिद्वेशास great hater Rv. VIII-75-9, परिक्रोश great reviler I-29-7. परिराप great enemy I1-23-3. Or *Pairi*=severally.

The passage put into italics in my translation may be rendered as simply referring to the apparent motions of the sun and the stars. At any rate we find that the writer once again turns his eyes towards the sky.

But Ha 50-2 is not the only passage in the Gathas which mentions the conjunction of the sun with Taurus; for in Ha 32-10 there is a passage which is even clearer than Ha 50 2. The passage runs thus *Ye achishtem vaenanghahe aogedâ gâm ashibyâ hvarechâ* "who (=that wicked man) called it wicked to see the sun and the cow with the eyes." With regard to this passage Prof. Harlez remarks that this is the only meaning but it is a queer proposition to be put forward by any man.

No doubt if we take *gâm* in the sense of the "earth" or "animals," the passage marks no sense at all. What is called wicked and inauspicious is the sight of the conjunction of the sun with Taurus.* This phenomenon which was looked upon as auspicious by people in general was called inauspicious by the wicked Grehma. Viewed in this light the passage makes perfectly good sense. The allusion to the astronomical phenomenon is irresistible. It was not an ordinary phenomenon but one which was looked upon as auspicious by the people, since it was connected with the commencement of spring.

Astronomical facts in the Tir Yashta.

In Tir Yashta § 12 we find that the asterism *Upa-paoirya* (subsequently called Pesh-Parvin) has been praised first and then the asterism Paoiryaeinya (=Parvin) the Pleiades or Krittika. It is clear from the root meaning of Paoiryaeinya that it must mean "the first asterism." How is it then that it is mentioned *second* after Upa-paoirya "the one before the first?" It seems that just like Krittika, Paoiryaeinya was formerly the first asterism and in due course some other constellation became first and was justly called the "one before the first." Thus in the days of the Tir Yashta Upa-paoirya was the first asterism.

Now we have seen above that the Krittika was the first asterism in 2500 B. C. (See Arctic Home in the Vedas p. 420); and it remained first between the years 2500 B. C. and 1550 B. C. It was second between the years 1550 B. C. and 600 B. C. Thus the Tir Yashta must have been written between these two latter dates. It seems likely that it may have been written a few centuries before the cuniform inscriptions of Darius, that is, about 600 B. C.

(2) In the 2nd para of the Tir Yashta it is said "I praise the star Tishtar...and the waters of the big ocean, and the good one (Ardvisura) famous from afar, and the name of the Cow created by Ahuramazda and the great Kyâni glory and the Farohar of the pious Zarathushtra Spitama." It is indeed interesting to know why all these different and heterogeneous matters have been grouped together in a single paragraph.

Tistar is a luminary in the sky which has been called the *ocean* by the ancient writers. R. Brown says "The Deep in archaic idea has a far wider and profounder meaning than is contained in our word *ocean*. It is formed by the undefined blending of the *over-sea*—*the mare magnum sine fine*—in which the solar and the lunar barques sail, the *ocean-proper* which, of unknown and awful vastness enrings the world, and the *under-sea* invisible and fathomless to man and into which the heavenly bodies sink (see Prim. Const. Vol. I, p. 89). Also we read "the watery deep, the Okeanos of Homer . . . . surrounds the earth like a coiled serpent

* Similarly even to-day the Hindus call it in auspicious to see the moon on the Ganesh Chaturthi.

(idem p. 42). The waters* of the ocean are the splendours in the sky" (idem p. 87).

A gaze towards the sky would attract one's notice to two important objects, (1) the river Ardvisura which takes its origin in the sky, and (2) the constellation Taurus. Taurus was, as we have already seen, closely connected with the beginning of spring. This again suggests to the author two important facts (1) that the Kyani kings were crowned on the day of the vernal equinox and (2) that Zarathushtra was born about the same time of the year.

The above passage must have been written long after the time of Zarathushtra and the expiration of the Taurus age, because the writer does not praise the Cow but the *name* of the Cow, not Zarathushtra but the Farohar of Zarathushtra. Thus we find that the author has grouped together certain facts which were closely inter-related in point of time, namely the birth of Zarathushtra, the day when the Kyani kings were crowned and the time when the Taurus ushered in the spring. Can we not conclude that in this passage the author wants to give us the date of Zarathushtra? For why otherwise has the writer connected the Farohar of Zarathushtra with the *name* of the Cow?

(8) In the para No. 33 of the Tir Yashta it is stated that Tishtar first makes the wind blow and then causes the rain and hail to fall in the towns. In the para No. 34 it is said that Apâm Napât distributes the waters in the cities. We have already seen that Plunket has explained the Apâm Napât myth as referring to the "sun in the celestial water of the Aquarius," and I fully agree with that view. In Jamyâdha Yt. § 52 and other places Apâm Napât is said to be *aurvat-aspa* (—"possessed of quick horses") which is a special epithet of the sun. This clearly shows that Apâm Napât was a luminary in the skies.

We find that among the Babylonians certain planets were said to be closely connected with certain constellations; for instance "the Solar Marduk who in a planetary phase is Jupiter, was called 'the star of the Fish of the god* Ea." Simlarly in Tir Yt. § 4 it is said that Tishtar has *Apâm-nafedhrat hacha chithrem* "its source from Apâm Napât." In other words the planet Tishtar is said to be connected with the Aquarius with the sun in conjunction with it.†

* In Rv. IV-28-1 "waters" means "celestial waters."

* The lord of the watery region of the skies (see Prim. Constellations Vol. I, p. 87(.

† Some constellations were mentioned as belonging to the watery portion of the skies. R. Brown says "the watery part of the celestial sphere occupied by the Dolphin, Demi Sea-horse, Goat-fish, Water-pourer, Southern Fish, Zodiacal Fishes and Sea-monster formed in the Euphratean scheme the region of Ea, the lord of the deep" (Vol I, p. 84). I think that Tishtar is called *afsh-chithra* for the reason that it belonged to the watery portion of the sky, to which Aquarius and the sun in Aquarius (Apam Napat) also belonged.

The celestial regions were divided into three parts between the Gods Anu, Bel and Ea......The sphere of Anu extended from the Bull to the Crab, that of Bel from the Lion to the Scorpion and that of Ea from the Sagittarius to the Aries (Prim. Const. Vol. II. pp. 161-176).

Now Anu was the lord of the *heaven*, Bel of the *lands* and Ea of the *deep* (see Jastrow's Baby. Reli. p. 147).

In the Scandinavian mythology the universe was conceived of as a *tree* whose top reached the heavens (see Eagle and Captive Sun by Mujumdar p. 90).

We thus see that the stars called *afsh-chithra* (bearing the seed of water), *jemas-chithra* (bearing the seed of land) and *urvarão-chithra* (bearing the seed of trees) probably belonged to the watery, earthy and herbal portions of the sky.

The *Airy* signs are Gemini, Libra and Aquarius.

The *Fiery* signs are Aries, Leo and Sagittarius.

The *Earthy* signs are Taurus, Virgo and Capricornus.

The *Watery* signs are Cancer, Scorpio and Pisces. (See Chaldean Astrology by G. Wilde, pp. 14-15).

We have already stated that in Lat. 40° N. the rains commenced in September-October. From the para No. 84 of the Tir Yashta and the preceding passages, it appears that the rainy season had advanced a good deal and consequently we may well assume that in these passages we have the description of the rains of December.

Thus the ApÂm NapÂt myth (— the sun being in conjunction with Aquarius) belonged specially to the month of December.* Now if the sun be in conjunction with Aquarius in December, the constellation Taurus would be the first constellation of the year; so that the above ApÂm NapÂt legend would belong to the Taurus age, that is 4698 B. C. to 2540 B.C.

Date of the Prophet Homa from the Homa Yashta.

We shall now consider the Homa Yashta § 26 in which it is stated that *Fra te Mazdâo barat paurvanim aivyâonghanem steherpaesanghem mainyu-tâshtem vanghuhim daenâm Mâzdyasnim* "Mazda brought forth† to thee the *belt* of (or belonging to) the Paurvanya‡ adorned with stars made in the sky§ and MÂzdayasni religion."

The word *frâ-barat* ("brought forth") suggests that Parvin and the Mazdayasnian religion which had up till then remained in the back ground were brought forth into prominence by Mazda, and presented to Homa; in other words it was in the days of Homa that Parvin became the first asterism and that the Mazdayasnian religion became conspicuous.

Now Parvin was the Pleiades or Krittika,* a portion of the Taurus and was the first asterism between 3600 to 2500 B.C. It was a few centuries before the latter date that Homa lived.

Date of Homa from the Meher Yashta.

The date of the Prophet Homa can be also determined from the Meher Yashta § 90. Before we discuss that passage, it is important to know what was the conception of sacrifice among men of ancient times. I give the following quotation from Mr. Majumdar's book named "the Eagle and the Captive Sun" pp. 161-168. "The Vedic conception of sacrifice is three-fold ——spiritual, celestial and artificial or symbolical——and the ingredients and ramifications of the three are considered to be similar whether within the human body or in the heavens or on the earth. Creation is conceived as a great sacrifice (see Purushasukta Rv. X-90) or rather the primeval original sacrifice in the image of which, the other sacrifices have been formed (see Rv. X- 130); and as this creation is typified in the heavenly body in which all the gods are represented and VÂk resides as the word of God and the sym-

* "The *Water-pourer* belonged specially to the rainy season......and hence became appropriated to the rain-giving sun." "Aquarius is a re-duplication of the sun of storm and rain." (Pri. Const. Vol. I, p. 84).

†*Fra* might mean "first;" cf. the comp. and superl. forms *fratara* and *fratema* used adverbially. In Sk. प्रभृति (Av. *fra-bereti*) gives the sense of commencement; as शैशवात् प्रभृति "commencing from childhood." Also cf. प्राह्ण "fore-noon."

§ *Mainyutâshta* might mean made of heavenly substance.

‡ As *aghra* has the adj. *aghrya* ("belonging to the top") so *Paurvana* has *Paurvanya*.

* The usual representation of the कृत्तिका is a razor and in the choice of this symbol is to be recognized the etymology of the name which may be derived from the root कृत् "to cut;" in the configuration of the group too may be seen by a sufficiently prosaic eye, a broad-bladed knife (see Burgess' Surya Siddhant). The *aivyanghan* or belt of Pleiades would thus be an appropriate word. The exact Sk. equivalent of *aivyaonghana* is अभ्यसन = *cluster*. The Pleiades were regarded as a *cluster* of stars (see Easy Star Lessons by Proctor, p. 71). They were called the *clusterers* by the Greeks (see Prim. Const. Vol. I, p. 11).

phony of the Divine machinery within, the best, truest and purest form of sacrifice is considered to be going on within man himself and his spiritual advancement is considered proportionate to his knowledge of this sacrifice. The spiritual Hindus have never lost sight of this spiritual sacrifice and have always tried and still try to gain a knowledge of it by conquering and subduing the evil genii within, which darken their inner vision and casting off the अविद्या or ne-science which covers them. This is their Atmavidyâ or science of self.

"The idea of this spiritual sacrifice was first of all drawn from the celestial sacrifice, the great sacrifice that is carried on in the universe by the nature gods, headed by their solar chief and is regulated by the God's law or *rita*. Now, although the main principle of this heavenly sacrifice remains constant, its nature varies according to circumstances. The sacrifice is on the whole annual but its elements vary according to the varying seasons of the year and the changing conditions of light and darkness. The object of the sacrifice is the destruction of darkness and the evils appertaining thereto.

"To the Vedic rishis inhabiting the arctic regions, the principal element of the annual heavenly sacrifice was that portion of it which represented the long continuous day—the *Brihat-diva*. Like Dirghatamas, *Brihat-diva is conceived as a rishi*. See Rv. X-120-8 in which it is said 'Brihat-diva, the foremost of light-winners, repeats these holy prayers, this strength to Indra.' Brihat-diva is the rishi and Indra the god of the hymn, in which this verse is contained. Of the heavenly sacrifice representing the long continuous day, the heavenly rishi or performer is the Long Day. . . . . The object sacrificed is Soma or moon caught in the clutches of the heavenly bird Syena, the constellation Aquila and the sacrifice is enjoined by all the gods (Rv. X- 65-4).

"The artificial sacrifice which men perform is mainly a symbolical representation of this heavenly sacrifice."

The passage No. 90 of the Meher Yashta is as follows:—

"Mithra first (*paoiryo*) prepared (*us dasta*) Homa in the mortar (*hâvana*) bedecked with stars, and made of heavenly substance (*mainyu-tâshta*); and Ahuramazda and the Ameshaspents praised him on account of his disk (*lit.* body, *kehrpa*) of good-size (*hu-raodha*); whom the sun of the quick horses makes a salute from afar."

Here we have a vivid description of a certain heavenly sacrifice (= astronomical phenomenon) performed by the angel Mithra as a Zaoti. The object sacrificed is the Homa, and the receptacle of the sacrifice is Hâvana, in which the Homa is pounded.

We shall try to see what this heavenly sacrifice is and what are Mithra, Homa and Hâvana.

MITHRA—As to Mithra we have already seen that he was the angel who presided over the vernal equinox.

HOMA—Hillebrandt believed that Homa was identical with Soma (= moon) in Yasna IX-26, X-10, LVII-19 and Yt. VIII-33. It appears to me that in the above passage the word *Homa* may with much better reason be assigned the sense of *Soma*, the moon.

In ordinary Sanskrit, the word Soma means the moon. But according to the Vedic commentators, it always means in the Rigveda, a plant the juice of which is drunk by gods, and especially by Indra, for refreshing themselves for the great contest with Vritra. There is no doubt that many of the Soma hymns were recited during the performance of certain ancient rites of the Vedic people and that a plant known as Soma was used in them. But this does not preclude us from thinking that these rites symbolised certain great and unique astronomical facts (see Eagle and the Captive Sun p. 57).*

In Rv. IX-86, IV-28-1 and 2, &c., the word Soma is clearly used for the plant as well as the moon. In Rv. X-85-2 we have सोमेन पृथिवी मही । अथो नक्षत्राणां एषां उपस्थे सोम आहितः ॥

"The earth is mighty by Soma, thus in the midst of these constellations the Soma is placed." Here the word Soma is clearly used in both the senses.

In several passages in the Rig-veda, Indra is represented as being strengthened by copious draughts of Soma, which, as observed by Plunket, means "the bright light of the *full moon* flooding the heavens with radiance."

In the Avesta passage before us we are clearly given to understand that the disk of the moon (*kehrpa*) is of full size (*hu-raodhas*). Also we are told the sun bows to the Homa from afar, meaning that the sun is in opposition to the Homa† or the full moon.

The Homa plant is pounded in a *hâvana* (=mortar). In the present passage the Hâvana is, as we shall see hereafter, an asterism in the sky. The passage before us contains a legend about an astronomical phenomenon of the by-gone times. The expressions and ideas connected with the preparation and ceremonial of the Homa juice are skilfully interwoven with those of the legend.

Usually a priest prepares the Homa juice by crushing the plant in a mortar; in the legend in question it is the head priest Mithra (= angel of the vernal equinox) who in the past prepared the Homa juice in the mortar, that is to say, Mithra placed* (*us-dasta*) the Homa (=full moon) in the Hâvana (=asterism of the mortar). In other words at the vernal equinox (of which Mithra is the presiding divinity) the full moon was in conjunction with the asterism of the mortar.

HAVANA—The Hâvana or the Mortar in the legend is the front portion of the constellation Scorpio. It seems to be identical with the Accadian constellation Zibânituv, which is equivalent to the Arabian *As-subânay* (the Claws). (See Prim. Constellations by R. Brown Vol. I, p. 70; see also Vol. II. p. 15, and p. 140).

In Albiruni's Asâr-ul-Bakie Sachau p. 347) the 16th Arabian lunar mansion is called *Al-subânâ*† which consists of two brilliant stars separated from each as far as five yards and standing in a place where the two claws of Scorpio might be.

This Asterism was identical with the 17th lunar mansion अनुराधा δ β π Scorpionis, the divinity presiding

---

* Mr. Majumdar commenting on certain expressions in Rv. IV-28-1 and 2 says "These expressions show beyond doubt that Soma whatever it might be in the allegorical ceremonies of priests was not originally an invigorating draught in the ordinary sense of the word. It is, again, distinctly called by the name Indu or moon in this and many other hymns. This hymn, therefore, confirms the identity of the moon and the Soma" (see Eagle and the Captive Sun p. 68).

† The form *Haomâm* (fem. acc.) deserves to be carefully noted. It is found in many manuscripts and strongly supports the meaning I have put forward here. The form shows that the sense is unusual.

* The word *usdasta* is clearly used in two senses. Usually it is applied to the preparation of the juice; here it also bears another sense from *us*+*dhâ* ("placed on high"); see Kanga's Gr. p. 200. *Hâvana* is also used in two senses.

† The *Av.* word *Hâvana* is derived from *hu* = to press juice + the termination *ana* which shows the instrument with which the action is performed. *Hu* undergoing vriddhi becomes *hâu* + ana = *hâvana*. In the Arabic *hu* + *ana* take *v* in the middle (cf. *vi* + *âpa* = *vivyâpa*); thus we have *huvana* which becomes *zubâna*.

over which was Mithra (see Surya-siddhant p. 336)——exactly as we find in the passage before us.

It is easy to see that the shape of the Hâvana must have closely resembled that of the Altar or the Censer, with reference to which Mr. Brown says "Altar was the original zodiacal constellation, afterwards superceded by the Claws of the Scorpion. It was called Altar-Censer or Censer . . . which was grasped in the huge Claws of the Scorpion. . . . . The gigantic size of the Scorpion is reduplicated in the Zodiac where it occupied two signs and thus gave rise to the mistake of Servius that the Chaldean Zodiac consisted of only 11 constellations" (see Vol. I, pp. 67, 113, 180, 218, also Vol. II, pp. 44, 232).

The Altar is represented as the seventh constellation from Aries; but as it is situated within the Claws of the Scorpion, its end coincides with the head of the Scorpion. Now as the full moon was placed within the Hâvana (= Mortar, *or* Censer) it well nigh touched the end of the Altar or the head of the Scorpion.

Thus from the Avesta passage we gather that at the time to which the legend refers, the full moon was in conjunction with the head of the constellation Scorpio at the vernal equinox. It would follow that at the time, the sun was in opposition to first point of Scorpio and in conjunction with the end of the Taurus.

From what has been said above it would appear that the legend presupposes the existence of the Homa ceremonial, which was first instituted by the prophet Homa. In the passage No. 88 of the Meher Yashta it is stated that Homa praised Mithra who (according to § 90) had placed the full moon in conjunction with the asterism of the Mortar. We thus see that it is in connection with Homa that this legend of Mithra is mentioned. This prophet therefore flourished in the Taurus age.

Signification of Draona, etc., offered to Homa.

From Yasna XI-4 to 7 it appears that it was an ancient custom among us to offer to Homa "a *draona* with the tongue and the left eye of a cow (*geush*) that was sacrificed." This ritual seems to be a remnant of the well-known Mithric representation which is depicted as under. In the centre stands Mithra the sun-god with large outspread wings. He stabs the Bull near whose head is a *Bucranium* and whose tail at the end is divided into two *Ears-of-corn*. The Bull is surrounded by a *Dog* which springs to lick his blood, a large *Serpent* which bites him, and a *Scorpion* which seizes on his *genitalia*.

As we have already seen this Mithric picture beautifully symbolises the disappearance of the constellation Taurus by the light of the sun on account of his conjunction at the spring equinox. We thus see that the Cow that is sacrified for the Homa ceremony is a symbolical counterpart of the Cow (= Taurus) sacrificed (= made to disappear from the skies) by Mithra, the angel of the sun's light. The tongue and the left eye signify the head of the Taurus. As a matter of fact only the *left eye* of the Taurus is visible to the observer—thus, the expression used by the Avesta writer is very appropriate. The *draona* offered with the tongue and the left eye of the Cow symbolises the circular disk of the sun in conjunction with the head or the front portion of the Taurus. This *draona* is offered in honour of Homa (= the full moon caught within the clutches of the Scorpio).

We thus see that whereas, on the one hand, the celestial Homa ceremony referred to in Meher Yt. § 90 (= the conjunction of the full moon with the Scorpio at the vernal equinox) takes place in the western portion of the sky, just a short time before the sun rises in the east,* on the other hand the celestial Cow sacrifice (— conjunction of the sun with the Taurus) takes place in the easter portion of the sky.

If I am right in the above interpretation, what a happy idea is contained in our ritual of the Homa ceremony—a ceremeny which so vividly reminds us of the important phenomena, which it was the privilege of our ancestors to witness—a ceremony which it is our pious duty to pass on to our descendants in all its purity and sanctity.

The ten Constellations in the Beheram Yashta.

In the Beheram Yashta it is stated that "Verethraghna (— Beheram) goes for the benefit of the worshipper in ten *Kehrpa*," namely (1) *Vâta* (2) *gao* (3) *aspa* (4) *ushtra* (5) *varâja* (6) *nar* (7) *meregha* (8) *maesha* (9) *bûja* and (10) *vîra*. It is supposed that these *kehrpas* are the different phases of the planet Beheram or Mars but it is difficult to believe that in ancient times, people could see the phases of the planet with their naked eyes. I am inclined to think that in the Beheram Yashta, we have an allusion to the ten constellations, some zodiacal and others non-zodiacal, which at a certain time were all visible to the observers.

In my opinion the word *kehrpa* significes the body or shape of a constellation. It is not the planet Beheram, but the angel presiding over it, who goes (rides) on the body of the constellations (*kehrpa âjasat*).

We shall now try to identify the constellations in the Beheram Yashta.

The first constellation is *Vâta*, which in Avesta usually signifies "the wind." In view of the fact, however, that all the remaining *kehrpas* are the names either of animals or men, it would be reasonable to infer that Vâta, must convey a similar idea. In Sanskrit जार means "paramour," and on looking at the starry chart with find that most probably it is the constellation Andromeda who is depicted in an amorous posture with her right hand kept horizontal and with her left arm raised vertical. It cannot be seriously contended that all the ancient constellations were imagined exactly under the forms by which we have learnt to know them from classical representations. The Avestan author might therefore have conceived the figure to be that of a bold man (*dereshis*) with his hand raised up as if to make a fight.

(2) The second constellation is *Gao*, the Taurus, who with his most prominent horns rushes to fight. Our author appropriately calls the ears yellow and the horns golden; for, they no doubt bear those colours at night. The bold front presented by the Bull has led the author to say that he carries Ama, the angel of courage on his horns.

(3) Next we have the Horse, the constellation known as Pegasus. The *saranyo aividâna* (golden caparison) is most probably the beautiful wing of the Horse, which looks like an ornamental covering thrown on its back.

(4) The next constellation is *Ushtra*, the Camel. No such name is found in the classical literature, but it seems to me to be the Sagittarius (— archer), which is represented as half man, half beast and which very nearly resembles a camel.

The expression *mashyo-vanghahe* "living with man" is highly significant. On some cylinders the Sagittarius appears in the usual type except that his wing ends in a Gryphon's head;* in other words it is a combination of a man in the front attached to a gryphon at the back. This gryphon very nearly resembles a camel and lives as if combined with a man. In the para

* *Yahmâi durât Hvarenemo baodhaeiti.*

* See Primitive constellations Vol. 2 p. 46.

No. 12 we have the expression *shmarshno-daem*, which according to Harles means "having beard श्मश्रु." This expression is quite in keeping with the fact that the man in the Sagittarius is represented with a beard. Further up we read *yâm he dûrae-sûkem durae frajavaiti, hitahe tânthrâyâm aipi khshapanem* "whom (= the angel of courage) the far reaching light of that white one (*hitahe*) inspires (*ju*) greatly (*durae*) in the dark night." This description closely resembles the Accadian name of the constellation which has been rendered by Sayce as "the light of the white face."*

(5). Then we have the mention of *Varaza* (boar), S K. वराह crocodile. It seems to be the constellation Cetus, the Sea-monster. In old astronomical maps it is represented with sharp teeth and wide jaws. The Avesta epithets *tizi dânsrahe* (of sharp teeth) and *tizi-asurahe* (of sharp jaws) would thus be quite suitable.

(6) The sixth constellation is *Nar* "man," which I identify with Aquarius, the man with the pitcher. The expression *kasu-pâshnahe* is taken to mean "having small heels," but I am inclined to take the word *pâshna* as equivalent to Sk. पाषाण "a stone or spear." Aquarius holds in one hand a small pitcher and in the other a spear. It might well be that we have an allusion to either of these things. The pitcher would appear to some as a small jar of stone.

(7) We now come to the constellation *Meregha* "bird" which, is the Aquila or eagle. We are told that it flutters its wings (*vâraghna*), is strong in the lower part of its body and smiting in the upper part; it is the only bird which moves the swiftest like an arrow flung with great force. In the early morning it goes rejoicing wishing that non-night were night that sun-light were non-sunlight (or darkness.)* All this graphic description is quite in keeping with the representation of Aquila.

(8) Then we have the constellation *Maesha*, the Ram or Aries with its horns bent down.

(9) The ninth constellation is *Buja*, the Goat or Capricornus, which has sharp horns and which runs to make a fight.

(10) Lastly we have *Vira*, the Hero, who carries a sward with a golden handle. This seems to be identical with the constellation Perseus (the rescuer) who bears a sword-like weapon in one of his hands

Having identified the ten constellations, we might well ask why the author mentions only these. I refer the reader to the Plate No. 24 given in Plunket's Book named. Ancient Calendars and Constellations,—from which it will be seen that only the abovesaid constellations were visible to the observers of Latitude 40° N at night on the summer solstice in about the 42nd century B.C. It cannot be seriously contended that the Beheram Yashta was written at that early period. All that we can affirm with confidence is that the phenomenon above referred to, which must have been viewed with great interest by the Avesta people of those days was handed down as a legend to the writer of the Yashta.

The Eagle in the Beheram Yashta.

We have already seen that *Meregha*, the Bird is one of the constellations

* Idem Vol. I. p. 78. The word *suka* usually means "the sight," but it is also = शुचिस् light.

* The reading adopted by Geldner is *asuiri suirim isemno* (= wishing that non-sunlight, *i. e.*, darkness would become sunlight) is evidently incorrect, because it contradicts the reading *akhshafni khshafnim isemno* (= wishing that non-night *i. e.*, sunlight would become night *i. e.*, darkness). The constellation wishes for darkness so that it might appear conspicuous in the sky. I therefore prefer the reading *suiri asuirim isemno* (= wishing that sunlight were darkness) which is found in many Mss.

mentioned in the Beheram Yashta. It is represented as wishing that "light were turned into darkness." This shows that it rose a little before the day-dawn; in other words, it is the heliacal rising of the sun that is alluded to in the above passage. This constellation is otherwise called Saena Meregha.

In the Rashne Yashta § 17 it is said that a large tree belonging to the Saena stands in the middle of the sea Vourukasha. This tree might well be compared with the Scandinavian tree Yggdrasil and the Vedic Varuna's tree. "In the Scandinavian mythology the *universe* is conceived of as a tree called Yggdrasil. Its roots are in Niflheim the region of the deadly cold at the northern end of the chaotic world. Its top reaches Asgard the highest heaven where the gods dwell"... "The stem of Varuna's tree is sustained erect in the baseless region (Rv I—24-7) and its top is inhabited by gods (Rv.—X- 135-1), In its crown sits Shyena, the eagle or Aquila."*

The sea Vourukasha is, I think, here as in several other places, used for the open space between the earth and the sky.

Thus we see that the tree of the Rashne Yt is the universe looked upon as a tree on the top of which sits the Saena constellation.

The Saena is also mentioned in the Beheram Yt § 41, which runs thus: "Verethraghna covers (protects) this house with his glory by means of cow-shaped weapons, just as *that* big bird Saena and just as *those* watery clouds cover big mountains." The big bird which covers mountains could not be any ordinary bird; it is evidently the constellation Aquila.

We have seen that in the Beheram Yt. § 20 the heliacal rising of the Aquila is referred to, which means that the sun was in conjunction with the Aquila which was the northern paranatellon of the Capricornus (see Prim. Const. Vol. II. p. 18). Also in § 41 the author points out the "*watery* clouds," which might indicate the commencement of the rainy Season. We know that in Persia, the rains commence in September-October. If we assume that the Aquila (or Capricornus) was in conjunction with the sun in October, the Taurus would be in conjunction with the sun at the spring time. This phenomenon would thus belong to the Taurus age. If however the watery clouds belonged to November we would have a reference to the Aries age. It seems to me that on linguistic grounds the writer of the Beheram Yashta cannot be assigned a date earlier than the end of the Aries age; in short the date of the Beheram Yashta would be about the same as that we have assigned to the Tishtar Yashta.

* See Eagle and Captive Sun pp. 90-91.

The date of Jamshed.

The date of the King Jamshed is given in the ShahnÂme, in which it is said that the King Jamshed came to the throne when the sun entered the Aries at the vernal equinox on the Roz Hormuzd of the Maha Fravardin.

We have already tried to show that Zarathushtra was a contemporary of Jamshed and belonged to the *end* of the Taurus age. It follows that the statement of the ShahnÂme must mean that Jamshed lived in the commencement of the Aries age.

Zarathushtra's date from other sources.

Pliny (79 A. D.) and Suidas (10th century A. D.) believed that there were two Zoroasters. Suidas says that one of them lived 500 years before the Trojan war, which took place in 1160 B.C. Thus 1600 B.C. would be the date of one of the Zoroasters. This could not be our prophet.

The other lived in the age of Ninus, an Assyrian king who had come to the throne in 2086 B.C. According to Ctesias, however, it was Hukhshathra the last Kayanian king who was killed by Ninus. If so, the time of Zarathushtra will have to be taken back about three or four centuries.

Dr. Haug in his Lecture on Zoroaster says :—"Close connection of the ancient Iranian religion with that of the Vedas and Zoroaster's antagonism to the latter necessitate us to seek the age of Zoroaster in remoter antiquity, since he must have been living at the time of the separation of the Iranians from the Indians and the immigration of the latter into Panjab which must have occurred about 2000 B.C. . . . According to Synkello's Chronographia, the king who founded the Dynasty of the eight Median tyrants over Babylon was called Zoroaster.* Since Zarathushtra is no proper name but that of a high priest, and the founder of the Parsi religion is called Zarathushtra Spitama, it is clear that he was not the prophet. If the prophet had conquered Babylon and founded this dynasty, that would have been referred to in the Avesta....That Zoroaster was living before the Median conquest of Babylon (2234 B. C.) may be gathered from some statements regarding the earliest settlements of the Aryans and Ragha in Media in particular. In Yasna 19 § 18 we have Ragha Zarathushtrish, which must mean Ragha governed by Zarathustra or high priests, not Ragha where Zarathushtra* was born. They were a kind of priest kings, since there was no *danyhu-paite* or king at Ragha, but the highest head was Zarathustra....We must assign to Zarasthustra Spitama a date prior to the Median conquest of Babylon.... Zarathustra lived about 100 or 200 years before the Median conquest" (see pages 21-26).

The date arrived at by Dr. Haug very nearly corroborates the date of Zarathushtra proved by us on quite different grounds.

---

* In the writing of Berosus (B.C. 280) preserved in the Armenian translation of Eusebius it is found that from Xisuthros and from the deluge and until the Medians took Babylonia there were 86 kings. Eusebius allows 224 years to the first Median kings. Muller and Rapp have observed that Zoroaster and the seven Chaldean kings were the Medians referred to by Eusebius (see Eastern Iranians II pp. 186-188). Rawlison referring to the chronology of Berosus states that the period of the eight Median kings extended from 2458 to 2284 B.C. Mr. Pallonji B. Desai in his Tavarikhe Hakhamanian p. 128 gives the dates as 2284 to 2210 B.C. which seem to be more accurate.

* I cannot agree with this view.

PART VI.

In this Chapter I have put together a few subjects which are remotely connected with the previous chapters and are more like appendices to them.

No. I.

Date of Zarathushtra from the Aban Yashta.

The Ardvisura.

According to the Aban Yt. § 3 and Fravardin Yt. § 6, &c., the Ardvisura was a river which proceeded from the Hukara mountain belonging to the Alburz range and fell into the Vourukash ocean. From the Aban Yt. § 96 and Rashne Yt. § 24 it appears that the river flowed from a height equal to the aggregate height of 1000 persons. If we take the average height of a man to be 5½ feet, it seems that the river proceeded from a height of about 5500 feet.

From Bundehishna 13-4 and Dadestane Dini 92-5 it appears that water got collected on the top of Hukara mountain forming a lake from which the Ardvisura began to flow. It will be seen that this description is very appropriately applicable to a river on this earth.

Let us consider some other passages of the Yashta. In § 85 Ahuramazda says to Ardvisura "Go away from these stars to the earth." In § 120 the river is represented as having four horses, namely, wind, rain, cloud and hail.

These passages leave us in doubt as to whether the writer refers to the great height from which the river takes its origin or whether the river is some river-like starry phenomenon.

In § 90 however we are told that "Ahuramazda made the Ardvisura flow not on the earth but towards the sun." This and certain expressions in §§ 126-127 (to be discussed hereafter) lead us to believe that the river was also the constellation Eridanus or the Stream. The author writes about the river and the constellation in a rather loose and confused manner, and the reader is left to find out for himself what description applies to the river and what to the constellation.*

A Lively Description.

We have a lively description of the Ardvisura in the paras Nos. 126 to 129, 11 and 64 of the Aban Yashta. On reading these passages we are at first somewhat surprised at the comparison made by the writer between the Ardvisura and a young maiden; for, the question naturally arises "what earthly comparison could there be between a river and a maiden?" The answer is easily given if we but turn to similar comparisons in the Sanskrit literature. The comparison or the rather the figure of speech consists only in this that the anthor uses words and expressions, which are applicable both to the river and a maiden, though in different senses. In short, we have here what is known in Sanskrit as शब्दश्लेष "a pun upon words."

We shall give here a few instances of this figure of speech from the sprightly description of a "cook" given by Kāshipati Mukundānanda.

(1) कृष्णमिव क्षालितकंसमालिन्यं — "(The cook) who has washed off the impurities of a pot is like Krishna (who has removed the impurity in the form of Kamsa)."

(2) राममिव मारीचमथनं = "(The cook) who has reduced chillies to powder is like Rāma (who killed Mārīcha)."

---

* Robert Brown says (p. 208 Vol. II): "It must be remembered that in sacred and semi-sacred accounts geography and uranography are at times intermingled and the mythical and mystical intrude upon the actual; whilst things on earth are frequently named after and are supposed to correspond occultly with things celestial."

(3) वैय्याकरणमिव विदितस्वरसव्यंजनप्रक्रियं —" (The cook) who knows the process of preparing *Chatni* of good flavour is like a grammarian (who knows the vowels and the etymology with the consonants)."

(4) पंडितमिव परिचितसकलरसपरिपाकं = " (The cook) who is acquainted with all the sauces and the cooking is like a Pandit [who is well versed in all the poetic sentiments (such as Shringâra, Hâsya, &c.,) and their perfection."]

(5) सिंधुमिव जडाशयं—" (The cook) who is stupid like an ocean (which is the bed of water)."

(6) जलदमिव पयोवाहं = " (The cook) who is the carrier of milk is like a cloud (which contains water)."

(7) जलदकालमिव घनमषीमलिनांबरं = " (The cook) whose garment is soiled by thick lamp-black is like the rainy season (in which the sky is black on account of the soot-like clouds)."

A few instances of similar homonyms from English riddles would be interesting :—

(1) When is a lawyer like a horse? When he draws a conveyance.

(2) Why is a house like the sun? Because it has beams.

(3) Why is a beggar mending his clothes like a landlord? Because he is making up his rents.

(4) Why is a naughty boy like a chair without a seat? Because both require a good caning.

A wrong belief.

It is generally believed that the passages of the Aban Yashta above referred to are meant to give us a vivid representation of the female Yazata, *Anâhita*.* If that be true, we shall have to assume that the Avestan people made idols of their Yazatas, just like the Greeks and the Assyrians who made idols of their goddesses Aphrodite and Milita respectively. It would be certainly wrong to suppose that the ancient Avestan people indulged in idolatry. No doubt, Arta-Xerxes II erected idols in honour of Anâhita and placed them in the temples; but it is quite clear that he acted in direct opposition to the teachings of the Avesta.

* Mr. Jamshedji D. Nadarsha tried to show that Nâhid was the planet Venus which was pictured as a naked female with a crown on her head in a Persian book named Jamaspi.

Para 126th.

We shall now consider the 126th para of the Yashta. Both the meanings of the common words and expressions are given together. The meaning applicable to the river is given in italics.

Translation : The pure Ardvisura, the knowing one stands in the form of a maiden.

Sriraydo — beautiful—*beautiful.*

Ashamaydo — possessed of great courage—*being cloudy.**

Huraodhaydo—of good appearance —*riding in the heavens* (स्वर्+रोध); or *of good banks* (सुरोधस्).

After *huraodhaydo* the sentence runs thus :—

Uskât yâstaydo frazushem adhkem vanghânem pouru-pakshlem zaranayanem — who has put on from above pleasant garment (and) dress fully-embroidered (and) golden—*who has at a great height put pleasant lightning*† *as well-decorated (and) golden dress.*

Eregvaithyo—Holy—*pure.*

* Cf. Vedic अश्म "cloud." Or the word *askamaydo* might mean "not quiet, boisterous" (अ + शम). In the above passage all the MSS. read *askamaydo* as one word; in § 64, however, five MSS. give the reading as here but one MS. gives the reading *ask-maydo*. This last reading is important. As applied to the maiden *askmaydo* means "of perfect wisdom," and as applied to the river, it means "full of water."

† *Adkka*—Sk. अत्क

Raevat chithrem â zâtayâo (=*â raevat &c.*)—Born of glorious seed—*which is produced near the shining* (*asterism*) *Chitrâ.* *

Para 127th.

Bâdha yatha-mâm baresmo-zasta= Verily (the pure Ardvisura stands like a maiden with Barsam in her hand in the proper manner†—*having the* (*asterism*) *Hasta* ‡ *for Barsam.*

Frâ-gaoshâvara sispemna chathru-karana = with a pendent, four-cornered ear-ring—*carrying thunder*¶ *which is swelling* (sispemna § (*and*) *which has* (=*is situated in*) *four corners* (=*directions*).

Zaranaeni-minum$ *barat*=Bearing a golden necklace—*carrying* मीन (*Pisces*) (*the 12th sign of the Zodiac*).

---

* *Chithra* is, I think, the 14th asterism चित्रा (lit. "brilliant"). It is the beautiful star of the first magnitude a Virgines or Spica constituting an asterism by itself and figured as a pearl or lamp (see Surya Siddhanta p. 334). If *raevat chithrem* is taken to mean "the brilliant Raevat," this might be a reference to the 27th asterism Revati. But the objection against this interpretation is that the Revati is not a brilliant asterism. The passage might also mean "produced in the sky (चित्र);" we have seen elsewhere that *afsh-chithra*, *zemas-chithra* &c., were portions, of the sky. Or it might mean "produced brilliantly."

† *Yatha-mâm* or *yath-mâm*; *Cf.* यथावत् "in the proper manner."

‡ *Zasta* (हस्त "the hand") is the 13th lunar mansion It is figured as a hand and contains 5 stars corresponding to the 5 fingers. These are the 5 principal stars in the constellation Corvus (see Surya Siddhanta p. 334.)

¶ *Gaoshâvara*-from *gaosha*, "ear" and *bere* "to carry;" hence "ear-ring" *Gaosha* is also= घोष = "thunder" which applies to the Ardvisura.

§ In Yt. 19-67 we have *spaetinish varemish sispemn* =" (Hilmand) throwing up its white billows."

$ I adopt the reading of 8 MSS. which read *zaranaeni-minum* as one word. In Râm Yt. § 57 we have the word *zaranyominem*, which is an adjunct of *Vava* (wind). I think that the word *minu* is another form *mina* (मीन = fish). Ervad Kanga says the same in his Dictionary.

NOTE:—As already seen in §§ 90, 126, 127, &c., the Ardvisura is the constellation known as the Eridanus or Stream. Brown says that in Lajard's plate XVI-5 the Stream is shown with a *Fish* above and another *Fish* below it. These Fishes are the constellation Pisces.

From the Median representations of Mithra, &c., it seems that the Avestan people were very fond of grouping in a single picture several constellations from the different quarters of the celestial globe; *e. g.* (1) We find the Bull, Dog, Scorpion and Crow in one picture. (2) In another Ear-of-corn, Eagle, Arrow, Tortoise and Dolphin are seen together. (3) In the well-known figure of Mithra, we find an animal having the head of the Lion, tail of the Scorpion, wing of the Eagle and body of the Bull.

Similarly the Ardvisura (= Eridanus) is here pictured along with the constellations picked up by the writer from all the four quarters of the heavens.

One of the most favourite ornaments of women is the necklace, which when worn, has the shape of a *fish*. Now as the Ardvisura is a female, the contellation Pisces is readily imagined as her necklace.

It also appears that the women of the Avestan times carried Barsam in their hand (*Zasta*). Very likely the *Zasta* suggests to the author's mind the asterism *Zasta* (=Hasta) which he connects with the Eridanus. Similarly the asterism *Chitrâ*, (=*Chithra*) which in the Avesta means the "Source" is represented by the writer as the source of the Ardvisura.

We shall presently see that in § 128 the *Sato-stranghâ* (शतभीषज = Aquari) is supposed to be the crown of the Ardvisura.

It will thus be seen that the author groups together Chitrâ and Eridanus which are opposite each

other*. and Shata-Bhishaja which is at right angles to them.

Hvâjâta (*Aredvisura anâhita*) — (The pure Ardvisura) nobly-born—*nobly-born.*

Upa tâm srirâm manaothrim = (Bearing nicklace) on that beautiful neck—(*Carrying Pisces*) *on that beautiful celestial strap* (*mana*+वध्रि).†

NOTE.—The Eridanus looks like a strap in the skies; hence the expression used by the author is very appropriate.

Hâ he maidhim nyâjata yathacha hukerepta fshtâna, yathacha anghen nivâzana —She (the maiden) has girt her waist in such a manner that her two breasts are ‡ of good appearance and pleasant—*She* (*the river*) *carries her middle part in such a manner that the watery expanses are*¶ *well-arranged* § *and in such a manner* (*that they*) *have become pleasant* $

Para 128th.

Upairi pumsâm bandayat Aredvisura anâhita sato-stranghâm— (Like a lady who) has put on on her head (*upairi*) a crown which has a hundred brilliants—*the Ardvisura has in the sky* (upa ri) *put on the Hundred-stars* (*constellation*) (*as her*) *crown.*

NOTE—The constellation *Sato-stranghâ** appears to be the same as the शतभीषज (—the asterism of 100 stars; *lit.* of 100 physicians). The Avestan word carries a clearer meaning with it. Of course the number 100 is not to be taken as an exact one. The exact Sk. word is शततारका

Zaranaenim — Golden—*of golden colour.*

Ashta-kaozdâm — Which has eight folds (see Harlez)—*which has eight rays* (*see Dar.*).

Ratha-kairyâm — which has the shape of a chariot—*belonging to Ratha and Kara*† (*the constellations Chariot and Hasta*).

Drafshakavitim — which has frills (or small flags) — *which has drops of water* (द्रप्स *or sparks of fire*).

S'riram — Beautiful—*beautiful.*

Anupoithvaitim—which is of proper size—*which posess good nectar.*‡

Hukeretâm—Of good make—*well-arranged.*

Para 129th.

Bavraini vastrâo vanghat Aredvisura anâhita,&c.—(Like a lady who) wears a garment of beavers, of thirty beavers giving birth to four young ones—*the Ardvisura wears moving* § *garment of thirty moving* (*clouds*) *rising* (जन्) *in four* (*directions*).

---

* Similarly in the Mithric art, the Scorpion and the Bull are seen grouped together in one picture.—the Scorpion biting the *genitalia* of the Bull.

† व of वध्रि becomes ओ. Or the word may be *mana—aothra* =“celestial covering” (see Kanga's Gr. p. 6). *Manothri* is another reading.

‡ *Anghen*—plural for dual, *fshtâna* the subject being in the dual.

¶ *Pshtâna* is, I think, a corruption of *afsh*+*tâna* (अप्+तानं); तानं — expanse. Cf. *afsh-tachin* अ is dropped as in वगाश also in Nâhid &c. One MS L 18 reads *afshtâna*, which word clearly shows that the writer understood the sense of the word as applied to the river. This reading also indicates the derivation. *Pshtâna* as applied to the lady is dual whereas as applied to the river it is plural.

§ *Hukerepta* — सुकॢप्त “well arranged.”.

$ *Nivâzâna* or *Navâzâna.*

* “Cf. the word *Hapto-iring*; *iring* = ऋक्ष and ऋषि all mean “the bright ones, the stars;” so far as the etymology is concerned, it is difficult to see why ऋक्ष (= Gr. *arktos*, Lat *ursus*) should mean the ‘bear’” —which is also one of the meanings of this word. Dr. Haug says that the word ऋक्ष occurs in Rv. I-24-10 and according to Shatapatha Brahmana II-1-2-4 was afterwards changed into Sapta rishayah “seven sages.”

† *Ratha* is this para and *Vâsha* in § 11 seem to be the constellation Chariot. *Kara* may be the constellation Hasta. For the form *kairya* from *kara* cf. nairya, Naotairya &c. Or *rath-kairya* might simply mean “causing pleasure” (*ratha*—रत.)

‡ *Poithva*—पेत्व “nectar” अनु— good; Cf. अन्वर्थ.

§ Bavraini from वर्व् “to move.”

Yat asti......gaonotema=The beaver is the best and of the best colour—*the moving cloud is the best and of the best colour.* *

Bavrish bavaiti upâpo=The beaver lives in water—*the moving cloud is watery.*

Yatha keretem, &c.=When at the proper time (there is) the cutting (of the beavers) (their) leathers become brilliant and shine much like a silver (and) golden ornament—*When at the proper time there is the seperation (of the clouds)* (their) *latter parts* (चरम) *become brilliant, &c.*

Para 11th.

Yâ paourva vâshem vazâite=(Like a lady who) drives a car in the front—*She* (= *Ardvisura*) *drives the* (*constellation*) *Chariot in the front.*

Ankhnâo drajaite vâshahe—(and) holds the reins of the car—*holds the reins* † *of the Chariot.*

Ahmya vâshe vazemna, narem paitish maremna avat manangha mainimna = Driving in this car, remembering the man (=her lover?), and thus thinking in her mind—*Driving in this* (*constellation*). *Chariot, remembering the man,* ‡ *&c.*

A glance at the starry map will show that the constellation chariot stands in front of the Eridanus. Our author is, therefore, quite right in imagining that the Ardvisura drove in the chariot. This passage removes all possible doubts about the identification of the Ardvisura (= Eridanus).

Para 64th.

This para is almost the same as § 126; only the passage "*nizanga aothra paitishmukhta zaranyo-urvikhshna bâmyâ*" is not found there.

Translation of the passage quoted above. (O you) who have put on shoes on the feet, who have a golden crown and who are beautiful—*You who are overspread with moving covering,* * who have golden aspect (ऊरू + ईक्षण) (and) who are beautiful. †

* This and the following clauses are parenthetical and explanatory.

† The stars of the Auriga present a resemblance to an ancient Roman Chariot, so that the title "Chariot" seems to be more appropriate than "Charioteer" ...... Ideler thinks that the original figure was made up of 5 stars *a b*, &c. The driver (represented by the star Capella) is imagined as standing on an antique sloping chariot, marked by *b*. The other stars represent the *reins* (see Star Lore of all Ages by Olcott p. 65). It will thus be seen that the expression used by our author is quite appropriate.

‡ Could this man be Mithra?

* *Paitishmukhta* = प्रतिमुक्त "overspread." *Nizanga*—Cf. जंघा from गम् or हन् "to go." *Aothra* from *av* "to protect."

† In Fr. Yt. § 107 Ashi Vanghuhi (the angel of wealth) is compared with a maiden as in Aban Yt. §§ 126 &c. Similarly in Hadokhta Nusk II-9 the Daenâ or Kerdâr (= the sum total of the righteous actions of a deceased pious man) is compared with a maiden. I say that the above passages also contain homonymous words and expressions. They confirm the views put forward by me as regards the passages in the Aban Yashta which have been already considered, in as much as many of the words and expressions used in the Fr. Yashta and the Hadokhta Nusk are different from those in the Aban Yashta. I shall give the translation of the passages in the Fr. Yt and the Hadokhta Nusk, which are applicable to the Ashi and the Daenâ.

Fr. Yt. § 107:—Ashi (= wealth) which is *srirayâo* full of glory, *ashamayâo*, boisterous (= making great noise while ringing), *huraodhayâo* of good growth (= grown much), *erezvaithyo yâ uskât stayâo*, beautiful because standing on high (= occupying high dignity), *raevat chithrem âzâtavâo* produced from brilliant source (= obtained by good means).

Hadokhta II-9:—The Daenâ (=action) is *srirayâo* glorious, *khshoithnyâo* brilliant *aurush-bâzvo* both the sides of which are fair, *amayâo* full of courage, *huraodhayâo* of good growth = fully developed), *huzarshtayâo* very pleasant (सु हृष्ट), *eredvafshnyâo* straight and prosperity-giving (= from *fshu*), *sraotanvo* of upright nature, *âzâtayâo* well-produced, *raevatchithrayâo* brilliant and shining, *pancha-dasyâo* containing 15 (virtues), *raodhaeshva, &c.*, so prosperous in (its) development that it is the best of all wisdoms (*dâman*).

Note. It is difficult to say what were the 15 virtuous actions referred to above. I am of opinion that they were those mentioned in Vendidad III-41 and 42 and IV-44.

The Eridanus.

W. T. Olcott in his "Star Lore of all Ages" (pp. 195-198) says "According to Eratosthenes, this imaginary river of the stars (Eridanus) winding its devious way across the winter skies, represented the river Nile....‡.The constellation Eridanus is so extended that it has been divided into the northern and southern stream. *The former has its source near the first-magnitude star Rigel in the foot of the Orion*.......The Arab name for this constellation was *Al-Nahr* meaning the 'river' ...... The river Jordan, the Red Sea, and the River of the Judge are other names for this stream. It also bears the name 'Oceanus' and the 'River of the Ocean.' "Brown says that "the constellation *Stream* was originally 'that *great* river' the classical Euphrates which in the Old Test. is simply called 'the river'" (Vol. I., p. 240.)

Brown suggests that as an Aryan name, *Eridanus* would mean "the strong-flowing" but he has strong reasons for believing that it is also a Turanian river-name, meaning "the strong river." I think that "Aredvi-sura" also means the "strong moving one" from ऋ "to go." "Aredvi" may also be connected with *erethvi* or *eredvi* which means "lifted up on high." The Pahlvi form of the word Aredvi might have been wrongly read *Ardni* (= Eridanus).

Date of Zarathustra from Aban Yt. §§ 88 and 90.

In § 85 we are told that Ahuramazda asked the Ardvisura to go from the stars and reach the earth. According to §§ 88 and 89 when the Ardvisura began to flow from the stars to go to the earth, she said "O holy righteous Spitama (Zarathushtra), Ahuramazda *created* thee as the lord of the corporeal world and *created* me as the protectress of all the holy creations."

Then we have this important statement in § 90:—*Kana thvâm yasna yasâne......yase tava mazdâo Kerenaot tachare, noit tachare antare arethem, upairi hvare khshaetem.* "With what Yasna shall I praise thee, because Ahuramazda made thy flowing; the flowing was not on the earth but on to the sun."* The statement that the river Eridanus flowed towards the sun means that the Eridanus was in conjuction with the sun. This passage cannot bear any other sense, unless the word *upairi* ("on or upon") is twisted to yield some other meaning.

The constellation Eridanus is situated at the foot of the Orion with which the Hindus connected Aldebaran the red star in the eye of the Taurus (see Star Lore of all Ages by Olcott pp. 278 279).

It will thus be seen that according to § 90 of the Aban Yashta, the sun was in conjunction with the Eridanus and its companion-constellations Orion and Taurus. We have been also told that when the river began to flow towards the sun (that is to say, when the Eridanus was in conjunction with the sun), Ahuramazda created Zarathushtra. Now we have already seen that Zarathushtra was born at the commencement of spring. Thus we conclude that when Zarathushtra was born, Eridanus and Taurus were in conjunction with the sun at the beginning of spring. Here also we see that Zarathushtra belonged to the Taurus age and very likely to its end (2500 B C.)

‡ Among the Babylonians "*the river of the sun-god*" was that of Ningersu-Tammuz "the river of the Orion," the Eridanus (see Brown II-205).

No. II.

Gathic, Pahlvi, Pazend and Sanskrit Ashirvadas.*

At the commencement of the nuptial ceremony the bride and bridegroom are made to sit in front of each other with a screen between. After the raw thread is tied round the couple, incense is burnt on the fire and rice is thrown by the male and female on each other. Then follows a clapping of the hands by the assembly, indicating that the marriage contract is complete. But this is clearly a wrong belief.

Three elements of marriage.

The three important elements of the marriage ceremony among the Zoroastrians are: (1) the meeting of an assembly of friends and acquaintances; (2) the consent to the marriage given by the couple or by the witnesses on their behalf; (3) the benedictory prayer recited by the priests, namely, *Har do tân râmishna avjoon bâd* "May you both be very happy." At this point the marriage contract becomes complete, and therefore I think, the people assembled should clap their hands after the abovementioned recitation.

Gathic Ashirvada.

The Gathic Ashirvadas are contained in the Yasna Ha 53 §§ 3 to 8. I shall first give my translation of the 3rd and 4th strophes.

Ha 53 § 3:—" O Pourichista of the family of Haechataspa and descendant of Spitama, the youngest of Zarathushtra's daughters, Ahuramazda has given (*or* appointed for) thee as thy husband that man who is devoted to the good mind and righteousness. Therefore we two (priests) together ask† thee dost thou with (thy) bounteous intellect of piety love* (him) with good wisdom?"

Ha 53 § 4:—(Pouruchista answers) " Verily I love him, I will vie (with him in love), when father (*fethro*) gives me away."

(The two priests recite):—" For thy pious husband, pious tillers and relatives, may Ahuramazda for ever give (thee) brilliant blessings † (*khenvat-hanghush*) (and) desires to attend (on them) (*mebet-ush*) for the advancement of good religion."‡

In this strophe Pouruchista gives her consent and immediately the priests commence to invocate blessings.

Pazend Ashirvada.

I shall now give literal translations of the first portions of the Pazend, Pahlvi and Sanskrit Ashirvâdas.

Translation of the Pazend Ashirvâda:—

"May the Creator Hormazda grant you a long progeny of sons and grand-sons, plentiful riches and cordial friendship, active body from strong seed, long life and existence for 150 years. On the day (so and so) of the month (so and so) in the year (so and so) of the King of King Yazdagard Sheheriar of Sâsân dynasty, in the city (so so) in auspicious Iran an assembly has met for the husbanding of (= supplying husband to) this lady and for her daughter-giving (= marriage ceremony) in accordance with the law of

* This subject was read before the Gatha Society and is only remotely connected with Zarathushtra and his age.

† *Perashvâ*—from *pares*, which becomes *feras*, as in *ferasâ* (= question"). Now *feras* + *hvâ* (termination dual first person) = *ferashvâ* (see Kanga's Gr. p. 26). The dual shows that two priests were necessary.

* *Hudânu* + *vareshvâ*. The latter is imperative At. 2-1 from *vere* (वृ) "to choose"; Cf. स्वयंवर

† Similar blessings are found in Rv. 10-85-26 and 28: " Speak as a lady to thy gathered people......well thrive the kinsmen of this bride."

‡ *Khenvat-hanghush*—compound noun 2-8; Cf *bareshnush gâtush*, &c.

Mebet-ush—Compound noun 2-8 from मव्" to attend." The pre. part. of मेव् would be *mevet* on the analogy of *hâget* from *hach*; subsequently *mevet* would become *mebet*—a reading adopted by Dr. Mills. *Ush* is indeclinable (=" wish").

the Mazdayasnian religion, on a contract of 2000 *dirams** of pure white silver and 2 *dinârs* of real gold of Nishâpuri coinage. Have you with your family with true mind, with three *gavashnis* and for the increase of your righteousness agreed to give (this bride) in marriage to (this husband) up to the end of life † ? Have you (=bride and bridegroom) preferred the contract of marriage with true mind up to the end of life ?" ‡

Then the priests recite :—*Har do tân râmishna asun bâd* " may you both be very happy."

Pahlvi Ashirvada.

The Pahlvi Ashirvâda § is found in a book printed by Kavasji Nusserwanji Kanga in 1859. It closely resembles the Pazend Ashirvâda. It appears that in more recent times some one has transcribed the Pazend into Pahlvi and in doing so has committed good many blunders. I do not propose to give the translation of this Ashirvâda, as it would be a mere repetition of the Pazend. The only difference that we find between these two Ashirvâdas is that in the Pahlvi, the amount is stated to be 2000 *dinârs*. This is very likely a mistake, as otherwise the sum to be paid would be very heavy.

Sanskrit Ashirvada.

This Ashirvâda* may be literally translated as under :—

" May the Creator, the Omniscient Lord grant you great progeny of sons, much prosperity, hearty friendship, continued advance of body, (good) appearance and a long life for 150 years. An assembly of the best persons having met in the city of——on the day——of the month——of the year——of Yazdagard Sheheriar *of old, with these bene-*

---

* A *diram* was a silver coin equivalent in value to two pence; and a *dinâr* was a golden coin equivalent to about 4 shillings.

† The reply is " agreed."

‡ The reply is "preferred."

§ I give here the text of the Pahlvi Ashirvâda, the Pazend of which is given within the brackets wherever necessary :—

Yehbunt (dihât) tân Dâdâr Auhormazda (Hormazda) frahist frazandân zakra (nar) o nârikân (Pazend has, nabirengân), frâkh roxi o dosti labmeman (dil) rotâk (ravâ) tan men (az) chitar (chihar) lobâk (ravâ) dir zivashni natrund (Pazend has o pâyandi) sad o panjâh shânt (sâl) barâ (ba) yume (roz) [vahmân (falân)] barâ (ba) binâ (mâh) [vahmân (falân)] shant (sâl) madam (avar) [vahmân (falân)] men (az) malkân malkâ (shâhân-shah) Yazdgard Sheheriâr Sasân tokhme barâ (ba) shatrostân (shaherastân) khajasta o shapirân (Pazend has not got this word) Airân (Irân) hanjaman jasta ekvimunet (ested), madam (avar) dâd âine Dine Mâzdayasni barâ (ba) kad khadâi banâ nishmane bentman (dûkht) debashni; denman (in) nishman (kanik) [vahmân (falâni)] shamvar (nâmvar) barâ (ba) paeman talin hazâr (do hazâr) dinâr zabâi (Pazend has diram sim spet vejah va do dinâr zar surkha sarh) Nishâpuri makdaluntam o yahvunt (padiraftan o budan); tân levatman (avâ) nafshman (khesh) dudmân barâe zani hamdadastâni barâ (pavan) (pa) râsta minashne (manashni) pavan (pa) se gobishne (gavishni) nefshman khesh) kerfe vakhshashni vahmân (falân râ) andâk (andâ) zindagi paeman barâ dâi (bi dâdet); vad andâk (andâ) zandagi paemân pavan (pa) râst minashne pasand kardet. Kola (bar) do tân râmishne avazun bâd.

* The text is as follows :—

देयाद् वो दाता सर्वज्ञानी स्वामी प्रभूतां पुत्रसंततिं विपुलां विभूतिं मानसीं प्रीतिं तनो रूपप्रवृतिं दीर्घां च जीवितस्थितिम् (पंचाशदधिकं शतं वर्षाणां) ॥ संवत्सरेषु (अमुक) शतेषु संवत् (अमुक) वर्षे (अमुक) रोजे (अमुक) मासे (अमुक) नगरे प्राक् यज्दगर्दे शेहेरिआर अर्वाक् वाग्भिः आशीर्वादाभिराभिः विंशतिशतजरनिशापुरिमौवर्णिकाभ्यां (पूर्वाचार अस्य अतीता) वो प्रवर्तामि उत्तमानां हंजमने संप्राप्ते उपरि अहनन्यायेन यद् माज्दयस्न्याः दीन्याः परिणीतकलत्रतया कन्यादानं (यदि कुमारी भवति) इयं कुमारी (यदि द्वितीयनारी भवति) इयं नारी (अमुक) नाम्नी (युग्मार्थे) युष्माभिः निजान्वयसमालोचन ऐकमत्येन सत्येन मनसा त्रिसृभिः वाणीभिः आत्मनः पुण्यवृद्धये यद् (अमुकाकस्य) आजन्मसीमं प्रदत्ता ?

(द्वितीयोपाध्यायः कन्यापक्षप्रतिनिधिं पृच्छति) प्रदत्ता ?

(वधूपक्षप्रतिनिधिः ब्रूते) प्रदत्ता ॥

(प्रमुखोपाध्यायः वरपक्षं पृच्छति) युष्माभिश्च आजन्मसीमं सत्येन मनसा प्रतिकृता ?

(स ब्रूते) प्रतिकृता ॥

(मुख्योपाध्यायः ब्रूते) उभयोः अपि कल्याणवृद्धिः भूयात् ॥

dictions containing ancient speech ——(as) the Ashirvâda is included in the ancient custom*——I *declare to you* that in accordance with the law of the rite which is of the Mazdasnian religion, there is the giving of the girl in marriage (*lit.* by way of married-wifehood) with 2000 coins and 2 golden coins of Nishapura. † Is this maiden (or woman—if a widow) given by you with one accord (ऐकमत्येन) with true mind and with three speeches for the increase of your righteousness with a view to (the continuation of) your family up to the end of the life of so and so?

(The second priest asks the witness on the bride's side): Is she given?

(The senior priest asks the witness on the bridegroom's side): Is she taken by you with true mind up to the end of the life (of this man)?

(The second priest asks the bridegroom): Is she accepted?

(He says): Accepted.

(The senior priest recites): May there be the increase of happiness to you both."

The above is recited thrice.

Difference betwean Pazend, Pahlvi and Sanskrit Ashirvadas.

It will be seen that the passages and expressions underlined in the Sanskrit are not to be found in the Pazend.

As already seen, the Pahlvi is practically the same as the Pazend.

From both the Pahlvi and the Sanskrit we find that it is essential to call an assemblage.

In the Pazend the first question is put to the witness on the bridegroom's side, whether he has agreed to take the bride on a contract of 2000 dirams and 2 dinars. In Sanskrit the first question is put to the witness on the bride's side whether he has agreed to give the bride, &c.

Some of the Sk. manuscripts agree with the Pahlvi in stating that the amount to be paid was 2000 golden coins. In one manuscript belonging to my friend Ervad Mancekji R. Unwalla and written about 175 years ago, the clause relating to the payment of money has been altogether omitted.

From the Pahlvi, Pazend and Sanskrit texts at hand it is difficult to decide whether the money was to be paid to the bride or by the bride. In the Pahlvi and the Pazend it is asked whether the girl is accepted *on a contract of* 2000 dirams, &c. The expression "on a contract of" (*ba paemân*) might mean either "contracting to pay" or "contracting to receive." Similarly in Sanskrit the expression "with coins" (सुवर्णाभिः) might mean "along with coins" or "in exchange for coins."*

Turning to the Avestan times we find that a ear-ring (*gaoshâvare*) was presented to the bride by her brother or father at the time of her marriage; for, in Vendidad 14 § 15 it is said that "a sister or a daughter wearing a ear-ring should be given in marriage with a pious man."

In Apastamba II-6-13-12 we are told that it is declared in the Veda that at the time of marriage, a gift ......should be made (by the bridegroom) to the father of the bride in order to fulfil the law: "Therefore he should give a hundred cows besides a chariot."†

---

* पूर्वाचारे आशीः अनिता It is difficult to determine what the correct reading is.

‡ विंशातिशतनिशापुरिसावर्णिकाभ्यां If we take the reading सुवर्णाभिः the passage means "with 2000 Nishapuri golden coins."

* In Sanskrit the instrumental case yields the sense of accompaniment. It also shows the price at which a thing is bought: *e. g.* कियता मूल्येन क्रीतं पुस्तकं at what price was the book brought?"

† In the Institutes of Sacred Law of Gautama IV-6 to 12 we find that in the Arshâ wedding the bridegroom presented a cow and a bull to him who was the guardian

It will thus be seen that the Vedic and the Iranian customs as to the nuptial donations were entirely different.

In the Pazend and Pahlvi the witnesses and also the marrying couple are asked to give their consent; in the Sanskrit the bride's consent is not asked for.

From all the Ashirvâdas we find that the marriage is *madam dâd âine dine Mâzdayasni*, (*avar dât âin dine* Mazdayasni) (अइन न्यायेन यद् माज्दइ-अस्न्याः दीन्याः) *i.e.* "according to the rule of the rite of the Mazdayasnian religion."

Three elements of Marriage.

From a careful study of the different Ashirvâdas it appears that in a wedding ceremony it is essential *firstly* that an assembly shall be called, *secondly* the consents of the parties shall be taken and *thirdly* that the priests must express their approval of the contract by the reciting the benedictory prayer "May you both be very happy."

As to the third element the following passage in the Sk. Ashirvâda is very important: —अर्वाग्वाग्भिराशीर्वादाभिराभिः &c. "With these benedictions containing ancient speech I declare ....the wedding, &c." In some MSS. instead of the above passage we read गंभीराशीर्वादभिराभिः "With these *solemn* benedictions &c.' It seems that the priest is to declare the sealing of the wedding bond by reciting the solemn Ashirvâdas and not otherwise. In other words the recitation of the benedictory prayer is a *sine qua non*. For the reason that the Sanskrit Ashirvâda contains this important note

of the maiden; in the Brahmâ wedding however the father gave his daughter dressed (in two garments) and decked with ornaments to a person possessing (sacred) learning, of virtuous conduct who had relatives and who was of a good disposition. Thus among the Hindus themselves the customs were different.

I think that we should not discontinue its recitation as some propose to do.

Gathic Ashirvada.

All the abovementioned elements are found in the Gathic Ashirvâda also. As we shall see hereafter the 7th strophe of the Ha 53 is an address to the assembly, which was essential in the Gathic times also. In Ha 53 §§ 3-4 only the consent of the girl is taken. For ought we know to the contrary the consent of the bridegroom was not asked for*. In the latter portion of the 4th stanza of Ha 53, immediately after the consent of the girl is taken, the priests begin to recite the Ashirvâda which end with the stanza No. 7.

Ha 53 § 5.

We shall now discuss the strophes Nos. 5 to 8 of Ha 53.

Ha 53-5:—" (The senior priest says) I speak (*i. e.* invoke) (these) blessings, for (on) the bride who is being married and for (on) you (*i. e.* bridegroom). By (reason of) my invoking these blessings, may you rejoice. Being well acquainted with religious laws, may you obtain the life which is of the good mind. May you love each other with righteousness, so that there may be a happy home."

I think that *kainibyo* and *khshmaibyâ* are used for Pouruchista and her husband—the nouns and the verbs being used in the plural for showing respect. Similarly in Vend. 14-15 the word for the husband is used in the plural.† In the strophe No. 3

* In Rigveda also we find that the consent of the bride only was necessary. Cf. Rv. X-85-9 "The Sun-god bestowed his consenting (शंसंती daughter Suryâ on her Lord." The reason for taking the girl's consent is evident, namely that she has to reside with another family.

† The passage runs thus: *Khangha vâ dugaha vâ........ mat gaoshâvare nerebyo ashavabyo upavâdhayen*; "a sister or daughter with a ear-ring shall be given in marriage to a pious man." Here *nerebyo ashavabyo* is used in the plural for respect. Cf. इति शङ्कराचार्याः "So says Shankara." In Sk. दारा (wife) is always plural.

the singular is used for Pouruchista, because she is spoken of *alone.*

The word *vasyamnâbyo* is very important. It is a present passive participle showing that the woman is "*being married*" and that her marriage ceremony is not yet complete. The strophe before us cannot possibly be an address to the married couples in the assembly, because the word *vasyamnâbyo* ("who are being married") cannot apply to the *already married* couples. Neither can we suppose that Pouruchista was married along with some other maidens at the same time, for the reason that there is no reference to the marriage of any other lady or ladies. The word *vasyamnâbyo* must, therefore, refer to Pouruchista alone.

Mânsdazdoom is a compound verb from मंद्+दा (मंद् — rejoice) meaning "may you rejoice." With this we might compare *Har do tân râmishna avasun bâd* "may you both be very happy."

The expression *daenâbish abyastâ* ("being well acquainted with religious laws") might be compared with the following from the Pazenda Ashirvâda: "*Hamishah hudin huhim bât*" (Sk. सदैव दीनिशीलोभव) "May you be always religious and full of knowledge"

Ha 53 § 6.

Translation :—"Thus, O men and women, may you truthfully stop in restraint (*yeme*) the increase (*frâidim*) of the Druj with (its) path. I desire that you may untie (=deprive) your bodies of the Drujs † May ill-honoured fame (*dush-kharethem*) reach (*nâmsat*) the supporters (*i. e.* followers) of Vâyu, ‡ the Dregvants (and) those who destroy righteousness—by these you destroy the spiritual life."

This strophe is addressed to the assembly. Similarly the initial passage in the Pazend, Pahlvi and Sanskrit Ashirvâdas—(*namely* "may Hormazda grant you a long progeny of sons and grand-sons") is addressed to the married persons in the assembly; it cannot apply to the marrying couple, since their consents have not yet been taken.

This strophe may be compared with different passages in the Pazend and Sanskrit Ashirvâdas: *Sbasgi ma-kun, khishmagi ma-bar...... âz kâmi ma-bar* (मा पैशुन्यं कुरु । मा क्रोधं वह । ... मा लोभं वह) &c. "Do not indulge in scandals, avoid being angry......Do not be avaricious."

Ashahi satâeât, jâdui nigaendât (स्तुहि पुण्यं निंद दैत्यान्): "praise righeousness, hate the Demons (the sorcerers).

Ha 53 § 7.

Translation: "And may there be to you the fruit of the pleasure (*maga*) (of marriage), when the love (*âjush*) which is seated in the heart (and) at the bottom of devotion* goes (*mraochâms*) up and down (*parachâ aorâchâ*) (in a place) where the spirit of the Dregvant (*i. e.* the evil thought) totally disappears (*bard anâmsat*). May you fan (*ivijyathâ*)† that pleasure (*maga*) so that your last word may be *vayo* (—Ah)."

This stanza might be compared with the following passage from the Ha 54 § 1 of the Yasna, which is quoted in the Pazend Ashirvâda and the translation of which occurs in the Sanskrit Ashirvâda :—*A Airyamâ ishyo rafedhrâi jantu nere-*

---

* Cf. *pazdayanti* (See Kanga's Gr. p. 255).

† The Drujs are the evil thoughts, evil passions, &c.

‡ *Vayoo-beredu*=supporter or follower of the good of Wind known as वायु or मरुत probably referring to the Vedic people. I think that *Vayu* is used in good sense and *Vayoo* in a bad sense.

* *Hakhti* (सक्ति) means (1) devotion, and (2) abdomen. If the latter, there is an indecent allusion. We find many such passages in the Vedas.

† *Ivijyathâ*—from वीज् to fan, increase

byaschâ nâiribyaschâ Zarathushtrahe vangheush rafedhrâi manangho.
"May the desired (angel) Aryaman come for the joy, of (for the joy of the good mind of) the Zoroastrian men and women."

The stanza seems to be an address to the assembly and also the couple.

Ha 53 §8.

Translation:—"May the evil workers be foiled along with these* and may all (of them) shriek through ridicule. May he who is in chain† know (or receive) from the good rulers injury (*jenerâm*), hardship (*khrunerâm*) and rest (*râmâm*) out of (*i. e.* may they be banished from) the cities and villages. May he move (*iratu*) with chains (*deresâ*) and may he quickly be the greatest of (the demon of) death (*i.e.* may he quickly die.")

The first line in the above passage might be compared with the following passage in the Pazend: *Aheema deva avshindi* (Sk. आह्रेमनं च दैत्यान् निर्दल च) "Destroy Ahreman and the Demons."

It will thus be seen that the Pazend and the Sanskrit Ashirvadas are practically based upon the Gathic Ashirvada and that the important elements of our nuptial ceremony have remained the same during more than 44 centuries.

* That is, the Dregvants referred to in § 6. We might also translate *andish* as "by these" that is to say, the good rulers referred to below.

† *Drafsho;* It might also mean "the deceiver.

No. III.

Did the Zoroastrians borrow their dcotrine of monotheism from the Jews?

In his "Theosophy or Psychological Religion" (p. 48) Prof. Max Muller says "There is another point on which we can observe an even more striking similarity between the Old Testament and the Avesta, namely the strong assertion of the oneness of god. Here, however, it seems to me that if there was any change of thought between the followers of Moses and of Zoroaster, it may have been the latter who were influenced. The sudden change from the henotheism of the Veda to the monotheism of the Avesta has never been accounted for, and I venture to suggest though not without hesitation, that it may have taken place in Media in the original home of the Zoroastrian religion. It was in the cities of Media that a large Jewish population was settled, after the King of Assyria had carried away Israel and put them in Halah and in Habor by the river Gozan and in the cities of the Medes (2 Kings XVIII-11). Now however difficult an exchange of religious ideas may be between the people speaking different languages, the fact of their worshipping one god or many gods could not fail to attract attention. The Jews impressed their neighbours with the conviction that there was but one god."

It is much to be regretted that such a careful *savant* as Prof. Max Muller should have put forward the opinion that the Iranians borrowed their doctrine of monotheism from the Jews in the 6th century B.C. or thereabouts. It is some satisfaction however that other scholars thought otherwise.

Prof. Hommel in the March No. for 1899 of the Proceedings of the Society of Biblical Archæology calls attention in his Assyriological Notes to the name "Assar Mazas" appearing in a list of Assyrian gods. The section of the list in which this name appears contains "a number of foreign sounding names" belonging to gods honoured presumably in the outlying portions of the Assyrian dominions.

Prof. Hommel claims that "this god (Assar Mazas) is no other than the Iranian Ahuramazda" and he thus concludes his arguments in favour of this opinion: "Concerning Assur Mazas, I should like to remark in closing this paragraph that we have the same older pronounciation of Iranian words as in Kassitic Surias (later Ahura and Hvarya, but Comp. Sk. Asura and Suria) which is of the highest importance for the history of the Aryan languages. In the same Kassitic period between 1700 to to 1200 B. C., I suppose, was borrowed by the Assyrians the Iranian word Assar Mazas."

That the Jews were indebted to the Zoroastrians for some of their important doctrines even Prof. Max Muller has admitted without doubt. On p. 47 of his book, he says "The chief doctrines which the Jews are supposed to have borrowed from the followers of Zoroaster are a belief in the resurrection of the body, a belief in the immortality of the soul and a belief in future rewards and punishments. It is well-known that these doctrines were entirely or almost entirely, absent from the oldest phase of religion among the Jews."*

Again as regards the word Asmodeus, Prof Max Muller says (on p. 187).

"There is only one really Persian name of one of the evil spirits attached to Ahriman, which actually has found its way into the Old Testament in the apocryphal book of Tobit III-8, namely *Asmodeus* which is the Persian (? Avesta) *Aeshma daeva*, the demon of anger and wrath. This name could have been borrowed from a Persian source only, and proves the existence of a real historical intercourse between Jews and Persians at the time when the book of Tobit was written."

In his "Zoroaster in the Gathas (p.p. 82-87) Dr. Geiger tries to show that the nature and attributes of Jehovah, in the Old Testament are exactly similar to those of Ahuramazda in the Gathas. Nevertheless he declares that it is an *entirely mistaken assumption* that Zarathustra borrowed the Jehovah idea directly or indirectly from the Israelites. We find nowhere else in the entire Avesta any traces of actual contact between the Iranians and the Semites, which would justify a theory of a borrowing of religious notions or conceptions from one another."

In another place, the same scholar says "The Iranians had in a very olden time and without any influence from without, independently acquired through the Zoroastrian Reform the possession of a monotheistic religion."

I have endeavoured to show in this book that the rishis of the later Rigvedic period were influenced by the doctrine of monotheism propounded by Zarathushtra. I am however conscious of the fact that in the earlier hymns of the Rigveda, there are a few passages in which the rishis have assigned to a single god-head such as Varuna, the highest position among the deities. For example, in Rv. II-27-10 we read त्वं विश्वेषां वरुणासि राजा ये च देवा असुर ये च मर्ताः । "O Varuna Asura, thou art king of all, be they gods or be they men."

Also in Rv. I-25-20 we read त्वं विश्वस्य मेधिर दिवश्च ग्मश्च राजसि "O Wise one, thou art the lord of the heaven and the earth."

* See also Zoroastrianism and Judaism by K. R. Cama.

It is important to note that in the former passage, Varuna is called असुर (lord), and in the latter मेधिर (wise). These two words असुर and मेधिर (cf. सु + मनस्) have become *Ahura masda.* *

In Ṛv. I-164-46 we read "They call him Indra, Mitra, Varuna, Agni. ...... To what is One, sages give many a title."

It will thus be seen that the monotheistic concept was not altogether absent from the minds of the Vedic writers of the earlier times. One point however is quite clear that the later rishis had not the courage to break with the polytheistic notions which had been handed to them from generation to generation. Zarathushtra and his follower made an entirely new departure in this that they are never tired of placing before us the doctrine of the supremacy of one god.

The Zoroastrians were not, however, the only people who were the first to preach the doctrine of monotheism. The Egyptians were also well aware of this doctrine, which has been summarised by Dr. Sayce in his Religion of the ancient Egypt and Babylonia (p. 244) as under:

"The Egyptians adored a being unique, perfect, endowed with absolute knowledge and intelligence and incomprehensible to such an extent that it passes man's powers to state in what he is comprehensible. He is the one of one, he who exists† essentially, the only one who lives substantially, the sole generator in heaven and earth, who is himself not generated."

We have reason to believe that the first Zoroastrians had come into contact with their neighbours the Egyptians. The calendars of the Zoroastrians and the Egyptians were exactly similar; the Ka of the Egyptians was akin to the Farohar of the Iranians; the Divine Law of the Egyptians "which governed the universe and to which the gods themselves had to submit" was closely allied to the Avestan Asha and Vedic Rita. *

I do not for a moment suggest that the Egyptians borrowed several of their religious dogmas from the Zarathushtrians; all that I say is that in all probability both the Egyptians and the Zoroastrians borrowed their doctrines (including monotheism) from a common and much older stock.

---

* *Ahura* असुर *Masda* मत्थ — मधम् — मेधम् Dr. Mills translates *Masda* by सुमधम्.

† In the Avesta, one of the names of Ahuramasda is *Ahmi yat ahmi* "I am that I am." Exactly the same name is given to Jehovah in the old Testament. The word *Ahura* literally means the *existing one*, rom *ah*, to be.

* See also the Egyptian and Zoroastrian Doctrines of Fatth by Dr. Roth translated by K. R. Cama.

No. IV.

The Roval Stars and the Constellation Ahura.

We have assigned to our Prophet Zarathushtra the date 2500 B. C. This date is further corroborated from another source which is as follows:—

In Siroza Yashta § 13, Bundehishn Ch. V, &c., we have the mention of the four Royal Stars Tishtrya, Satavaesa, Vananta and Haptoiringa. These Avestan stars have been identified by Dr. West with Sirius, Antares, Fomalhaut and Ursa Major. Dr. Geiger is of opinion that Satavaesa is Vega, the chief star in the Constellation Lyra.

Flammarion thinks that "Fomalhaut was known as Haptoiring in Persia about the year 3000 B.C. It was called the magnificent royal star and was one of the 4 Royal stars ruling over the four cardinal points of the heavens, the other stars being Regulus, Antares and Aldebaran. These four stars were also regarded as the four guardians of Heaven, sentinels watching over the other stars." (Star Lore of All Ages, p. 40).

W. T. Olcott in his Star Lore of All Ages (p. 234) says "The Persians had a tradition that four brilliant stars marked the four cardinal points *i.e.*, the colures and that these Royal stars were Regulus in Leo, Aldebaran in Taurus, Antares in Scorpio and Fomalhaut in the Southern Fish. These four stars were celebrated throughout all Asia. The brilliant star in the Eagle, Altair, has been suggested as the fourth Royal star instead of Fomalhaut. Thus as in the vision of Ezekeil, so in the constellation figures, the Lion, the Ox, the Man and the Eagle stood as the upholders of the firmament, as the pillars of heaven.' They looked down like sentinels upon all creation and seemed to guard the four quarters of the sky."

"Bailly, a brilliant scholar and eminent astronomer, contends that the phenomena of astronomy had been closely observed before the great races of mankind separated from the parent stock. He claims and few would dispute him, an *antediluvian* race as the originators of astronomical science. In proof of this he cites the fact that there are ancient Persian records which refer to the four famous 'Royal stars,' as having marked the four colures (the meridian points of the solstices and equinoxes) a fact possible in *antediluvian* times only." (Star Lore p. 7).

"Many of the authorities hold that the Zodic was planned while the spring equinox fell in the constellation Taurus......The date of the Zodic is given as 3000 B.C. which agrees very well with the significant position of the four Royal stars previously mentioned which marked the four cardinal points" (idem p. 8).

We also read in the Star Lore of All Ages (p. 329): "Antares was one of the four Royal stars of Persia 3000 B.C."

Let us now turn to a Pahlvi Revayet wherein it is enjoined that a charm shall be written and posted on the front door of the house on the day Spendarmat of the month Spendarmat. The charm runs as under:—

Pavan sham-e Dâdâr Auhormazda; yum Spendomat men binâ Spendomat bastum safra hamâk khrafastarân shedaân va darujân &c., &c., *pavan gadmane Yasata, pavan gadmane tug Faridun, pavan gadmane Tishtar stârak, pavan gadmane Satavesi, pavan gadmane Vanand stârak, pavan gadmane valmanshân stârkân Haptorang.*

"By the name of the Creator, the Omniscient Lord; on the day Spendârmat of the month Spendârmat I enclose the mouth of all noxious creatures, the demons, the drujas &c., &c., by the glory of God, by the glory of brave Faredun, by the glory of the star Tishtar, by the glory of Satvaesa, by the glory of the star Vanant, by the glory of the stars Haptoiring."

We find in this charm the names of all the four Royal stars mentioned along with the name of the king Faredun, the first physician of Iran. The reason why Faredun has been mentioned along with the four Royal stars seems to be that it was probably he who was the inventor of the charm at a time when the four Chief Stars were the objects of great adoration. If so, we must assign to Faredun the date 3000 B.C.

Now from the traditional account given by Bundehishn we see that Zarathushtra was born exactly 500 years after Faredun. Thus also we see that our Prophet lived about 2500 B.C.

The Constellation Ahura Berezat.

In Yasna Ha 1 § 11, Ha 2 § 11 Ha 3 § 13, &c., we find that immediately after Ahuramazda, Mithra is adored; and then the Stars, Tishtar, Moon and the Sun. On the other hand in Meher Yt. § 113, Khurshed Nyaishn § 7, &c., the prayer runs thus:

Tadha no jamyât avanghahe Mithra-Ahura beresanta.

"May the luminous (*beresanta*) Mithra and Ahura come to our assistance." Are we to understand that here Ahura is the same as Ahuramazda and that he occupies a secondary position? I do not think. The passage of the Khurshed Nyaishn makes the point very clear. There Ahurmazda is adored before all His creations, then the Ameshâspents are adored (§ 1); then follows the adoration of the Sun, then of Mithra (§ 6); then the assistance of Mithra and Ahura is invoked (§ 7); then Tishtar is adored and so on.

We cannot see our way to identify Ahura with Ahuramazda first because he is Ahura-berezat (not Ahuramazda), secondly because Ahuramazda has been adored *before* all his creations and thirdly because Ahura is mentioned with the Sun, Mithra and Tishtar which are the luminous objects in the sky. This leads us to think that Ahura also is some celestial object. For reasons stated below I am of opinion that he is the constellation Sagittarius or to be more accurate the front portion of Sagittarius.*

In connection with this subject we shall quote here at some length, the very convincing arguments of the Hon. Emmeline M. Plunket in the Ancient Calendars and Constellations (pp. 64, 75 to 83):

"In the ruins of Persepolis, ruins of buildings designed, erected and decorated by the worshippers of the supreme God Ahura Mazda and of his friend and representative Mithras, Tauric symbolism abounds...... In the bas-reliefs adorning the walls we find a collosal being (Mithras) thrusting his dagger into the body of a mystic creature......combining in one instance at least the attributes of Bull, Lion, Scorpion and Eagle; and frequently those of two or more of these animals."

Plunket concludes that the progenitors of the Assyrians at an early date of the world's history borrowed Tauric and other religious symbolisms from the ancestors of the Medes. In proof of this theory she says: "Tauric symbolism......points us back to a very remote date for its first institution, to a date considerably earlier than that at which the existence of the Assyrian people as an independent nation is generally put......Tauric symbolism must, at the latest, have been originated about 2000 B.C. Of the Assyrians as a nation we have no monumental proof earlier than 1700 B.C.

"But further in the symbol of Ahura and Assur, I believe, an astronomic reference may be traced to the position of the colures among the constellations, a reference which points us back not merely to a date

* The *Ushtra* in the Beheram Yt. is probably the back portion of Sagittarius. *Note*:—I may state here what I should have stated elsewhere that the Arabs called Cassiopeia the "kneeling camel," and Dolphin the "riding camel" (see Star Love of All Ages, pp. 126, 181).

between 4000 and 2000 B.C. but rather......to the furthest limit of time mentioned, namely to 4000 B.C.

"To penetrate into the meaning of this symbol of Ahura we must study both the Median and Assyrian representations of the figure presiding over the winged disc......Ahura presiding over winged circle holds in his hand a ring or crown; Assur in some examples is similarly furnished but more often he appears armed with a bow and arrows. In this figure I believe that the heavenly Archer, the Zodiacal Sagittarius is to be recognized—in which constellation the autumnal equinoctial point was situated......from 6000 to 4000 B.C."

As regards the crown or wreath or ring which often replaces the bow and arrows in the hand of Ahura and of Assur Plunket says: "A glance at the celestial globe shows that in it......we find close to the hand of the Archer the ancient Ptolemaic constellation Corona Australis (the Southern Crown) actually incorporated with the zodiacal constellation Sagittarius."

Plunket adds: "True it is that speaking generally Gemini and not Taurus is the constellation of the zodiac opposed to Taurus but owing to the irregularity of the shape and size of the portions assigned in the ecliptic to the Zodiacal constellations, the extreme western degrees of Sagittarius are opposed to the extreme eastern degrees of Taurus. Therefore about 4000 B.C. the equinoctial colure passed through the constellations of the Archer and the Bull.

"In the Assyrian standard (depicted in Layard's Monuments of Nineveh Plate 22) we see the figure of an Archer above that of galloping Bull and in another Assyrian standard, that of Sargon II (King of Assyria 722 to 705 B.C.) the Archer and the Bull, the two constellations, which 4000 B.C., marked the *equinoctial* colure; but we may also clearly trace a reference to the two constellations which at the same date marked the *solsticial* colure, namely those of the Lion and the Waterman. Here the Archer dominates over a circle in which symmetrically depicted Bulls appear and duplicated Lions' heads emerge out of what appears to be a low vessel resembling a Water jar...... This standard of Assur may (like the Persepoletan monster above described) be considered as an astronomic monogram representing the four constellations which marked the four seasons of the year and the four quarters of the earth. The monogram of the standard refers us back to an earlier date for its origin than does the monogram of the composite animal in the Persepolitan bas-relief, for in the standard the Archer is opposed to the Bull, in the bas-relief the Scorpion takes the place of the Archer and the Eagle takes the place of the Waterman. The precession of the equinoxes advances from east to west among the stars. Therefore the Scorpion marked the colure at a later date than did the Archer......At 4000 B.C. suggested with such curious accuracy by this Assyrian standard, we have absolutely no trace of the Semitic nations of the Assyrians in Northern Mesopotamia. In Babylonia 200 years later the Semitic Sargon I. ruled at Accad."

Then Plunket proceeds to show on the authority of Hirodotus (though Prof. Sayce is opposed to this view) that the Manda or Medes came to rule the land and that these Medes were the worshippers of Ahuramazda. "It is for the Lord Ahura......called Asura in the early times (about 4000 B.C.) by the Aryan Manda or Medes that I would claim at the date of 4000 B.C. the original conception of the astronomic monogram, in which may be so plainly read an allusion to the four constellations of the Zodiac, which at that date marked the four seasons and the four cardinal points, *i.e.*, Sagittarius and Taurus, Aquarius and Leo."

"I would claim that the Assyrians borrowed not only religious symbolisms but the very name of their god Assur from the Medes; for, I look upon Assur as a loan-word adopted from the Aryan Asura.

At pp. 151-153 Plunket observes that Prof. Hommel maintained the high probability of the Median god Ahuramazda having been the representative of Vedic Varuna. She however considers Rudra to be a close parallel to Ahuramazda in view of the following passages :—

(1) Rv. II-1-6 त्वं रुद्रो असुरो महो दिवः । "Thou Rudra art the great Asura of heaven." Here असुर मह् closely resembles the Avesta *Ahura Maz(-da)*.

(2) Rudra is not only the wise and great Asura, he is above everything else celebrated in the Rigveda as an archrer. "He has the sure arrow and the strong bow"; (स्विषुः सुधन्वा) see Rv. V-42-11.

(3) He is "the divine Rudra armed with the strong bow and fast-flying arrows" (इमा रुद्राय स्थिरधन्वने गिरः क्षिप्रेषवे देवाय); See Rv. VII-46-1.

I quite agree with Plunket that Rudra affords a closer parallel to the Avastan Ahura rather than Varuna, because Ahura Berezat was not an omnipotent lord like Ahura Mazda, much in the same way as Rudra was not an all-powerful god like Varuna.

In Meher Yt. § 96 Mithra is represented as "having a *vasra* or mace" in his hand and in § 102 he is depicted as having a sharp lance (*tisi-arshti*) fast flying arrow (*khshviviishu*) and piercing weapon" (*paro-kevidha*). All these epithets show that Mithra was also an archer like Ahura.

We have already seen that Mithra, besides being the sun-light preceding the rise of the sun, was also an angel of the spring equinox. Thus Mithra (—sunlight) is represented as shooting his arrows (—rays) from the east and Ahura Berezat (—Sagittarius) shooting his arrows from the west at the vernal equinox; and as we see in the Mithric representation, the arrows are evidently flung against the Bull (—Taurus).*

It certainly seems very plausible that the primitive man should have chosen to record the great and important events for the benefit of posterity with reference to certain important phenomena in the heavens.

Classical evidence.

Let us here briefly summarize the evidence of the classical writers on the question of the date of Zarathushtra.

Pliny the elder (A. C. 23-79) cites the authority of Eudoxus (B. C. 368), of Aristotle (B. C 350) and of Hermippus (B. C. 250) for placing Zarathushtra 6000 years before the date of Plato or 5000 years before the Trojan War (1100 B.C.). Pliny also expresses uncertainty as to whether there were two Zoroasters.

Plutarch (A.C. 1st century) adopts likewise the same general statement.

Diogines Laertius (2nd or 3 century A. C.) quotes Hermodorus (250 B. C.) the follower of Plato as an authority for placing Zarathushtra's date at 5000 years before the fall of Troy and he adds on the authority of Xanthus of Lydea (B C. 500 to 450) that Zarathushtra lived 6000 (some MSS. 600) years before Xerxes.

All the above authorities assign to our Prophet a hoary antiquity.

In view of the astronomical evidence found in the Avesta and the evidence afforded by the writings of the Greek and Roman authors who flourished several centuries before Christ, it is much to be regretted that our own co-religionists, the Pahlvi writers, (and after them the Mahomedans) should have seen their way to assert that Zarathushtra lived only about 300 years before Alexander.

---

* I seriously ask the readers to consider whether the weeping Bull in Meher Yt. § 88 is not the Taurus, and whether the *Mithro-druj mashya* in that passage are not men-shaped constellations in whose possession (*darena* धरण) the Bull is kept.

The traditional date assigned to our Prophet by Bundehishn, Arda-Viraf-nâme and Zadsparm seems to have been based upon a misconception of some important fact. It is not to be wondered at, that when once a misconception had taken a firm root in the minds of the people, it was readily believed as a fact by persons who came on the scene after several centuries.

There is not the slightest doubt that a great religious upheaval had taken place in Iran in the seventh century before Christ, when the *reformed* calendar was introduced. It was a pious custom both among the Avesta and Pahlvi people to ascribe any great event or deed to the Prophet Zarathushtra. The belief seems to have been handed down to posterity that it was Zarathushtra who had introduced the reform in the calendar. The date of this great reform always remained green in the memory of the people for many years because it was arranged among the Persians "to add an intercalary month every 120 years by transferring the five Epagomenæ and putting them at the end of that month, to which the turn of intercalation had proceeded on the last occasion of intercalating." And as a matter of fact this arrangement remained in force until 8 (or 9)* such intercalations had been made. The Iranians thus easily knew how to find out the date of this reform in the calendar, and as the name of Zarathushtra was associted with it, his date could be determined without much difficulty.

I do not believe that our Prophet could have had any hand in this reform, because from the testimony of the Gathas we can see that during his lifetime, Zarathushtra could at best have gathered round him but a small band of followers; and to talk of a reform in the calendar, when the religion itself was not established on a firm footing, seems a bit strange, if not absurd.

It is painful to find that some European scholars have thought it fit to brush aside the almost unanimous testimony of the high antiquity of Zarathushtra furnished by the classical writers on very flimsy grounds. We wish that the scholars would direct their energies towards finding out whether and to what extent, ancient Astronomy in the Avesta and the allusions in the Rigveda bear out the writings of the Greek and Roman authors, who were in a much better position to speak on the subject—they having lived centuries before the Pahlvi writers, at a time when our scriptures had not suffered at the hands of fanatical obstructionists.

But it might be said that there is a considerable difference between the date we have assigned to Zarathushtra, namely, 2500 B.C., and that given by the Classical writers. The reason is that we have preferred to place the date of our Prophet at the end of the Taurus age; whereas if we place it at the commencement of that age, it would have to be shifted back some 2100 years. Also some allowance must be made for the fact that the ancient people had not any correct notion of the precession of the equinoxes and that the sizes of the portions assigned in the ecliptic to the Zodiacal constellations were quite irregular.

---

* The intercation of the ninth month was done in anticipation, as we shall see hereafter.

No. V.

Why the Avestan people watched Taurus with delight?

We have already seen that the Avestan people took special delight in watching the conjunction of the sun with Taurus. In Ashi Yt. § 56 it is said that the boys and girls were much rejoiced to watch the said conjunction. The following passage from Albiruni (tr. by Sachan p. 211) supports our contention: "The most lucky hours of this day (BahAr-Jashn) are those during which Aries is the horoscope. People consider the hour of morning as of good omen......On the morning of the *Fox-day* the Persians thought it a good omen to look at the clouds; and from the fact whether they were clear or dark, thin or dense, they drew conclusions as to whether the year would be prosperous or not, fertile or barren."

The above passage of Albiruni leads us to believe that in *olden* times the lucky hours of the BahAr-Jashn must have been those in which *Taurus* (not Aries) was the horoscope; and that is what we find in Ashi Yt. § 55, Yasna Ha 50 § 2 and 32 § 10—passages which have already discussed at great length.

The following remarks of Albiruni in connection with the 16th day of the month Dae are important: "On the same day the weaning of Fredun took place. It was the first day when he rode on the ox in a night, when the ox appears which drags the carriage of the moon. It is an ox of light, with two golden horns and silver feet, which is visible for an hour and then disappears. *The wish of him who looks at the ox* when *it is visible will be fulfilled in the same hour.*"

The passage underlined corroborates the translation we have given in respect of Yasna Ha 50 § 2.

No. VI.

Dasyu in Assyrian History.

I have tried to show that Dasyu was the name given to Zarathushtra by the Vedic people in the early Rigvedic times. This identification receives complete support from the History of the Assyrians. I quote the following from Prof. C. P. Teile's Religion of the Iranian People translated by Mr. G. K. Nariman (new edi. pp. 47-48).

Commenting on the different countries mentioned in the first Fargard of Vendidad, he says "Next follow......the Hapta Hindu in the south east and Ragha, which latter, a land of inclement cold must have occupied more northern latitudes. Be that as it may, the document the editor of the Fargard employed to his instructive end bears every trace of hoary antiquity. It exhibits the geographical horizon of the original writer in its entirety. His Iranian world did not extend beyond. Media and Persia, were situate outside these limits. The above exposition derives corroboration from the records of the wars of the Assyrian kings. Several times they made incursions and prior to the Babylonian conquest far into Media. Though they did not completely overthrow it, they pursued the object of terrorizing the populace by ceaseless raids and predatory inroads and there founded spordic colonies. Now well nigh all the names of the Median localities and tribes they mention have a non-Aryan ring about them, at any rate till the reign of Sargon II. This evidences that the bulk of the Aryans before the 8th century B.C. had not pressed forward so far to the west. Still we encounter stray exceptions. In near propinquity to the eastern border of Assyria, the country or the clan of *Parshuas** is spoken of, which appear to have dwelt east of Elam at the

* Cf. पर्शवः in Rv. I-105-8, VIII-6-46 which we have already considered.

time of Senacherib. Perhaps they were the Persians, though the name might equally be an Assyrian disguise for the Parthavas or Parthians. In the annals of Salamanassar II. ninth century B. C., he relates a victory over a certain Artasar,* who lived not far from Parshuas and speaks of a certain prince Hubushka † now called Data and again Datana. Both the names are certainly Aryan. Tiglatpeisar III, names as the lord of Kummukh, *i.e.*, Kommagene far in the west a Kushtaspi, in which uncouth expression we recognize unmistakable Vishtaspa. Sargon II captures in Man a *Dayaukku* which *he considers a proper name* but which signifies a landgrave *Dahyuka.* A similar oversight we discover in Herodotus who calls the founder of the Median Monarchy *Deiokes.*"

We cannot agree with, Prof. Teile that KushtÂspi was the VishtÂspa of the Avesta. On the analogy of KaspÂi (= Av. Hvaspa, HvaspÂi) I should think that *Kushtaspi* was identical with *HvashtÂspa* (= *Hu-ashta aspa* ‡ —with well-obtained horses). It is also possible that *Hvashta* = *Hu* + *vashta* = well-tamed.

It is true we do not come across such a name in the extant Avesta, but such a name is not impossible. As Tiglatpeisar III ruled between the years 745 and 728 B.C., we are not in a position to identify Kushtaspi, with regard to whom however we can say this with the greatest confidence that he must have been an Iranian.

Prof. Teile says that Dayaukku who was captured by Sargon II (722 to 705 B.C.) and Deiokes (708 to 655 B. C.) who founded the Median monarchy were *dahyus* or landgraves. That Dayankku and Deiokes (= Dahyu or Dasyu) must have been Iranian names is clear beyond any doubt whatsoever. I differ from Professor Teile in this that it is my opinion that some Iranians got the name Dahyu § (= Dasyu) after the name of the tribe known as Dasyus (= followers of the Prophet Zarathushtra) by the Vedic people, much in the same way as some of our Parsis to-day bear the surname Frenchman named after the Frenchmen or the inhabitants of France.

The theory that the Dasyus were the non-Aryan aborigines of Punjab carries little weight.

---

* Probably the same as Arta-Khshathra.

† Could this be the same as Hubaksha.

‡ *HvashtÂspa* = *Khushtaspa* = *KustÂspa.* Cf. *Hvare-chithra* = *Khurshed-cheher.* See Pallonji B. Desai's History of the Achæminides p. 67). Compare also *SatÂspis* = *Sata* + *aspa* = having 100 horses; and *Hvaspa* *Hu* + *aspa* = *Khuspa* = *Kuspa* = *Kaspa* (having good horses).

§ Cf. DaghestÂn (= DahyustÂn = DakhyustÂn) in Iran.

An explanation of the origin of the three Fires Adar Froba, Adar Gushaspa and Adar Burzin-Meher.*

In Bundehishn Ch. 17 § 4 it is said that "in the sovereignty of Tehemuraspa, when the people moved from Khaniras to the other Keshvars on the back of the Ox Saresaoka (= the leader of lights), on one night the wind extinguished a fire-place in the midst of the ocean—the fire-place within which there was fire, just in the same manner as there was (fire) on the back of the Ox in three places. The wind hurled that (fire-place) with the fire into the ocean. (At that time) three fires like three Khurehs grew up (= appeared) in the site and place of the fire on the back of the Ox, so that there might be light and men might pass again through the ocean."†

§ 5 :—"And Jamshed did all his work in his sovereignty in the best manner by the help of all these three fires, and for that reason (*ajash*) Adar Frobâ has been placed in a Dâdgâh on the mountain Gadman-humand in Khwarzm—which (Dâdgâh) was made by Jamshed."

§ 7 :—"In (*lit.* up to) the sovereignty of Kai-Khushru, Adar Gushaspa was protecting the world in the same manner. When Kai-Khushru dug out the idol-temples on the lake Chaichasta, it sat on the mane of the Horse and removed pitchy darkness and made illumination, so that he dug out the idol-temples. On the same spot he established Adar Gushaspa in a Dâdgâh on the mountain Asnavand."

§ 8 :—"In (*lit.* up to) the sovereignty of the King Gushtâspa, Adar Burzin-Meher came into the world and gave protection............ Gushtâspa established it in a Dâdgâh on the mount Raevant where there is what is called Pushte Vishtâspa."

In the para. No. 4 we have been told that in the days of Tehemuraspa, people moved from the central country known as Khaniras to the adjoining provinces on the back of the Ox Sare-saoka. In Bund. XV-27* the writer says that nine out of the fifteen tribes who descended from Mashi and Mashyâni moved to the *other* six regions over *the ocean Farahokant* on the back of the Ox Sare-saoka.† It is im-

* This and the following papers were read before the Society for the Promotion of Researches into the Zoroastrian Religion, while the preceding pages were in the press.

† In Zadsparam XI-10 the same story is thus given : "In the reign of Hoshang, when men were continually going forth to the other regions on the Ox Sruvo, one night, half-way, while admiring the fires, the fire-stands which were prepared in three places on the back of the ox *and* in which the fire was, fell into the sea, and the substance of that one great fire *which* was manifest, is divided into three and they established *it* on the three fire stands, and it became itself three glories whose lodgments are in the Frobak fire, the Gusnasp fire and the Burzin-Mitro" (S. B. E. Vol. V. P. 186). The Bundehishn story seems to be more accurate.

* Cf. also Bund. 19 § 13.

† This ox has been also named Hadhayos or Hadhayâvs or Hadhayâs (see Bund. 19 § 13, 30 § 26 and Dadestan reply 89). Dadestan says "Gopatshah.........*keeps watch over* the ox Hadhayâs on whom occured the various emigrations of men of old." Minokherd 61 § § 31 to 36 says "Gopatshâh remains in Airan-vej within the region of Khavaniras ; *from foot to mid-body he is a bull and from mid-body to top* he is a man ; *at all times* he stays on sea-shore and always performs the worship of God, and *always* pours holy water into the sea ; through the pouring of that holy water innumerable noxious creatures in the sea will die ; for, if he should not mostly perform that ceremonial and should not pour that holy-water into the sea and those innumerable noxious creatures should not perish, then always when rain falls, the noxious creatures would fall like rain."

It is easily seen that this cannot be the description of a mere man. In ancient as-possible to conceive how people could move on the waters, riding on the back of an ox. I think, that by using the expression "on the back of the Ox," the writer makes a pointed reference to "the Taurus Age"—the age when Taurus was the leader of the constellations at the vernal equinox. The epithet *Sare-saoka* (="leader of lights") is very important, and reminds us of the ancient Akkadians who called Taurus "The Bull of Light." For the space of 2000 years Taurus was the prince and leader of the celestial host. Its lucida is a star of the first magnitude called "Aldebaran," which means "the leader" (See Star Lore of All Ages, pp. 335-342).

We thus conclude from the above tradition that Tehemuraspa belonged to the Taurus age. We are further told that that when a party of men was journeying by sea, the fire on the back of the Ox was extinguished by wind on a certain night all of a sudden. The Vâta or wind was most probably some tempestuous storm which took place at the time. To make confusion worse confounded, a starry phenomenon occurred which may have been regarded as an ill omen and which may have increased the terrors of the people manifold. This phenomenon is described as the extinction of a fire on the back of the Ox—which fire was hurled into the ocean by the storm. This leads us to enquire as to what such a fire could be.

tronomy great men were represented as constallations. Evidently Gopatshah is some constallation here, probably a mixed representation of Sagittarius and Aquarius. Gopatshah being a constellation, we can readily understand that he keeps watch over Hadhayâs or Taurus. Hadhayâs is most probably—SK. सधिस् (ox). Mr. B. T. Ankfesoria reads Sare-saoka as *srisaok* (See S. B. E. Vol. 5. P. 62) meaning "the triangle" on the back of the Ox.

Temporary and Variable Stars.

In ancient and modern astronomy such expressions as the "temporary stars" and "variable stars" are well known. We shall try to know something about the characteristics of such stars.

W. T. Olcott has, in his Star Lore of all Ages (p. 449), given a long list of the famous temporary and variable stars. One of the most famous temporary star which appeared in the constellation Cassiopeia is thus described:—"No account of the star in the constellation Cassiopeia would be complete without a reference to the wonderful temporary star that flashed out in this region of the sky in November 1572 astonishing the world. It was visible in full day-light and said to be brighter than the planet Venus...The Chinese called it the 'Guest Star' and Beza thought, it was the same luminous appearance that guided the Magi, the so-called 'star of Bethlehem'... La Place says 'As to those stars, which, suddenly shine forth with a very vivid light and then immediately disappear, it is extremely probable that great conflagrations, produced by extraordinary causes, take place on their surface'...Dr. Good thus refers to the temporary stars: 'Worlds and systems of worlds are not only perpetually creating but also perpetually disappearing. It is an extraordinary fact that within the period of the last century not less than 13 stars...seems to have totally perished and ten new ones to have been created. In many instances it is unquestionable that the stars themselves, the supposed habitation of ...intelligent beings... have utterly vanished and the spots which they occupied in the heavens have become blanks'" (Star Lore, pp. 180-181).

One of the most famous variable star is Omicron Ceti, about which Olcott says: "No account of the constellation Cetus would be complete without a reference to that wonderful variable star Mira or Omicron Ceti. Historically it is the most interesting of all the variable stars. . . . D. Fabricius observed it early on the morning of 12th August 1596 as somewhat brighter than Alpha Arietis. In October it had disappeared. He observed it again in February and March 1609." (Star Lore, p. 145.)

Fires on the Ox.

The fire on the back of the Ox which was suddenly extinguished seems to me to be a temporary star in the constellation Taurus.

It appears from the tradition recorded by Bundehishn that at the particular time, the constellation Taurus was rising above the horizon and would thus appear to emerge out of the ocean. A storm was raging at the time when one of the bright stars on the back of the Taurus disappeared. The witer therefore very appropriately describes the phenomenon, when he says that the wind extinguished the fire on the back of the Ox and hurled it into the sea.

But the story does not end here. We are further told that shortly afterwards three fires appeared on the back of the Ox in the place of the fire which was extinguished. Are we to understand that these new fires were (to use an astronomical term) Novœ or new stars? We shall give the description of a couple of these Novœ.

"About midway between Beta and Delta Persei there appeared Feb. 21, 1901 a *Nova* or new star. It was discovered by Dr. Anderson of Edinburgh and when first seen was of 2·5 magnitute. It shone with a bluish-white light and two days after its discovery it was brighter than Kapella, having in three days increased its brightness 25,000 fold. All *Novæ* are temporary and rapidly diminish in brightness." (Star Lore, p. 805.)

"An exceedingly brilliant *Nova* is said to have appeared low down in Sagittarius in the year 1011 or 1012...The appearance of this star was recorded in the astronomical records of China. It was visible for three months." (Idem, p. 821).

Now turning to the subject in hand we find that the three stars which appeared in the Taurus could not be *novæ*, because our author states in §5 that Jamshed,* the successor of Tehemuraspa, did all his work by the help of these fires. They therefore appear to be permanent stars.

For a similar reason I think that the appearance of the three fires could not be a phenomenon like Aurora Borealis, Aurora Austrialis, Northern Lights, Merry Dancers or Lord Derventwater's Light. †

Aurora Borealis is a luminous meteoric phenomenon, which usually appears in streams ascending towards the Zenith. It appears in the following forms:—(1) Arcs or segments of circle; (2) Bands; (3) Rays; (4) Curtains; (5) Corona; (6) Patches; [during some displays the auroral light appears in irregular areas or patches, which sometimes bear a very close resemblance to illuminated detatched clouds]; (7) Diffused aurora.

On one or two occasions at Jan Mayen, auroral light is described as making the full moon look like an ordinary gas jet in the presence of electric light; while rays could be seen crossing and brighter than the moon's disk. Such extremely bright auroras seem very rare, however, even in the Arctic regions. (See Encyl. Bri., Vol. II).

It will also be seen that the auroral light occupies a very large space.

*This means that Jamshed lived in the Taurus age.

†This name was given after the Earl of Derventwater who was beheaded for rebellion on 24th Feb. 1716; it is said that the Northern lights were unusually brilliant on that night.

whereas the three fires referred to in Bundehishn appeared in a very small space, namely on the back of the Taurus. For this reason also I think that the three fires were not auroral lights.

Now if we assume that the three fires on the back of the Ox were permanent stars, we must inquire what they were. I am of opinion that very likely they were the three following stars:—

(1) *Alpha Tauri* or Aldebaran (="Leader"), a star of the first magnitude, and known as *Rohini* (=" the ruddy one ") to the Hindus. The rising of Aldebaran is thus described by Mrs. Martin: "In September a very little north of east, it shows its *fiery* face above the horizon with such unmistaken individuality that it catches the eye of even the least observing. It glows with a rosy light that demands recognition and at once pronounces it one of the most important heavenly bodies."

(2) *Beta Tauri*—a second magnitude star on the horn of the Bull. "This star is particularly white in colour. Between it and Psi Aurigæ was discovered on the 24th January 1891, the now celebrated[1] *Nova* Aurigæ, that has occasioned so much interest in the astronomical world. Among the Hindus, Beta Tauri represented Agni, the god of *fire* and *among the astrologers it portended eminence and fortune*. (See Star Lore, pp. 341-342.)

(3) *Alcyone*—The bright star of the Pleiades, a star of the third magnitude, which the Arabs called "the bright one."

We have already seen that Taurus was rising above the horizon when one of its stars suddenly disappeared. As the constellation would rise up gradually, its bright stars Alcyone, Beta Tauri and Aldebaran would shine out with great lustre. It is these three stars which are the fires on the back of the Ox. When during the storm the star disappeared, the people on the high seas regarded the phenomenon as a precursor of a great calamity, but shortly afterwards Beta Tauri, the star of good fortune, made its appearance, which must have dispelled all their fears. It seems to me that with a view to commemorate this important event, and also to express their gratitude to the Almighty, the people of those days erected the fire temple of Adar Frobâ, much in the same way as the refugees from Iran, who had met with a tempest on the high seas, erected an Atash Beheram at Div in token of their thankfulness to God, when they safely reached the coasts of India.

The three Fires, Froba, Gushaspa and Burzin-Meher.

The language of our author would make us think that the three fires Frobâ, Gushaspa and Burzin-Meher were all established at the same time; but I think that only the Frobâ was consecrated in the time of Tehemuraspa and the two others were established in the days of Kaikhushru and Gushtâspa respectively. The context requires that *vad Khudâie Khaikhushru* should mean *dayan Khudâie* &c., "in the time of Kaikhushru" (not "up to the time of that King.")

In § 7 we are told that when Kaikhushru dug out the idol-temples on the lake Chaichast, a fire was seen on the mane of the Horse *; in astronomical language we might say that a *Nova* appeared on the neck of Pegasus. We do not know of any temporary star having been noted in the constellation Pegasus; but we are informed that in Aquila which is very near Pegasus, a famous temporary star appeared in 389 A.C. Cuspinius stated that it equalled Venus in brilliancy. It vanished after three weeks' visibility. (See Star Lore, p. 50.)

* Dr. West and others insert the word "*his*" before "horse"; but there is no such word in the original.

Derivation of Froba.

The derivation of the word *Frobâ* cannot be given with great certainty. It may be the same word as Sanskrit प्रभा "lustre," the exact Avesta equivalent of which would be *Frabâ*. We are told that when the three fires appeared, there was a good deal of light; hence it would be quite appropriate to name the phenomenon प्रभा.

Derivation of Gushaspa.

The word Gushaspa is made up of Av. Ghosh ("ear") and Aspa ("horse"). A *Nova* may have appeared on the neck of the constellation Pegasus, and hence the name.

The derivation I have suggested above, derives great support from the Zande Bahman Yashta Chap. III §10——a passage which Dr. West has not correctly understood. I quote the Pahlvi text in full from the Book of Dastur Kaikobad Adarbad of the Deccan:—*Hamâk Airân matâyân-i li Auharmazd-dâd min gâs-i nafshman barâ val Padashkhvârgar yâmtunet humant yehvunt. Mun Atro-Gushaspa pavan var Chechast-i zafra-i garmo âv-i jvitshedâ humant; tameman chigun petâk humant yehevunt. Mun mâhik goft. Ataro goft aigh Kurchang; aidun pavan tâvishn yehevunet pavan denman Airân matâyân-i li Ahuramazd-dâd min Aeshm-tokhmakân, Spitama Zaratuhashta, âigh denman anashutâ val Padashkhvârgar va Pârs va sulâk-mânih kof-mân-i daryd mân adinash vâng barâ mânet.*

Dr. West translates the above passage thus:—"And all those of the countries of Iran, which I Ahuramazda created, come from their own place in Padashkhvârgar. owing to those of the race of Wrath, O Spitama Zarathushtra, so that a report of something of the cave-dwellings, mountain-dwellings and river-dwellings of these people will remain at Padashkhvârgar* and Pârs. Some have said, the fire Vishnaspa on the deep lake Chaichast, which has medicinal water, opposed to the demon, is there (in Padashkhvârgar) as it were conspicuous; some have said '*originating*' (*Mâhik*) so that they use *it* anew *and* the fire may become shining in these countries of Iran, which I Ahuramazda created."

Dr. West translates the word *mâhik* as "*originating*." He has put up the following note on it: "The most obvious meaning of the word is *mâhik* 'fish,' which can hardly be reconciled with the context......The writer was translating from an Avesta text and met with the word *chithra* which means *pedâk* ('clear') and *tokhmak* ('originating'), but to express the latter meaning he used the synonym *mâyakik* which can be written exactly like *mâhik*."

Dr. West has unfortunally failed to grasp the sense and therefore he has tried to explain away the difficulty. The learned Doctor has not seen that the Fish is not the terrestrial fish but the celestial Fish (=the constellation Pisces).

I translate the passage thus:—"All those countries of Iran which I Ahuramazda created will go from their own place to Padashkhvârgar. Some (say that) Adar Gushaspa, which is (established) on the lake Chaichashta, which is deep and which is hot (*garm*) will go towards (the place which is) free from the Dimon*—to that place (*tameman*) where it became apparent (*petâk*, that is, where it first appeared). Some (say) (it will go to) Pisces. Ataro said to Cancer (*Kurchang*), &c."

The author says that the people of the whole of Iran would be so much oppressed by the wicked foreigners—of whom we shall speak hereafter—that they would seek

*The mountainous region South of the Caspian according to Dr. West (S.B.E. Vol. 5, p. 214).

* This place is probably the sky.

refuge in Padashkhvârgar and that even the fire Gushaspa will, in order to escape the ravages, go back to its old place in the skies, namely in the constellation *Pisces* as some said, or *Cancer* as the commentator named Ataro said. The derivation of the word Gushaspa, however, leads us to think that the original place of the fire must have been near Aspa (Pegasus) which, is a northern companion-constellation of Pisces.

Origin of Burzin-Mitro.

As to Adar Burzin-Mitro, we are not told what its origin was; but I think that the derivation of the word helps us to deduce its origin.

Burzin Mitro is, I think, a corrupt form of the Avesta Berezat-mithra.

Ere of Avesta becomes *ur* in Pahlvi; for example, Av. *â-zere*—Pahl. *azurdan* ("to hurt"); Av. *spere*—Pahl. *spurdan* ("to give in charge"); Av. *mere*—Pahl. *murdan*. Thus *Berezatmithro* becomes *Burzat-Mitro*.

त् or द् while combining with म् becomes न्; as तद्+मय=तन्मय. Similarly *Burzat-mitro* becomes *Burzan-mitro* or *Burzin-mitro*.

I have shown elsewhere that Berezat or Ahura Berezat is identical with the constellation Sagittarius. It would thus appear that the *Nova* appeared in this constellation. We find that "an exceedingly brilliant *nova* appeared in Sagittarius in the year 1011 or 1012 which was visible for three months. The appearance of this star was recorded in the astronomical records of China" (See Star Lore, p. 321).

A similar *nova* appeared in the same constellation in 886 A. C. (idem, p. 449). Could it be that Burzin-mitro was the same *nova* or temporary star in Sagittarius?

History of Religion in the Zand-i-Vohuman Yashta, and the date of Zarathustra.

While on the question of the three fires above referred to, it is important to consider the historical value of the Bahman Yashta as a whole, and the passage No. 40 of Chapter III in particular.

Dr. West in his introduction to the translation of this Pahlvi work in the S.B.E. Vol. V says :—"Bahman Yashta usually called the Zand of the Vohuman Yashta professes to be a prophetical work, in which Ahuramazda gives Zarathustra an account of what was to happen to the Iranian nation and religion in future."

I am, however, of opinion that under the pretext of forecasting the future, the writer of the Bahman Yashta narrates the important events connected with the Iranion nation and the Zarathushtrian religion from its commencement. This method of narrating historical events was very common among people of olden times.

A good illustration of this is found in the P[illegible]z[illegible] Jama[illegible]i (see Peshotan Memo V[illegible]. p. 111 and Cama Memo. Vol. p 284). The King Gush[illegible]âspa asks Jâ[illegible]âspa as to who would rule Iran after him. Jâ[illegible]âspa in prophetic language names the Kaya[illegible]ian, Ashkanian and Sassanian kings known in history with the periods of their rule.

Another illustration is found in Minckherd Chap. 27 §§27 to 31, wherein we are told that the second benefit that accrued from Jamshed was that he built the Vare Jamkard. Then the writer, using prophetic language, says : "And when the rains would pour down, then (as is said in the religion) men and the creation of Ahuramazda would be destroyed Then the door of the cave made by Jamshed would open and men, animals and the other creatures of Ahuramazda would come out of the cave and the world would be reformed." We know that all this is history and yet the writer chooses to use the language of a prophet.

Swami A. Govindachârya in his Vade Mecum of Vedânta (p. 12) says:—"All the historical statements of the Puranas are given in the form of prophesy in order to maintain the appearance of great antiquity in the books, which in their oldest forms were certainly very ancient."

I also rely upon the prophetic statement in § 49 * of Chap. II of the Bahman Yashta itself, wherein the writer with the precision of a historian names the foreigners who would rule in Iran—namely, the Khivs, Turks, Aturs†, Chinese, Kopdars,† Romans and others. With still greater definiteness the writer says

---

*Dr. West translates the passage thus :—"And the rule and sovereignty come on to slaves, such as the Turk, the non-Turanian (Atur) of the army, and are turbulent as among the mountaineers; and the Chini, the Kavuli, the Softi, the Roman and the white clothed Karmak, then attain sovereignty in my countries of Iran." In the foot-note he says "Very little reliance can be placed upon the details of this sentence but it is difficult to make any other complete and consistent translation. Darmesteter suggests the reading *heno* 'army' but another possible reading is Khyon (Av. Hyaon) the old name of some country in Turkastan, as Arjaspa is called the king of Khyon in Yadgare Zarirân . . ." With reference to the Karmak Dr. West says, that they were "Probably the people of Samarkand, which place was formerly called Chin acccording to a passage in Tabari; see also Bund., XII—22."

Dastur Kaikobad gives the translation thus:—"And the rule and sovereignty shall go to the non-Aryan slaves, such as Khiv, Turk, Atur, Topid, Aniruk, Kopedar and Chini, Kabuli and Sopati, Arumaik &c.

Dr. West places little reliance upon this passage because he has failed to correctly identify the time, to which the Bahman Yashta relates.

†We shall speak about Aturs and Kopdars hereafter.

in Chap. II—68 that the Iranians would be so much oppressed, that their only recourse would be to move in a body to Padashkhvârgar, whence ultimately the enemies would be driven back. Is not all this history?

Let us proceed further and examine Chap. III §19 wherein we are told that a young enthusiast would arise, having made ready numerous warriors with banners and weapons, according to some from Sagistân, Pars and Khruâsân, according to some from the caves of Padashkhvârgar* according to some from Airyân and Kohistân and according to others from Tapristân. If all this is prophesy how is it that it is so very uncertain about the countries from which the warriors are to come? But if we take it that this is all history, we might well understand why opinions may differ about some uncertain details.

Bahman Yashta was originally in Avesta.

Dr. West thinks that "the Bahman Yashta is a literal translation of an original Avesta text" (see Intro. S. B. E., Vol. 5, p. 53). In another place he says "In speculating upon the contents of the Bahman Yashta it is necessary to remember that we are most probably dealing with a composite work whose statements may be referred to the three different ages of the Avesta, the Pahlvi translation and commentary, and the Pahlvi epitome of the latter" (idem, p. 53).

It is however easy to see that our writer has added a good many historical facts, which happened long after the time of the Avesta.

Chapter III, Para. No. 40.

We shall first consider the paragraph No. 40 of Chap. III. The writer narrates what would happen in the distant future long after the time of Zarathushtra. He says that certain demon races with dishevelled hair would attack the Iranian countries and harass the people. Then history would repeat itself. The tide would be turned against the demons, who would be beaten as in the days of Peshotan and the three sacred fires would be re-established in their places as before. Then, says the writer in Chap. III-40:—*Gurg ambûm barâ vazlunet, va Mesh ambûm dayan yâtunet, va Ataro Frobâ, Ataro Gushaspa va Ataro-i Burzin Mitro lakhvâr val gâs-i nafshman yetibund; va aesm va bod dâd-ihâ barâ yehbund.*

Translation:—"And the Wolf age would go away and the Ram age would come on, and the Fires Frobâ, Gushaspa and Burzin-Mitro would be re-established in their own places; and wood and incense would be put on them according to law."

The Wolf is the constellation Sea-monster, which is the southern paranatellon of Taurus. We gather from the above passage that after the expiry of the Taurus age, the Aries age came on and that the three sacred fires were first established in that age. These three fires were established, as we have already seen in the reigns of Tehemuraspa, Kaikhushru and Gushtâspa. Here then we have the most confirmatory evidence that our Prophet lived at the end of the Taurus age and the commencement of the Aries age, that is, about 2500 B.C. I have adduced several proofs which point to the end of the Taurus age as the time when Zarathushtra lived; but of all the proofs, the one furnished by the Bahman Yashta is the most important, coming as it does from a Pahlvi translator, not only because it is the most direct and indisputable testimony we meet with, but because it is adduced from some original Avesta writing translated into Pahlvi.

*The mountainous region South of the Caspian; See Bund. XII—2,17 (S. B. E. Vol. 5, p. 214.)

Contents of the Bahman Yashta.

But this is not all. The whole of the Bahman Yashta recasts and recounts the history of our religion, chiefly in the times, when most probably, the Avesta was a living tongue. There is some confusion in the order of events narrated by our writer, but in ancient writings, which are after all collections from several compilations of still older times, we cannot expect to have much of symmetry or harmony.

In Chapter II of the Bahman Yashta, Zarathushtra is supplied with omniscient wisdom for a week, during which he sees a tree with seven branches of different metals, which are explained as denoting the different ages of our religion. The first six ages were in the reigns of (1) the King Gushtâspa, (2) Kyani Ardeshir, who is also called Bahman of Aspandiar, (3) Ardeshir (Babegân) and Shahpur, (4) an Askhanian King who is not named but who was most probably Vologeses I., (5) Behram Gor and (6) Khushru Kobad, also called Khushru Anushehravân. These were the six ages of the triumph of our religion. The seventh was the age of adversity.

In the language of prophesy, the writer says that at the end of Zarathushtra's millennium, Iran would be invaded from the east by hordes of demons or idolators with dishevelled hair, who would work much mischief, so that they would destroy the greater part of the nation and mislead the rest until the religion becomes well nigh extinct. Does this last age refer to the time of the fall of the Sassanian dynasty? I do not think so. The demons with dishevelled hair could hardly be the Arabs. On the contrary, in Chap. II-50 we have been told that these people would gain sovereignty over the Taziks (Arabs) and Arumaiks (Romans).

The whole of the second Chapter of the Bahman Yashta describes the condition to which Iran and the Iranians would be reduced by the foreigners, whom we have already mentioned. In the third Chapter, we have the history of the demons of wrath with dishevelled hair known by the names Shedâspi (or rather Scitâspi) and Kilisyâki, who (to use plain language instead of the language of prophesy) were once the rulers of Iran (see Chap. III, § 8). Now who were these Scidâspis and Kilisyâkis? Our author is himself puzzled at the question; he, therefore, quotes the opinion of the commentator Mahâvandâd who thought that they were the Romans and also that of Roshan, who thought that they were the people who put on red hats, who had red weapons and red banners. In our own times Dr. West, Prof. Darmesteter and others have also tried to solve the question, but I am afraid, they were not themselves satisfied with their own solutions.

Dr West translates Chap. III-8 thus: "There is a fiend of Shedâspi of Kilisyâki, &c." In the footnote he says: "This fiend appears to be a personification of Christianity or ecclesiasticism, and the writer seems to place his appearance sometime in the middle ages probably at the end of the 13th century . . . . Darmesteter suggests that Shedâspa may have been intended as a modern counterpart of Bivarâspa (Azi Dahâk)."

The fac-simile of the Bahman Yashta, edited by Dastur Kaikobâd Adarbâd clearly reads *Shedâspi o Kilisyakih*, hence the translation given by Dr. West (who probably took *o* to be a misprint for *i*) cannot be seriously considered. Shedâspi and Kilisyâki must be the names of some people, whom we shall try to identify hereafter.

Chapter II, Para No. 19.

Chapter II §19 which is not found in Dastur Kaikobad's edition, has been thus translated by Dr. West "the age that was of copper is the reign of the Ashkânian king, who removes from the world the heterodoxy, which existed, and the wicked Akandar of Kilisyâkih is utterly destroyed by this religion." In the footnote the learned Doctor says: "I am indebted to Prof. Darmesteter for pointing out that Nerioshang in his Sanskrit translation of Yasna IX-75 explains *Kalasiyâkâh* as 'those whose faith is the Christian religion'; the original Pahlvi word in the oldest MSS. is *Kilisâyâik*, altogether a misreading of the Avesta name *Keresâni*, which it translates but sufficiently near the name in our text to warrant the assumption that Nerioshang would have translated *Kilisyâkih* by Christianity; literally it means 'ecclesiasticism, or the Church religion'. Akandar is probably a misreading of Alaksandar or Sikandar......The anachronisms involved in making Alexander the Great a Christian are not more startling than the usual Pahlvi statement that he was a Roman...... The name Kilisyâkih is given in Chap. III-3, 5, 8, to denote some Christian* enemy." (S. B. E. Vol. 5, p. 200).

The reason why Dr. West and Prof. Darmesteter identified Kilisyâki with some Christian is not far to seek. Many European scholars have disregarded all the classical testimony about the early date of our Prophet and have chosen to place him in the 7th century B. C.,—the result being that they found themselves encountered by anachronisms and absurdities, which they have tried to explain away by making all kinds of suppositions.

What age did Bahman Yashta relate to?

Should we however fix the date of Zarathushtra at 2500 B. C. the whole history recorded by the writer of the Bahman Yashta becomes clear as day-light. The author writes about the seven ages of our religion, six of which were ages of prosperity. These have been mentioned *almost* in their chronological order. The seventh age was the age in which our religion was reduced to an adverse condition. The history of this age forms the chief theme of the Bahman Yashta.

In Chap. III, § § 43-44 Ahuramazda thus speaks to Zarathushtra: "When the millennium of Zarathushtra would end, that of Hushedar would begin. As to Hushedar it is well known that he would be born 1600 years (after you). He would come to a conference with God at the age of 30 and would accept the religion."

It should be noted here that according to Pahlvi writings, Zarathushtra himself came to a conference with Ahuramazda at the age of 30 (see Dinkard VIII-51, Zadsperm XXI-1 to 4). History would thus repeated itself in the case of Hushedar.

It should also be noted that in the Bahman Yt. III §§18, 47, 48 Hushedar has been called *Hurshedar-i Zaratuhashtân* "Hushedar of Zarathushtra," and in §47 as* *Hurshedar-i-Dino rasto virâstâr*, "Hushedar the reformer of the true Religion."

In §14 it is stated that "a king (*Kae*) would be born, either in Chinistân or Hindustan—who would come to the help of Hushedar, who would collect a large army of troops and would defeat the demon races with immense slaughter. Then (see §§49-51) all the men would put faith in the Mazdayasni religion and the creation would come back to its original condition. When the millennium of Hushedar would come to an end, Peshotan of Gush-

---

* The usual Pahlvi word for the Christian is *Tarsâk* (See Shâyast la-Shâyast VI-7, Madigâne Hazâr Dâdestân, &c.).

*In Bundehishn 82-8 T.D. and D.H. read this name *Hushidar* which seems to be more correct.

taspa would appear and the Kyâni Khureh would reach him. In other words, history would again repeat itself. Then once again the Turks, Arabs, Romans and wicked people of Iran would extinguish the sacred fire and destroy law and religion. Then would come the millennium of Hushedarmâh and a third time history would repeat itself by the appearance of Peshotan".

Now what are these *hazâres* or millenniums? I do not think that the word here means an exact period of 1,000 years. I say, it simply means a very long period of time. We are, for instance, told in § 48 that Hushedar would appear after the *hazâre* of Zarathushtra comes to an end; and in the very next passage it is stated that Hushedar would appear 1,800 years after Zarathushtra. Here then the *hazâre* or millennium is a period of 1800 years.

At this place let us for a moment consider Dr. West's translation of Chap. III-44. It is as follows: "Regarding Hushedar it is declared that he will be born in 1600 and at 30 years of age, he comes to a conference with me Ahuramazda and receives the religion." In the foot-note the learned Doctor remarks: "There seems to be no rational way of understanding this number. According to this view, Hushedar was to be born in the 600th year of his own millennium and not at its beginning as § 18 seems to imply, nor nearly 30 years earlier as the Dinkard asserts. As the beginning of his millennium may be fixed about A. D. 593-685 the writer must have expected him to be born about A. D. 1193-1235, a time which was probably far in the future when he was writing. And as Beheram Varzâvand was to be born when Hushedar was 30 years of age (Cf. §§ 14 and 44)* and was to march into Iran at the age of 30 (§ 17), the conflict of the nations (§ § 8, 19-22) was expected to begin about A. D. 1253-1293 and to continue near the end of the millenmium about A. D. 1593-1685 when Peshotan was expected to appear (§ 51) and restore the good religion (§ § 26, 37, 42)" (S. B. E. Vol. 5, p. 231).

* We find nothing of the sort in the text. All that we find is that when the *Kae* (King) (not Hushedar) becomes 30 years old, Beheram would be born. This Kae was Astyages as we shall see hereafter.

As to the figure in § 44, we find that Dastur Kaikobad's edition reads 1800 instead of 1600. Dr. West supposes that Hushedar was born about the year 1193 after Christ, and at the time, 1600 years had elapsed since the commencement of Zarathushtra's millennium. Thus Dr. West assumes that Zarathushtra's millennium commenced somewhere near (1600-1193=) 407 B. C. Elsewhere Dr. West takes 630 B. C. to be the beginning of the tenth millennium when Zarathushtra came to a conference with Ahuramazda at the age of 30. (see Jackson's Zoroaster).

Should we take the date of Zarathushtra to be 2500 B. C., the date of the event above referred to would end somewhere about (2500—1800=) 700 B. C. It was during this long interval of 1,800 years that according to the statement in Chapter II-49 the non-Aryan foreigners such as the Khivs, Turks, Atur, Aniruk, Kopdâr, Chini, Kâbuli, Sopti, Romans and the Arabs ruled in Iran.

Foreigners who invaded Iran.

The Khivs were the inhabitants of Khiva, formerly an important kingdom of Asia, but now a much reduced Khanate dependent upon Russia and confined to the delta of the Oxus. Formerly it included Chorasmia, Khwarizm and Gurganj. Chorasmia is mentioned by Herodotus (See Encycl. Bri).

Dr. West translates the word Atur as the "non-Turanians", but that cannot be the meaning, because the non-Turanians would include the Iranians also. I am of opinion that Atur was identical with the country named Atur (read Athur=Assyria) mentioned in the Behistun inscription, Col. 1, line 6. This identification, however, is not altogether free from doubt, because in Chapter III-5, the country Assurik has been clearly mentioned. In that passage we read "The Drujs, Shedâspis and Kilisyâkis, would hold red banners and would hasten towards the Iranian countries, which I Ahuramazda created, up to the bank of the Arvand (=Tigris). Some have said up to the river Frât (=Euphrates), as far as Assuristân of Yunân,* which is the dwelling of the Yunâns (=Greeks). The reason why it is called the Assurik dwelling is that the men of Assurik (=Assyrians) *were* massacred † there.

It is a historical fact that in the 7th century B. C. the Sedâspis (that is to say the Scythians, as we shall see hereafter) inflicted a severe defeat on the Assyrians; subsequently they were overthrown by the latter and became their allies.

The Assyrians and also the Scythians wore dishevelled hair. As regards the Assyrians, we read the following in Rawlinson's Second Oriental Monarchy, p. 200: "The thick hair carried in large waves from the forehead to the back of the head and then carefully arranged in 3, 4 or 5 rows of stiff curls was regarded as a sufficient protection both from the sun and rain. No head covering was worn......Sometimes if the hair was very luxuriant, it was confined by a band or fillet."

The history of Assyria can now be traced back to 2500. B. O. though it did not rise to political eminence until 2000 B. C. (See Ency. Bri.).

* Mr. B. T. Anklesaria reads it as Duvân—a district of Persia.

† Mr. Anklesaria thinks that here the word is *Katrunt* (=dwelt) and that *Zaktalunt* (massacred) is a mistake.

Turning to the Chronology of Berosus, we find that 8 Median kings ruled between 2458 to 2284 B. C., 11 Chaldean kings between 2234 to 1976 B. C., 49 Chaldean kings between 1976 to 1518 B. C., 9 Arabrian kings between 1518 to 1273 B. C., 45 Assyrian kings between 1273 to 747 B. C., and 8 Assyrian kings between 747 and 625 B. C.

It is these Assyrians and Arabs who have been mentioned in the passages Nos. 49 and 50 of Chapter II.

Now who were the Kopdârs? The Pahlvi word which has been read as Kopdâr by Dastur Kaikobad can also be read as Kavpdâr, or Kavpdakhar. Could it be that these Kavpdakhars were the Cappadocians (Grk. Kappadokia)? Herodotus tells us that the name of the Cappadocians (Katpatouka) was applied to them by the Persians. In the Behistun Inscription, one of the countries subjugated by Darius was Katpatuk (Cappadocia). The Pahlvi word before us bears a closer resemblance to Cappadocia than the word in the cuniform inscription.

The kingdom of Cappadocia which was still in existence in the time of Strabo as a nominally independent state was divided according to that geographer into 10 districts...... *Cilisia* was the name given to the district in which the capital of the whole country was situated. (See Ency. Bri.).

As indicated above, we have to direct our attention to the 7th century before Christ and find out the condition in which our religion then was. We must also endeayour to see, who the Shedâspis and the Kilisyâkis were.

Who were Shedaspis and Kilisyakis?

The Pahlvi word for *Shedâspi* could also be read as *Sitâspi* or *Skitâspi*. [*Skitâspi*=*Skit*+*aspi*.] I am of opinion that the *Skitâspis* were "the Scyth horsemen." In the Behistun Inscription we find a country named *Saka (h)* which has been identified with Scythia; but the word *Skit* or *Skith* is a still nearer name.

The Kilisyâkis were the Cilicians and not Christians, as Dr. West suggested.

I cannot do more than giving here bare outlines of the history of the Assyrians, Cilicians and Scythians in the 7th century B.C.

The Scythians or Scyths as a people were coarse and gross in their habits, with large fleshy bodies, loose joints, soft swollen bellies. They never washed themselves; they merely applied a paste to their bodies. They lived either in waggons or felt tents of a simple and rude construction, and subsisted on mare's milk and cheese, to which the boiled flesh of horses and cattle was added as a rare delicacy. In wars their customs were barbarous. The Scythian who slew an enemy in battle immediately proceeded to drink his blood. * He then cut off the head, which he exhibited to his king in order to obtain his share of the spoil. Sometimes he flayed his dead enemy's right arm and hand, and used the skin as a covering for his quiver.......*The greater part of each day he spent on horseback.* † (Note: This explains why they were called *Skitâspi*) in attendance on the huge herds of cattle which he pastured. His favourite weapon was a bow which he used as he rode, shooting his arrows with great precision. He also carried a short spear or javelin, and sometimes also a short sword or battle axe......

Their principal religious observance was the worship of the naked sword......Course and repulsive in their habits, not individually brave but powerful by their numbers and by the mode of warfare which it was difficult to meet... ...they were an enemy who might well strike alarm even in a nation so strong and war-like as the Medes. Pouring through the passes of the Caucasus, horde after horde of the Scythians blackened the rich plain of the South. Neither age nor sex would be spared. The inhabitants of the open country and of the villages would be ruthlessly massacred.* According to Herodotus the Scythians were masters of the whole of Asia from the Caucasus to the borders of Egypt for the space of 28 years †. This is doubtless an exaggeration but still it would seem to be certain that the great invasion, which he speaks of, was not confined to Media but extended to Armenia, Assyria, Syria and Palestine (Second Ori. Monarchy, pp. 510-514).

* See also Rawlinson's Herodotus, Vol. III, p. 45.

† The Scythians were accustomed one and all to shoot from horse-back. (Rawlin's Herodotus, Vol. III, p. 84).

The following extracts have been taken from the Encyclopædia Britannica 11th Edition :—

"The representatives of the nomad Scythians on objects of Greek art show people with full beards and *shaggy* hair...The men are said to be in appearance very much like eunuchs.

The oldest inhabitants of whom we hear in Scythia were the Cimmerians...In the 7th century B. C. they were attacked and partly driven out by a horde of *new comers* from Upper Asia called Scythæ...About the same time similar peoples harassed the northern frontier of Iran where they were called Saka (Sacæ).

Their religion was nature worship. They reverenced Tabite, Paperus, Apia, &c......They set up no images or altars or temples save to Ares only. To Ares they made a heap of faggots three stades square......

* Cf. *Gehân-zivo zektelund* (as Dr. West reads), "they slay those living in the world," Chap. II-26.

† From about 660 to 682 B. C.

Upon the top is set up a sword which is the image of Ares; to this they sacrifice captives pouring their blood over it."

With the above historical extracts, it is interesting to compare the passages Nos. 24 to 29 of Chapter II, in which we are told that "a hundred kinds, a thousand kinds, a myriad of kinds of demons with dishevelled hair, of the race of wrath would rush into the country of Iran.......They have uplifted banners, they slay those living in the world......They are mostly a small and inferior race, forward in destroying the strong doer....Through witchcraft they rush into these countries of Iran which I Ahuramazda created, since they burn and damage many things; and the house of the house-owner, the land of the land-digger, prosperity, nobility, sovereignty, religion, truth, agreement, security, enjoyment and every characteristic which I Ahuramazda created... would encounter annihilation and direct destruction and trouble would come into notice....They would lead these Iranian countries of Ahuramazda into a desire for evil, into tyranny and misgovernment......so that what they say, they do not do; and they are of a vile religion, so that what they do not say, they do. And their assistance and promise have no sincerity, there is no law, they preserve no security, and on the support they provide, no one relies; with deceit, rapacity, and mis-government they would devastate these my Iranian countries." (S. B. E. Vol. V, pp. 202—203).

As stated above, the Kilisyâkis were the Cilicians, who were the inhabitants of a district in Asia Minor. The Cilicians appear as *Khilikku** in the Assyrian inscriptions and in the early part of the first millennium B. C., were one of the four chief powers of Western Asia...Under the Persian empire, Cilicia was apparently governed by tributary native kings. (Encycl. Bri.).

The Assyrian King Sennacherib fought with the Cilicians and Greeks in 689 B. C., and defeated them (Rawlinson's Second Ori. Monarchy, p. 454). The Cicilians whom Sennacherib had subdued...re-asserted their independence in the reign of Esar-haddon, who therefore made a campaign in Cilicia and inflicted a severe defeat on the Cilicians (idem, p. 468).

Assur-banipal (B.C. 667) entered into communication with the Cilician monarch and took to wife a daughter of that princely house (idem, p. 487).

Emperor Cyaxares and his Successors.

It is the monarchy of the Median emperor Cyaxares (B.C. 682 to 593) which is the most important for our purpose. I am of opinion that it was this emperor who has been called Hushedar. This my opinion is based on the fact that the name Cyaxares is the exact equivalent of Av. *Huvakhshatra**, Pahl. Hushedar (about which we shall speak hereafter). My opinion is also based on Chap. III—14 in which it is stated that "at the age of 30 Hushedar would come to a conference with Ahuramazda. According to some in Chinistan and according to others in Hindustan, a Kai (=king) would be born—the father of that king from whom would come the descendants of the Kyânis (*Kyân tokhmak*)†. He (=Kai) would help Hushedar."

* This shows that the word Cilicia should be pronounced with an initial *K*. not *S*.

* The name of Cyaxares in the Behistun Insc. II-5 is (H) uvakshatra.

† The expression *Kyân tokhmak* means "the descendants of the Kyânis." On the strength of the writings of Firdusi and other Mahomedan authors on the one hand and the Greek authors on the other hand, Sir John Malcolm thought that the Achimenedes

These Kyâni descendants were the Achiminians, whose founder was Cyrus or Kurus (558 to 529 B.C.). The father (or rather the maternal grand father) of Cyrus was the last Median emperor Astyages, the son of Cyaxares. The father of Cyrus was also a king, known as Cambysis I, the son of Chishpâish Hakhamanish. Cambysis I, was a king as is seen in the inscriptions of Cyrus and Darius.

I am inclined to think that it is Astyages and not Cambysis I, who according to Chap. III-14 went to the help of Hushedar, for the following reason. In the same passage we are told that "this king, when at the age of 100, would desire to have a wife; and from him would be born the Kai (or King) of the religion known as Beheram Varzâvand. This last named king would defeat and destroy the Skithâspis and other enemies of Iran and bring the countries of Iran to their original condition."

Now history tells us that Astyages who had no male issue, married wives even in very old age. This is quite in keeping with what is stated by our author when he says that the king desired to have a wife at the age of 100. Our historian is so very accurate that in §16 he gives the precise day and month (the day Govâd of the month Aban) when the last mentioned king died.

Cyaxares was the real founder of the Median empire. This is proved by the fact that in the time of Darius, a Median usurper Fravartes pretended to be his offspring (See Behistun Inscr. II, 5). Cyaxares renewed the war against the Assyrians, in which his father Phraortes had perished, but while he was at Nineveh, he was attacked by the Scythians army. After their victory over Cyaxares, the Scythians conquered and wasted the whole of Western Asia and ruled for 28 years, till at last they were defeated and expelled by Cyaxares. Afterwards Cyaxares renewed his attack on Assyria and in 606 B.C. destroyed Nineveh. He conquered all Asia up to Halys (See Rawlinson's Third Ori. Mon., pp. 187-196).

It was the emperor Cyaxares who *established Magism as the state religion.* He was a man of considerable ability and a rare tenacity of purpose, which gained him his chief successes (idem, pp. 215-216).

Scyth Invasions.

As to the Scythians, we are told that they, on and off, attacked Media (Second Ori. Mon., p. 512). They were the great allies of the Assyrians; for, says Rawlinson: "Assyria, when the Scythians quitted her, was but the shadow of her former self" (idem, p. 517).

The last campaign of the Scythians into Media deserves special attention. Rawlinson says: "The Scythians defeated Cyaxares, who agreed to pay an annual tribute. The Scythian conquerors, not content with the fixed tribute which they had agreed to receive and which was paid them regularly, levied contributions at their pleasure on the various states under their sway....The barbarous Scythians would press heavily upon the more fertile tracts, and remaining at them until the region was exhausted. The chiefs would not be able to restrain their followers from acts of pillage; redress could be obtained with difficulty and sometimes even the chiefs themselves may have been sharers in the injuries committed. The insolence of the dominant race was very course and rude...The Scythians dispersed themselves over a wider and wider area invading Assyria, Mesopotamia, Syria, Palestine, Armenia, and Cappadocia,

---

were identical with the Kyânis. Our author simply states that they were the Kyân tokhmak. The point has been elaborately argued by Mr. Pallonji B. Desai in his Tarikhe Hakhâmanian, pp. 105—115.

elsewhere plundering and marauding, conducting seizes and fighting battles.

"The Medes took heart by degrees ...Cyaxares and his Court invited a number of the Scythian chiefs and massacred them remorselessly...At last they were expelled...Herodotus believed that from their defeat of Cyaxares to his murder of the chiefs was a period of 28 years" (Third Ori. Mon., pp. 181-183, 188).

Cyaxares—Hushedar.

Now as to the derivation of the name Cyaxares, Rawlinson and Paul Horn think that the Persian of this word was *Uvakhshatara**—from *u* or *hu*=good, *akhsha*=eye, *tara* being the termination of comparative degree—[the whole, meaning "more beautiful eyed."] Mr. Pallonji B. Desai derives it from the Avesta *Hu+vakhsha+tara*=well-‑prospering (See Tavârikhe Hakhâmaniân, p. 57).

The Pahlvi writers have known *Ukhashyat-ereta* (*lit.* "growing or high exalter") of Fr. Yt. § 128 as Hushedar. Now Av. *ere* becomes *ar* in Cuniform and also Pahlvi: Cf. Av. *teres (teresmaite)*, C. *atrasa(h)*, Pahl. *tarsidan*; Av. *kereta*, C. *kart*, Pahl. *kard;* Av. *ereghant*, Pahl. *argand;* Av. *gerema*, Pahl. *garm*. Thus *ereta* becomes *arata* in C. and Pahlvi.

Then *ra* and *ta* change places † (Cf. Av. *karana*, Pahl. *kenâre;* Av. *gereva*, Pahl. *gevar;* Av. *chakhra*, Pahl. *charkha* (See Dastur Peshotan's Gr. p. 28). Thus we get *atara*, and *a* being dropped we get *tara* (in fact *a* is not found at all in C. and Pahl., though it is pronounced).

Ukhshyat + *tara* — *Ukhshyatara* (*t* merging into *t*), which is practically the Cuniform word, but according to phonetic rules *u* takes *v* after it; Cf. Av. *anu*, C. *anuv;* Av. *hâu*, C. *hauv*. Thus we have the Cuniform *Uvakhshyatara* —*Uvakhshatara*. Or it may be that Av. *Ukhshyat* is the short form of the reduplicated *Vavakhshyat—Uvakhshyat* (from *vakhsh;* cf.) उवाच-उवच from वच्.

Again as Av. *Ereksha* and *Yimakhshayeta* become *Arsha* and *Jamshed* respectively in Pahlvi, so *Ukhshyatar* becomes *Ushedar* or *Ushetar*. Then phonologically the initial vowel takes *h;* cf. Av. *ushi*, Pahl. *hush*. Thus we have *Hushedar*.*

From the Behistan inscription Col. II—5, we find that a Median named Fravartes, who claimed to be the descendant of Uvakhshatra revolted against Darius. Uvakhshatra has therefore been correctly identified with Cyaxares. Thus we see that the Avestan *Ukhshyat-ereta*, (=Cuniform *Uvakhshatra* and Pahlvi *Hushedar*) was the name of Cyaxares, the Median emperor.

Tradition has it that Hushidar *would* be born at the time of the Ristakhiz, or the resurrection. Turning however to the Fravardin Yashta §§128—129, we find it stated *only* about Soshiosh that he would be born in the future and that he would bring about the resurrection of the world, but no such statement has been made in respect of Ukshyat-erat (Hushidar) or Ukshyat-nemangh (Hushidar Mah). Could it be that tradition has confounded the story of Soshiosh with that of Hushidar and Hushidar Mah? Could it be that Hushidar

* Third Ori. Mon., p. 144, and Dastur Peshotan Memorial Vol. p. 247. See also Rawlinson's Herodotus Vol. III, p. 448.

† This appears clear from the Pahl. form *Hushit-dar* (also read *Hushid-dar*) in Maneckji Unwalla's Bund. XXXII. Or *Ukhshyat+arata*=*Ukhshyatarata* and then the final *ta* is dropped. Cf. *Haraberezaiti*, Pahl. *Alburz;* Av. *parena*, Pahl. *par*.

*It must not be supposed that the word has passed through all the forms above indicated, any more than लिह्+ति becomes लेढि, or *Aurvat-aspa*, becomes *Lohrâspa* or *Paitizanti* becomes *Pâzand* by passing through different forms.

(—Cyaxares) the so-called son of Zarathushtra was confounded by the later Pahlvi writers with the Zarathushtra who reformed the Calendar?

I have already stated that the King, referred to in Chap III-14 who went to the help of Hushidar, and who desired to marry wives at the age of 100, was Astyages. It was from him that the King who was the progenitor of the Kyânian (—Achimenian) Dynasty was born. This latter King was the world-famous Kurus (or Cyrus). He was the son of Mandâne, the daughter of Astyages. I am of opinion that it is this Kurus who had been called Beheram Varzavand by some and Shâhpur by others, as our author says. These were not the proper names but only titles earned by the great emperor after the conquest of the wicked demons. The Avesta equivalent of Beheram Varzâvand would be *Verethraghna Varechanghvant* meaning "the killer of the enemies, the illustrious." Similarly Shâhpur simply seems "the ruler of the country."

I do not propose to say anything about Hushedar Mah, since our author helps us very little in identifying him.

Ashvins in the Avesta and the Rigveda.

In Yashta 2 § 8 we have the passage, "*Aspinâcha yevino yasamaide,*" which also occurs in Yassa Ha 42 § 2 and elsewhere. It has been correctly suggested by Mr. B. T. Anklesaria in Cama Memorial Volume (p. 219) that the *Aspinâ* represented the asterism Ashvini; but I do not agree with him when he says that the *Yevino* stood for the asterism Bharani. The *Aspinâ* were the well-known Ashvins of the Rigveda. What they were, we shall try to see hereafter.

The conjunction *cha* (=and) in *Aspinâcha yevino* joins two sentences and not the two words. This is clearly seen in Yashta 2 § 8, where we have "*Aspinibya yaonibya*" without the conjunction "and" between the two words.

I would translate *Aspinâcha yevino yasamaide* thus:—"And we praise the two young Ashvins." I prefer the reading *yavana* (instead of *yevino*) which is found in 2 MSS. in Yashta 2 § 8; similarly I prefer the variant *Yavanabya* (instead of *Yaonabya*) which is found in 1 MS. in Yt. 2 § 8; because in Rv. I-117-14, VII-69-8, &c., we find that the special epithet of the Ashvins is युवाना, "the two young ones."

The only references to the Aspins in the Avesta are the passages in which the two young Aspins are praised. Indeed, the material at our disposal for their identification from the Avesta is very scanty and limited.

Turning however to the Rigveda, we come across quite a number of hymns which are dedicated to the laudation of the Ashvins. It is impossible to conceive that the Iranians could have borrowed this devotion to the Ashvins from the Hindus after the Indo-Iranian separation. Either the worship of the Ashvins must have been the common property of the Vedic and the Iranian people long before they separated, or the Ashvins must have been the objects of such absorbing interest that these two nationalities (and probably many others), though dwelling in different places, spontaneously took to the worship of these objects.

What were the Ashvins?

Now what were these Ashvins and what was the epoch that to led their worship? These are the two important questions which we shall try to answer.

The exact identification of the Ashvins has been a matter of considerable difficulty to the scholars of the past, as well as of the present days. In his Science of Mythology Prof. Max-Muller has devoted quite a number of pages to show that the Ashvins were the representations of the day and the night. We however fail to see why such phenomena as the day and the night had received such an elaborate treatment at the hands of the Vedic bards. Lassen called them "the agents behind the rays of light preceding the dawn." Roth stated that "they were the first messengers of light." Myriantheus thought that they were the "twilight," Weber "the double star of the Dioskouroi," and Benfey "the morning and the evening stars". Yâska, the celebrated lexicographer and commentator of the Veda, who flourished about 500 B. C., said: "The Ashvins bide in the sky, they appear after midnight, when light approaches slowly on darkness." A similar idea is expressed in Rv. X—61—4: "I invoke you, O Ashvins, when the black cold(=night) sits among the red cows (=in the morning)," when the night is surrounded by the red clouds in the east. (See Science of Mythology, pp. 603-604).

Macdonell in his Vedic Mythology (p. 49) says:—"The Ashvins

are celebrated in more than 50 entire hymns and in parts of several others, while their name occurs more than 400 times. Though they hold a distinct position among the deities of light...their connection with any definite phenomenon of light is so obscure that their original nature has been a puzzle to Vedic interpreters from the earliest times. This obscurity makes it probable that the origin of these gods is to be sought in a pre-Vedic period... The Ashvins are *young*—the Taittiriya Samhitâ even describing them as the youngest of the gods. They are at the same time ancient. They are bright lords of lustre, of golden brilliancy and honey-hued......In the Ait. Brâ. the Ashvins as well as Ushas and Agni are said to be the gods of Dawn and in the Vedic ritual, they are connected with sunrise."

I am of opinion that the correct view about the Ashvins has been put forward by Plunket followed by Olcott, which is as under:—"In the Rigveda the first lunar station in the Indian series is named Ashvini. The two chief stars in the station are Bita and Gama Arietis. Joyous hymns were addressed to the twin heroes, the Ashvins which may be properly called the new year's hymns, composed in honour of these stars, whose appearance before sunrise heralded the approach of the great festal day of the Hindu new year" (Anc. Calendars and Constellations, pp. 186—187, and Star Lore of All Ages, p. 57).

Support of the Rigveda.

This view is no doubt supported by several passages in the Rigveda, which we propose to consider here.

In Rv. I—22-1 and 2 we read "Waken the Ashvin pair, who yoke their Car at the early morn. We call the Ashvins twain, the gods borne in a noble Car, the best of charioteers who touch the heaven." (प्र सुग्मा रथीतमोभा देवा दिविस्पृशा । अश्विना ता हवामहे ॥).

Here the car appears to be the constellation Charioteer. In Rv. I-30-18 and 19 the poet thus addresses the Ashvins:—Your chariot yoked alike for both, immortal (अमर्त्यः), ye of mighty acts, travels, O Ashvins, in the sea (=aerial sea). High on the forehead of the Bull, one wheel of the Chariot ye ever keep, the other revolves round the sky." In Rv. V-74-1 the poet asks "Where in the heavens are ye to-day, Ashvins?"

How are we to understand these passages, if we adopt the view of Prof. Max Muller that the Ashvins represented the day and the night? What is the meaning of the statement, that the Bull (who as we shall presently see is yoked to the car) has one of the wheels of the car on his forehead? We have only to cast a glance at the starry chart for an answer. The Bull is the constellation Taurus; the Car, the constellation Charioteer. We thus easily understand the paradoxical writing of the Vedic astronomer that one of the wheels of the Chariot is always found on the forehead of the Bull and the other turns round the sky.

In Rv. IV-44-1 we read तं वां रथं वयमद्या हुवेम पृथुज्रयमश्विना संगतिं गोः Griffith thus translates the passage "We will invoke this day your car, far-spreading, O Ashvins, even the gathering of the sun-light." Prof. Wilson following Sâyana renders संगतिं गोः as "the associator of the solar ray," and observes that the translation is purely conjectural, founded upon the connection of the Ashvins with light or the sun. I am of opinion that संगतिं गोः should be translated as "the associator of Taurus," as we know that the Car or the Charioteer is the paranatellon or companion-constellation of the Bull.

The description of the Car is given in Rv. I-118-1 where it is said to be मर्त्यस्य मनसो जवीयान् "swifter than the mind of mortals" and वातरंहः "fleet as the wind," In

Rv. VII—69—1 it is a golden chariot invested with the rays of light. According to Rv. I—116—18 a Porpoise and a Bull are yoked to the Car (वृषभश्च शिशुमारश्च युक्ताः). The Shishumâra is, I think, the constellation Sea-monster. This and Taurus may be truly represented as drawing the constellation Chariot.

In Rv. X—64-8 the poet sings the praise of the sun, the moon, the two Moons (*i.e.* new Moon and full Moon), to Yama in the heavens, to Trita, Vâta, Dawn, Night and the two Ashvins. In this passage neither of the Ashvins could be the night; for, the night has been already mentioned.

We thus see that the Ashvins were the luminaries in the sky connected with Taurus, Charioteer and Sea-monster. They have therefore been correctly identified with the two important stars in Aries.

Ashvins connected with early dawn.

It should he noted that in quite a number of passages in the Rigveda, the Ashvins are connected with the early dawn. A few instances might be given here. In Rv. V.–77–1 we have प्रातर्हि यज्ञमश्विना दधाने "The Ashvins claim the sacrifice at daybreak." In Rv. VII—71—8 the poet prays: "May your Bulls strong and seeking bliss bring hither, Ashvins, your car at the earliest flush of morning (अवमस्यां व्युष्टौ)." In Rv. VII—72—4 we read: "What time the Dawns break forth in light, O Ashvins, to you the poets offer your devotion."

From all these passages we arrive at the conclusion that at a certain time, the sun was in conjunction with the Ashvins or the two chief stars of the constellation Aries.

Vartika Myth.

Several myths have been woven round the central figure of the Ashvins. Most of these myths can be satisfactorily explained as referring to the spring equinox. We shall first deal with what is known as the Vartikâ myth. Max-Muller says "We read that a quail (Vartikâ) had been swallowed by a wolf (Vrika) but was delivered by the Ashvins from their jaws.* Even if we took Vartikâ as the name of a real woman, her being saved from the jaws of a wolf would hardly have been of sufficient importance to inspire various Vedic poets, nor is it quite clear how the Ashvins could have saved her from being swallowed, unless with the Aitihâsikas, we took them for two ancient kings. *Vartikâ* in Sanskrit means 'quail', and corresponds to Greak *ortux*. The elymological meaning is the returning bird, the returning or revolving year...Vartikâ, the returning night might well have represented the return either of the day or of the *spring*. If she represented the return of the day, *i.e.* the dawn, she was indeed rescued from the jaws of the night; if she represented the return of the year, she might well have been the *spring*, rescued from the prison of winter...We have seen how these two ideas, the matutinal and the vernal, are constantly running together in ancient mythology. If then we find Leto was delivered of her two children, Apollon and Artemis in the island of Ortygia, the quail land, we can hardly look upon this as a mere coincidence but have to recognise here too a slightly altered repetition of the old story that the solar god was delivered at the return of the morning or at beginning of the spring. We can then understand why Apollon was called Lykoktonos, the killer of the wolf and why his sister Artemis was called Ortygia. That island Ortygia which was originally a mythical postulate rather than a geographical reality, is best known by the name of Delos and this again means the bright island or the morning island, that is, the Eastern sky...

* Rv. I-112-8, Rv. I-116-14, &c.

All this proves that the first germs of the myth had begun to break forth, when the ancestors of the Greeks and Hindus were still living in close contact together" (see Science of Mythology, pp. 584—586).

I agree with Prof. Max-Muller that Vartikâ was the return of the spring.

In Rv. I—116—14 the Ashvins are thus addressed: "Ye from the wolf's jaws, as ye stood together, set free the quail, O Heroes." From this passage we gather that up to the time of the writer the constellation वृक (Av. Veherka, Pers. Gurg) or the Sea-monster, (which is the paranatellon of Taurus) had swallowed (that is, had full sway over) the Vartikâ (*i.e.* the return of the spring), which the Ashvins set free from the clutches of the Sea-monster and over which they themselves acquired sway. In other words the Wolf constellation which had so far presided over the spring, was superseded by Aries. The close connection of the Ashvins with the early Dawn in the Rigveda shows that the sun was in conjunction with Aries. This becomes clear from passages like Rv. I—117—13 where we read: "The Daughter of the Sun with all her glory chose your car to bear her." In Rv. IV—44—1 is mentioned "the car which bears Suryâ." In Rv. VII—69—4 the poet says: "When night was turning to the grey of morning, the maiden Suryâ chose your splendour." We thus conclude that the Vartikâ myth is a poetical representation of the conjunction of the Sun with Aries at the spring equinox. Therefore, this myth carries us back to 2500 B.C.

Chyavana myth.

Another important myth connected with the Ashvins was that of Chyavâna. In Rv. I—117—13 the writer thus addresses the Ashvins: युवं च्यवानं अश्विना जरंतं पुनर्युवानं चक्रथुः शचीभिः। "Ye with your powers, O Ashvins, restored to youth the old Chyavâna". Again in Rv. I—118—6 we read पुनश्च्यवानं चक्रथुर्युवानं "Ye made Chyavâna young again." Max-Muller derives च्यवान from च्यु "to fall down," relying upon such passages as तारा अंबराच्च्यवंते "stars fall (or set) from the sky." He takes Chyavâna to be the setting sun (Science of Mythology, p. 589). I am however inclined to think that Chyavâna was the sun at the winter solstice, which has been represented as blind and lame. The sun becomes bright and brisk in spring. The Ashvins make the old and decrepit sun of the winter, young and vigorous in spring.

Ashvins the ruling stars.

That the Ashvins were the ruling stars in the Vedic times can be gathered from the following passages. In Rv. VI.—62—1 the poet invokes "the controllers of this sky" (दिवो अस्य प्रसन्ता अश्विना हुवे). In Rv. II—31—4 they are called the "ruling or unvulnerable lords" (अवघा पती). In Rv. I—116—16 we read आ वां रथं दुहिता सूर्यस्य कार्ष्मेवातिष्ठदर्वता जयन्ती। "The victorious daughter of Surya ascended your car, reaching as it were the goal of the race with the coursers." I should think that the goal is the commencement of the year. Dr. Wilson observes "Suryâ, it is related, was desirous of giving his daughter to Soma, but all the gods desired her as a wife. They agreed that he, who should first reach the sun as a goal, should wed the damsel. The Ashvins were victorius and Suryâ, well pleased by their success, rushed immediately into their chariot." Suryâ, sometimes called the daughter of the sun, was "the sun in her female character or the morning sun, the Dawn" (Sc. of Mythology, p. 582). This shows that the Ashvins were the *first* stars to come into conjunction with the sun.

In Rv. X—39—11 the Ashvins have been called "kings" (राजानौ), which word is very significant.

Ashvins the old friends.

That the Ashvins received homage from their votaries for many generations can be inferred from Rv. VII—72—2 युवोर्हि नः सख्या पित्र्याणि समानो बंधुः। "Betwixt you and us there is ancestral friendship and common kin." In view of the fact that the Ashvins were the ruling stars for more than 2,000 years, a later Vedic poet might well claim, that the Ashvins were the friends and helpers of his ancestors.

Ashvins ploughed the first heavenly harvest.

We have a very important statement in Rv. VIII-22—6 दशस्यंता मनवे पूर्व्यं दिवि यवं वृकेण कर्षथः which Griffith translates thus: "Ye with your plough, when favouring Manu with your help, ploughed the first harvest in the sky." In the foot-note Griffith explains the expression "ploughed the first harvest" as first ploughed the ground and sowed and reaped, that is, taught by example men to do so."

But the expression to be explained is "ploughed the first harvest in the sky", or (to be more literal) "first ploughed the barley in the sky." In Rv. I-117-21 we read of the Ashvins यवं वृकेण वपंता "sowing the barley with a plough." I understand the expression to mean, that just as oxen move on, drawing the plough in the earth in which barley is sown, so do the Ashvins move on ploughing the sky in which the stars are, as it were, sown.

The word वृक has two meanings, "the plough" and "the wolf"; and I think that in the Vedic passage above quoted, that word is used by the writer in both the senses. The wolf is the constellation Sea-monster, accompanied by which the Ashvins ploughed the first harvest in the sky, that is to say, were the first to move in the heavens. If among all the constellations, Aries was the first to make its march, followed by Sea-monster, it was the first constellation at the spring equinox—an event which carries us back to 2500 B.C.

Our poet further says that the Ashvins made their first march for Manu; in other words, it was in the time of Manu that they did so. Now who was this Manu. In the Shataputha Brahmana, Manu is represented as the man, who escaped from the flood. In Rv. VIII-52-1 he is called the son of Vivasvân. In Rv. X-62-11 he is called ग्रामणीः "hamlet's chief" or "leader of men." Manu originally meant the "man"; Cf. Rv. X-63-7. Turning to Rv. X-14-5, X-58-1 and X-60-10 we find that Yama is also called the son of Vivasvân. Manu who was the brother of Yama (=Yima or Jamshed of the Iranians), seems to have been confounded with the latter, for the reason that Yama was the "leader of men" or "the man" (Manu). It was therefore in the time of Manu or Yama that the Ashvins first ploughed the heavens. This corroborates our conclusion * that Jamshed of Ha 32 § 8 was a contemporary of our Prophet who lived about 2500 B.C.

Surya's Bridal.

No story about the Ashvins would be complete, unless we refer to the pleasant Myth about Suryâ's marriage recorded in the 85th hymn of the last book of the Rigveda. Suryâ, the daughter of Savitar (=the Sun) was given away by her sire in marriage to Soma. The Ashvins acted as the bridesmen. The marriage took place in the month of Phalguna.

We shall quote the verses Nos. 9 and 13:—

सोमो वधूयुरभवदश्विनास्तामुभा वरा ।
सूर्यां यत्पत्ये शंसंतीं मनसा सविताददात् ॥
सूर्याया वहतुः प्रागात् सविता यमवासृजत् ।
अघासु हन्यन्ते गावो (अ)र्जुन्योः पर्युह्यते ॥

"Soma was he who wooed her, the bridesmen were both the Ashvins, when Savitar (the sun) gave his willing Suryâ to her lord.

---

* See pp. 43–46.

"The bridal pomp of Suryâ, which Savitar started, moved along. In Aghâ (=Maghâ) days are oxen slain, in Arjuni (=Phâlguni) (she) is wedded."

The last sentence is important. The poet who all along writes as if the marriage was a matter of the past, abruptly turns round and refers to his own times. It is difficult to see what the writer means when he says that "in Maghâ days the oxen are slain." Could it be that oxen were slain in the month of Maghâ on the occasions of festivities held in honour of the long-past marriage of Suryâ? The writer further says that "the bride is wedded in Phalguni." So far as we can judge from the context, it is meant that the time of the year, namely Phâlguna, when Suryâ's marriage took place in the past was observed as an important festival by the people in the time of the author.

Thus we gather from the above myth that the marriage of Suryâ (=Dawn) with Soma (the Full Moon) took place in the month of Phâlguna, that the Sun gave away his daughter and that the Ashvins acted as the bridesmen. Elsewhere we are told that the Ashvins themselves became the husbands of Suryâ. As we have already seen: "Suryâ was desirous of giving his daughter Suryâ to Soma; but all the gods desired her as a wife. They agreed that he, 'who should first reach the sun, as a goal, should wed the damsel. The Ashvins were victorious and Suryâ, well pleased by their success, rushed immediately into their chariot (Rv. I—116—17)."

In astronomical language we might say, that the above myth relates to the time, when the sun *first* came into conjunction with the Ashvins (=Aries) on the full-moon day of Phâlguna.

There is a considerable amount of evidence for Phâlguna having been regarded as the beginning of the year, since the full moon in Phâlguni is often described as the 'mouth (मुख) of the year'; [cf. Tai. Sam. VII—4-8-1, 2; Panchvimsha Br. V-9-9; Kausitki Br. IV-4; Shata Br. VI-2-2-18, &c.]

Oldenberg and Thibaut maintain that the choice of Phâlguna as the 'mouth' of the year was due to its being the first month of spring. This view is favoured by the fact that there is distinct evidence of the correspondence of Phâlguna and the beginning of spring: (Cf. Shata. Br. I-6-3-36, Kau. Br. V-1, Shata. Br. XIII-4-1-2 to 4, &c. Also see Vedic Index of Names and Subjects by Macdonell and Keith, Vol. I, pp. 424-425).

Thus we see that the above myth relates to the time when the sun first came into conjunction with the constellation Aries in the commencement of spring—that is to say about 2500 B.C.

URUNĀ KHRAFSTRĀ.

Yasna Ha 34 § 9 which contains the important expression *Urunâ khrafstrâ* runs as follows: "From those (*ãibyo*) who (though) knowing bounteous devotion as thy beloved, live doing wicked actions in ignorance of the good mind, Asha flies away much, just as the wicked Varunâs fly away from us."

Dr. Mills following the Pahlvi translator renders *urunâ khrafstrâ* as "the foul demons"—the Pahlvi translation being *aharmok i khird stared*, "infidel of perverted understanding."

We also come across the word *khrafstrâ* in Gathas Ha 34 § 5 and 28 § 5. In the former passage we have the words *khrafstrâish mashyâish* (="by wicked people")—*khrafstrâ* being translated as *khird stared* in Pahlvi. In the latter passage *khrafstrâ* is a noun and is translated in Pahlvi exactly as in the above passages.

Ervad Kângâ translates the words *aurunâ khrafstrâ* as "wild noxious creatures," but as we have seen above, in the Gathas the word *khrafstra* seems to be used for persons only. No doubt as Ervad Kângâ suggests, the Sk. equivalent of *auruna* is अरुण "red"; (cf. Rv. I—106— 18 where we read of अरुण वृक "red wolf.") It is not, however, a fact that the *khrafstrâs* always *run away from* us; for, we have been told in Vendidad 7 § 2 that when a man dies the Druj *runs towards* (*upa-vâsaiti*) us from the north like *khrafstras*.

It thus appears that the Pahlvi translator has correctly rendered *auruna* by *Ashmog*. We shall try to determine the original sense of that word.

In Yasna Hâ 34 § 9 quoted above, nine MSS. read *aurunâ* while six read *urunâ*. The exact Greek equivalent of *auruna* is *ouranos*, which word has been identified with Sk. *Varuna*. Sometimes व् in Sanskrit becomes *u* in Avesta; for example, वश् (wish) =Av. *us*; Sk. वषट् = Av. *ushta*. In Sanskrit the comparative of उरु is वरियस् which shows that the positive must have been originally वरु, subsequently changed to उरु. We thus see that the Avesta equivalent of वरुण would be *uruna*—a form, which is found in six MSS.

The *Urunâ* (=Varunas) were the followers of वरुण, the Deity of the Vedic Aryans. These Varunas were the enemies of Zarathustra and might well be referred to by our Prophet as *running away from* the Zarathushtrians.

In the 28th Chapter of the Bundehishna, many Devas have been named, one of whom is Varuna. The name of this God may also be read Uruna. In § 25 we are told that, *Varuna shedâ sak mun avârun marzashnih vâdunet, chegun yemallunet âigh Varuna arâs*; "Varuna Deva is he, who is illegal intercourse, as it is said that Varuna is wrong path." "Ervad Tehemurasp Anklesaria's Bundehishn adds at the end, the word *areshkih*, "jealousy." We thus see that Varuna or Uruna was the God of the wrong path or wrong religion. This wrong path seems to be identical with the *drujo râthman* of Yasna Ha 53 § 6 and opposed to *ashahe râthman* of Ha 8 § 3.

Varuna was also the God of punishment; cf. Rv. I-128-7. He was a deity of very ancient times.

Prof. Max Muller says: "Next to Dyaus I look upon Varuna as one of the oldest names of Gods in the Veda; for,......there can be no doubt that Varuna was the prototype of Ouranos."...Then after pointing out certain comparisons between Varuna and Ouranos, he says: "We might vindicate to Varuna a date previous even to the Aryan separation...... Varuna is the king of all the worlds and the old title of the deity *Asura* is more frequently applied to him than any other Vedic God. It may account for his appearing under the name of Ahura in the Avesta" (Science of Mythology, pp. 546, 549, 550).

We know that Zarathushtra was the cause of the split between the Aryans and the Iranians. This view is quite in keeping with the statement in Yasna Ha 34 § 9, in which we are told that the followers of the deity Varuna "ran away from us," that is, separated from Zarathushtra and his diciples.

Prof. Hugo Winckler's discoveries at Boghaz-koi in Asia Minor, in the year 1907 may be referred to here. That scholar has deciphered, in an inscription of about 1400 B. C. found there, the names of certain deities as *mi-it-ra*, *uru-w-na*, *in-da-ra* and *na-sa-at-ti-ia*, which correspond to the important Gods Mitra, Varuma, Indra and Nâsatya.

Prof. Macdonell draws three inferences from the occurrence of these names. He says "Firstly, these names may have been derived from Vedic India; in that case the Vedic religion must have flourished in India considerably before 1400 B.C., even though the hymns that have came down to us may not have been composed before that date.* But that these names should have travelled all the way from India to Asia Minor is a hypothesis so highly improbable that it may be dismissed. Secondly, the names may belong to the early Iranian period after the Iranians had separated from the Indians but before their language had reached the phonetic stage of the Avesta. This seems the more probable theory both chronologically and geographically. It implies only that the Indian branch had separated from the Iranian, not that it had already entered India. Lastly, the names, being common to the Iranian and Indian languages, might be assigned to the Indo-Iranian period when the two branches were still one people living in Iran."

We cannot accept the conclusions arrived at by Prof. Macdonell. The second name *uru-w-na* in the inscription resembles the *ûruna* of the Gatha more closely than the Varuna of the Rigveda. All that we can infer from the materials at hand is that these Avestan names were in existance about 1400 B.C., and that therefore the Avesta language must have been in existence long before that date.

* Prof. Macdonell thinks that the Rigveda was not written earlier than 1200 B.C.

Gathic and later views about Dualism*.

One of the cardinal doctrines propounded by the Zarathushtrian religion is that there is only one God, Ahuramazda, that as stated in the Bundehish, He is omnipotent (*harvespa-kerdâr*), omniscient (*harvesp-âkâs*), and matchless in goodness (*pavan shapiria ahamki*). In the Gathas (Ys. 31 § 8) He is praised as *haithim ashahyâ dâmim angheush ahurem shyaothaneshu*, "the true Creator of Law and the Lord of the works of the world." In Ys. 31 § 7 He is *khrathvâ dâmish*, "the Creator by his wisdom." In Fr. Yt. § 78 He is *dathusho khshayato*, "the Creator and the Ruler." According to Ys. 43 § 1 He is *vase khshayâns*, "Ruler at will," As stated in Ys. 31 § 13 He sees every thing with his own eyes, in other words He is omniscient (*tâ chashmaneng vaenahi*). In Ha 33 § 12, 51 § 7, 43 § 2 &c. He is Spenishta Mainyu "most bountiful Spirit."

If Ahuramazda is the supreme God, how could he be thwarted and opposed by the Evil Spirit, Angra Mainya? And yet it is an undoubted fact, that many of our scriptural writers,—with but a few exceptions—in their attempt to solve the origin of evil in the Kosmos, have evolved a theory which places Angramino (the author of evil) in direct antagonism to Ahuramazda. It is a matter of deep regret, that many of our writers have not cared to see, that in trying to solve a difficult question which has engaged the attention of the writers of different religions, they have reduced Ahuramazda to the level of a thwarted and limited God.

If Ahuramazda is omnipotent and all merciful, how is it that He has consciously created a universe with various kinds of evil in it? The concept of Angramino as a separate and independent personality was meant to solve the problem, but we must admit that this sort of dualism is irreconcilable with monotheism. Khan Bahadur N. D. Khandalewalla says: "The dogma of an existence of an evil spirit accompanied by his numerous and vile brood, watching to ruin men and suggesting ever to them evil thoughts, has been hanging as a dark paul over the otherwise simple and grand teachings of the Prophet Zarathushtra......In stead of the pure worship of Ahuramazda, the sole and omnipotent maker of the universe, the meaningless imprecations against Ahreman and the imaginary Devas and Drujas constantly obtrude themselves in the prayers."

The Two Spirits in Bundehishn.

But the important question crops up, as to what our Prophet Zarathushtra thought about this doctrine. Before we consider that, we shall see what traditional account, the writer of the Bundehishn has to give about the subject. In the very first Chapter we are told that, *Auharmazda bâlest pavan harverspa-âkâsih va shapirih, dayan roshnih ahamki bud*; "Ahuramazda is supreme in omniscience and goodness, and is unrivalled in splendour." Now If Ahuramazda is the Beneficient Creator, how is it that we find evil mixed up with good everywhere? This question seems to have occured to the writer. He seems to have argued thus :—"If evil was created by Ahuramazda, He would not be a beneficent god. If on the other hand, evil was created by some other spirit, Ahuramazda would not be the omnipotent Lord". The writer is placed on the horns of a dilemma and seeing the difficulty of his position, he tries to get rid of it in the best manner he can. He says: "The two (spirits) act together—one is he

* This paper was read by me before the Gatha Society.

who is without rival (and) of unlimited time;* because Ahuramazda and the space, and the religion and time of Ahuramazda, were and are and ever will be; (the other is he who is) Ahriman in darkness, (who) with backward understanding and with desire for destruction was and is in the abyss and it is he who will not be; and the place of that destruction and also of that darkness is called *asar-târiki* 'endless darkness.' Between these two there was empty space, which is called *vâe* 'air,' in which there is their meeting."

If the two spirits act together (*ham kolâ do vaxârishne*), how can one be said to be without any rival in the same breath. Adopting a somewhat different text, Dr. West gives the translation thus: "Revelation (*din*) is the explanation of both the spirits together." The Gathas do contain an explanation of the doctrine of the two spirits, as we shall see hereafter, and that is what is referred to by our writer. Ahuramazda is without a rival and is independent of time. He Himself His place, time and religion† are eternal without beginning and without end; Angramino was and is but will not be,—that is to say, he existed without any beginning and he exists now; but his end is sure to come. Here then the writer lays down the important distinction between Ahuramazda and Ahriman, namely that the former has no end, whereas the end of the latter is certain. But it is easy to see that in spite of this subtle distinction, the writer has made Ahuramazda a thwarted and limited God—at any rate, a God not ruling at will."

* In Zadsparm I—24 it is distinctly stated that Ahuramazda produced the creature Zorvân (boundless time). We thus see that the Greek and Arminian writers who asserted that the two spirits sprang from Zravân were entirely wrong (S.B.E. Vol. 5 Intro.)

† Here we are told that Ahuramazdian religion existed from the commencement of the world. Cf. and Bund. I-25. The Zarathushtrian religion was a mere reform.

In § 5 the author says: "Both the spirits are limited (*kenâre-humand*) and limitless (*akenâre-humand*). Exaltation (*bâlest*) is that which they call endless light (*asar roshni*), abyss (*sarpahâ*) that which is endless darkness (*asar târiki*,)—so that there is a void (*tohik*) and one is not connected with the other. And again the two spirits are limited as to their own selves."

To call Ahuramazda a limited God is highly derogatory to his great dignity. Ahuramazda is infinite probably because of his omniscience and eternity. Ahriman is infinite because of his malice and because of the endless darkness in which he resides. The above passage of the Bundehishn was most probably taken from § 44 of the Jamyâd Yashta, wherein it is suggested that Spenâmino lived in brilliant heaven which is high up, and Angramino lived in foul-smelling hell which is low down.

The idea of two infinites is opposed to monotheism. The Eleatics rightly said "If there is an infinite, it is one; for if there were two, they could not be infinite but would be finite one towards the other. But that which exists is infinite, and there cannot be more such. Therefore that which exists is one" (See Max Muller's Theosophy p. 93).

§§ 6–7: "And secondly on account of the omniscience of Ahuramazda, both the things—the finite and the infinite—are in the creation of Ahuramazda; for, this is in the covenant of both the spirits. Again the complete sovereignty and creation of Ahuramazda will remain up to the time of future existence and the same would continue unlimited for ever and ever; and the creation of Ahriman will perish at the time, when the future existence occurs; and that (time) would be unlimited."

The covenant between the two spirits is explained as under:-Through his omniscience Ahuramazda knew that "Ahriman existed and that whatever he schemed, he infused with malicious intents." Angramino was not aware of the existence of Ahuramazda. He arose from the abyss, came to the light which he desired to destroy and fled back to his gloomy abode. He there created many demons and fiends. Ahuramazda knowing all this, went to meet the Evil Spirit and proposed to him peace, which the latter declined. Ahuramazda then proposed that for 9000 years there might be the conflict through the intermingling of good and evil. The Evil spirit, short sighted and un-observant was content with that agreement. But Ahuramazda knew through omniscience, that (during the above period), for 3000 years everything would proceed according to his will, for another 3000 years the desires of Ahuramazda and Ahriman would remain intermingled, and for the last 3000 years Ahriman would be disabled.

We thus see, that by virtue of this covenant, the wills of Ahuramazda and Ahriman are mixed up to-day, and hence good and evil are found together in this world. This state of things will not go on for ever, but only up to the time of resurrection. We also see that Ahriman is a weak, ignorant and timid spirit,—the creator of evil, whose end is certain. The argument of our author is elaborate but fails to produce the desired effect, since it gives after all a poor concept of the omnipotent God.

In Bund. Chap. 28 § 3 however, Ahriman is not only an antagonist of Ahuramazda, but is a cause of great anxiety to the latter; for, we read therein: "ever since a creature was created by me, I who am Ahuramazda have not rested at ease, on account of providing protection for my own creatures; and likewise, not even he, the Evil spirit, on account of contriving evil for the creatures."

Here the author has evidently committed a great blunder. It is, as we shall presently see, the angel Sraosha who has been restless since the commencement of the creation.

Views about dualism in Avesta.

If we turn to the Avesta writings, there also we find that Ahriman is the opponent of Ahuramazda. According to Vendidad Chap. I when Ahuramazda created the 16 prosperous countries, Ahriman in opposition produced diseases and maladies. The idea that Ahriman is the wicked enemy of Ahuramazda occurs in almost every prayer, where blessings of Ahuramazda are invoked and imprecations hurled against the Evil Angramino (*Khshnaothra Ahurahe-mazdao, taroidite Angrahe-mainyush*, "May Ahuramazda be pleased, Angramino hurled back").

But even in the Avestan times there were a few writers who held different views. In the Sraosha Yashta (Yasna Ha 57 § 2), we find that Sraosha first praised Ahuramazda, then the Ameshaspents, and then the two (spirits), the *protectors** and the creators, who created the whole creation (*Yo yazata Ahurem mazdam, yazata Ameshe spente, yazata payoo thvoreshtâra, yâ vispa thvaresto dâmân*). In the same Yashta (—Yasna Ha 57 § 17) we read that Sraosha does not sleep well, from the time that the two spirits, Spenta Mainyu and Angra Mainyu created the creation; (*Yo noit paschaet hushkhafa, yat mainyu dâmân daidhitem yascha spento yascha angro*). In Yasna Ha 42 § 2 we have: *Pâyoo-cha thvoreshtârâ yazamaide;* "We praise the two protectors and creators."

Here is indeed the glimpse of a new doctrine. Sraosha first praises Ahuramazda, then the Ameshaspents and then the two spirits, Spenta Mainyu and Angra Mainyu. Thus clearly Ahuramazda is not the same as Spenta Mainyu. Further the Evil Spirit is also praised as a *protector* along with the Beneficent Spirit. This seems at first sight somewhat strange, but it is, I submit,

* *Pâyu*, "protector" is one of the names of Ahuramazda in Yt. I § 12.

quite in keeping with the doctrine propounded by our Prophet Zarathushtra.

Gathic View about Dualism.

The doctrine of the so-called dualism is contained in the Gathas, (Ha 30 §§ 3 to 6 and Ha 45 § 2). I propose to take up each stranza and discuss it, giving my translation.

Yashna Ha 30 § 3.

Ha. 30 § 3 :—" Now those were the two spirits who, in the commencement, were known (lit. heard) as twins inactive (*Khafenâ*). They were (known as) good and wicked in mind, word and deed. And the wise rightly (*eresh*) discerned them (*dos**)—not the evil-talented ones"

[Note :—*Asravâtem*, 3/2 passive; see Dr. Mills' Gathas p. 438.

Eresh—used adverbially; Cf Ha. 30 §6 and 44 § 1: *tat thvâ peresâ eresh moi vaochâ*.]

The first line of the strophe is quite in keeping with what we find in Bundehishn Chap. I § 8: " He also produced spiritually the creatures which were necessary for those means and they remained 3000 years in a spiritual state, so that they were unmoving (*a-muitâr*), fixed (*a-ravâ*) and intangible (*a-geraftâr*)."

In the third line we have been told that the evil-talented ones did not discern the two spirits aright. In Ha 30 § 6, (as we shall presently see) we have been told that "the Daeva worshippers did not discern them properly." It appears that the passage before us refers to the evil-talented ones of the Mazdayasnian religion. Could it be that even in the time of Zarathushtra, there were some Mazdayasnians, who did not correctly understand the problem of good and evil in the world?

Yasna Ha 30 § 4.

Ha 30 § 4 :—" And when those two spirits came together at first, they produced life and lifelessness; and thus it will be, till the end of existence—(those two spirits namely) the worst one among the wicked and the one of best mind among the good."

[Note :—*Ashâune*, dat. used for gen.

Vahishtem-mano, a compound word.

The Pahlvi translator and Neriosang take *dazde* as a noun in the dative case. They translate the first two lines thus: "Thus both the spirits came together for the first production (in the creation) (namely Gyomard) with life and non-life, (Ahuramazda with the former action and Ahriman with the latter action)]"

Yasna Ha 30 § 5.

Ha 30 § 5 :—Prose construction: *Aydo manivdo dregvdo* (*ye achishtâ-verezyo*), *mainyush spenishto* (*ye aseno khraojdishteng vaste*), *ashem varatâ* &c.

" Of these two spirits, the wicked one who does worst actions, (and) the beneficent spirit who cuts off all pervading wickednesses, chose *Asha* (*Law*). They (*lit.* and who) pleased Ahuramazda faithfully (*fraoret*) by their appropriate actions."

[*Note* :—*Varatâ* is in the third person singular and *khshnaoshen* is in the third person plural; both these verbs should be in the dual. But it is a rule of the Avesta grammar that when a dual form is wanting, the singular or plural forms may be used; for the instances, see Kanga's Gr. p. 294.

The context requires that the relative pronoun *yae* should refer to the two spirits. *Yae* is the plural form here used for the dual. Similarly *yoi*, which is but another form of *yae*, is used in the Ahuramazda Yashta § 25 for the dual: *Idha Haurvata Ameretâta yoi sto mijdem*.

* With this form compare *aydo* in Ha 30 § 6.

It would have been more correct if the writer had used *spento* instead of *spenishto*—which latter is the special epithet of Ahuramazda.

The usual translation of *ye khraojdishteng aseno vaste* is given thus: "Who lives in the firm sky." But as the writer intends to bring out an antithesis, we cannot adopt this translation.

Khraojdishteng—from क्रुध् "anger" and दा "to give," (superlative form); "something that gives or excites anger most," hence "wickedness," "evil" &c. Cf. *khraojdat-urvân*.

Aseno—अश्न "pervading," "reaching all."

Vaste—from वस् "to cut off," "drive away by shining."]

The above strophe is very important, as it really contains the doctrine propounded by Zarathushtra. We would not much mind how the first two lines are rendered; it is the last line which is important for our purpose. "*Yae*" must refer to the two spirits, since the writer writes about them only, and nothing else.

Asha and its Vedic equivalent *Rita* are the "immutable laws of nature." The two spirits do their actions in conformity with these laws, each playing his roll in the world faithfully. "Evil is not an absolute thing; it is only relative*." Anxieties and adversities, maladies and diseases, plagues and famines appear evil, but they are quite essential for the upkeep and equilibrium of the world. We are not therefore, surprised that Ahuramazda was pleased with the actions of the two spirits.

The postulate of an Evil Being arises from the difficulty, at all times felt by a certain class of persons, of reconciling the existence of evil with the Divine attributes of perfect goodness, full knowledge and infinite powers. It was for this reason that John Stuart Mill, in his "Essay on Religion," preferred to disbelieve in the omnipotence of God, rather than forego the belief in his goodness.* In the Gathas Ahuramazda is undoubtedly Spenishta Mainyu "the most beneficent spirit" (Cf. Ha 33 § 12, 43 § 2, 43 § 16, 51 § 7) &c ; but He is not indiscriminately good to one and all. He has laid down the great law of Asha which is never violated. It is for this reason that we read about the Daevas in Ha 32 § 4 : *Mazdâo Ahurahyâ khrateush*† *nasyanto ashâat châ* ; "(The Daevas are) destroyed by the wisdom of Ahuramazda and by Asha." In Ha 51 § 9 Ahuramazda is thus addressed : *Râshayanghe dregvantem, savayo ashavanem* ; "May you (Ahuramazda) prosper the righteous for the wound of the wicked." And in Ha 43 § 5, He is thus addressed : *Hyat dâo shyaothana Mijdavân yâchâ ukhdhâ, akem akâi vanghuim ashim vanghaove* ; "You give rewards according to actions and words : evil unto the wicked, good benedictions unto the pious."

The same strain of thought is contained in Yasna Ha 51 § 6. The prose construction of this passage is as under: *Ye Ahuro Mazdâo khshathrâ vangheush vahyo vârâi dazdi, yaschâ hoi râdat. At (Ahuro Mazdâo khshathrâ) ahmâi akât ashyo angheush apeme urvaese (dazdi) ye hoê noit vidâite.*

"And as *(ye)* Ahuramazda through (His) sovereignty gives better than good to the chooser (of righteousness) *(vârâi)* who makes offerings *(râdât)* to Him, so *(at)* He (gives) at the last end of existence, worse than evil to him who does not make offerings (*vidâita*) to Him."‡

* See Sir Oliver Lodge's Substance of the Faith.

* See "Dualism" in the Ency. Brit. 11th edition.

† Gen. used for ablat.

‡ The latter half of the Stanza suggests the construction of the first half. *Ye* is, I think, correlative of *At* ; or *Ye* may be redundant as in ये यजामहे स्वाहाग्निं स्वाहा सोमं "We praise, Agni, and Soma with स्वाह. *Vârâi* corresponds with *ahmâi*, from वृ "to choose"—"a chooser of the right path."

Dr. Geiger rightly observes (C. E. I. Intro. p. 82): "Ahuramazda is the God, who rewards the good and punishes the bad, not only in this world, in which He sends blessings or misfortune to men, but also at the end of this world, in the next one."

The last line of Ha 30 § 5, which is quite easy, has been sought to be explained away by the oriental and occidental scholars, who were reluctant to make a departure from their preconceived opinions, formed from the traditional accounts of the two spirits. That the tradition has egregiously blundered is sufficiently proved from the passages in the Sraosh Yashta above referred to, where the two spirits have been called *protectors*. How the tradition blundered, it is not difficult to surmise. As already seen in Ha 33 § 12, 51 §7, 43 § 2, &c , Ahuramazda is called *Spenishta Mainyu*, "the most bountiful spirit," which seems to be at first His most distinctive epithet and which distinguished Him from the twin spirit, *Spenta Mainyu*.* In course of time, however, as we find in Ha 44 § 7, 47 § 5, 47 § 60 etc., Ahuramazda came to be called Spenta Mainyu instead of Spenishta Mainyu. This was certainly an undue license with the use of the latter term. Ahuramazda, though quite distinct from Spenta Mainyu became identical with the latter. The distinction between Spenta Mainyu and Ahuramazda being lost, the latter became an antagonist of Ahriman.†

Yasna Ha 30 § 6.

Ha 30 § 6 : "The Daeva worshippers (*lit.* seekers) did not properly discern these two, since deception (= deceptive error) approached these inquirers, (and) since they chose the worst mind and combined with Aeshma to harm the world (and) men."

From the above passage, we gather that the Deva-worshippers (= the Vedic people) came to inquire about the cause of good and evil in the world and that they erred in the solution of the problem.

Dualism in the Rigveda, &c.

Dr. Telle's observations in connection with this subject may be noted here. He says : * "The dualism of the Zarathustrians is no new dogma, is no product of mere scholastic speculations but it is the continuation of a philosophy, which all the Aryan peoples share in common... All the Aryan religions are of a dualistic nature. The struggle between light and darkness, life and death, good and evil is the main subject of all mythology or religious teaching . . . . The doctrine of the Avesta indeed was not arisen of itself by gradual evolution but it has borrowed from this primitive dualism a portion of its own material." In another place Dr. Teile says : "Between the dualism of the Gathas and that of the younger Avesta there exists, even in its principle features, a divergence, although the former has in itself the germ of all that, which was to have developed subsequently."

We cannot agree with Dr. Teile, when he says that the Gathas contain the doctrine of dualism, which was borrowed from the Aryan religion. We have nothing whatever to do with the later scriptural writings of the Hindus. The question is whether we have any traces of the doctrine in the Rigveda. To that, the answer is given in the negative by Professors Max-Muller, Rajaram Bhagvat and others. Prof. Bhagvat says : "The Avestan words *mainyu*,

* Ha 30 § 5 is probably the only place where *Spenishta Mainyu* is used for the twin spirit (the *Spenta Mainyu*).

† Max-Muller in his Science of Mythology Vol. I, p. 60 says:—"How the character of a god can change through the preponderance of one or other of his attributes, we can see in the case of Varuna, originally no more than the god of the dark covering sky, who, in the later Hindu mythology, became the god of the waters."

* See Mr. G. K. Nariman's translation, p. 136.

spenta and *angra* are identical with the Sanskrit words मन्यु, श्वेत and अघ. ......Both the words मन्यु and मंत्र are found in the Vedic literature, so also the words श्वेत and अघ; but the latter have no notion of dualism, no shade of antagonism in them. It should not however be supposed that no dualism is to be found in the ritualistic literature, on the contrary, it is quite rampant in that literature. But the ritualistic dualism is the Deva-Asura dualism with its units more or less antagonistic and combative. Though all these units in the earlier writings culminated in the two unities of Prajâputi father of Indra and Pralhâda (of Kayâdhu) father of Virochana, (Taitt. Bra. 9-5—I), and run parallel to one another in later writings, there is a decided attempt to make the two parallel streams meet in Prâjapâti, who is the father and the teacher of both the Devas and Asuras. (VII—7 Chhândogya Upanishad)" (Meher Yashta from the Brahmanical Standpoint, p. 42). Professor Max-Muller says : "Of all this, of the original supremacy of Ahuramazda, of the later dualism of Ahuramazda and Angra Mainyu, and of the councils of these two hostile powers, there is no trace in the Veda. Traces, however, of a hostile feeling against the Asuras in general appear in the change of meaning of that word in some portions of the Rigveda and the Atharvaveda and more particularly in the Brahmans" (See Theosophy or Psychological Religion, p. 187).

In the face of these authoritative statements, we should be careful not to put in a note dissent without strong proof. The fact remains that the Gathic writer says with great precision, that the Daeva-worshippers did not understand the doctrine correctly. This makes us look closely into the Rigveda. I have arrived at the conclusion that the Rigveda does contain traces of dualism. It appears that some of the Rishis conceived of two deities—one the beneficent god Indra and other the goddess of destruction Nirriti—who governed the world. Indra was a god of wisdom unattainable, who sped the good (Rv. 2-21-4). He was the sovereign of the whole universe (विश्वस्य भुवनस्य राजा, Rv. 8-46-2). He was the sovereign lord of the Earth and Heaven, the lord of the waters and mountains (इंद्रो दिव इंद्र ईशे पृथिव्या इंद्रो अपामिंद्र इत्पर्वतानां, Rv. 10-89-10). He created all the worlds and beings [य इमा जजान विश्वा जातानि Rv. 8-85 (96)—6]. Him passing wise, the gods Heaven and Earth produce--him who was fashion-by Vibhvan (the maker) to crush the Vritras. (यं सुक्रतुं धिषणे विभ्वतष्टं घनं वृत्राणां जनयंत देवाः Rv. 8-49—I). He was truly bounteous (सत्यराधाः Rv. 10-49-11).

Nirriti was a goddess who "reigned supreme around Indra" as we read in Rv. 7-37-7 (अभि यं देवी निर्ऋतिः चित् ईशे). In Rv. 10-59-1, 10-76-4 10—36-4, 6-74-2, &c., imprecations are hurled against Nirriti, while Indra is prayed to keep her at a distance. In Rv. 10-36-4 she has been mentioned along with Râkhshasas and voracious fiends. In Rv. 10-86-2 she has been called a malignant ruler. The passage runs thus : मा दुर्विदत्रा निर्ऋतिर्न ईशत तद्देवानामवो अद्या वृणीमहे.

"Let not malignant Nirriti rule over us. We crave this gracious favour of the Gods to-day." Is not this passage almost similar to "Khshnaothra Ahurahe Mazdâo, taroidite Angrahe *Mainyush* ?

According to this conception, the beneficent God created by the Great Maker, and Nirriti the malignant goddess, governed the world. This conception of the two antagonistic rulers of the universe did not meet with the approval of Zarathushtra. Thus we conclude that the dualism in the Rigveda is as complete as that in the Bundehishn. But it must be admitted that this was the view of only some of the Vedic writers: others looked upon Indra as the supreme god, who was the ruler irresistible (Rv. I-7-7); who ruled with *single* sway men, riches and the five-fold race; who was the maker of all things (विश्वकर्मा), mighty All-god (विश्वदेवो महान्), who was the lord of the heaven (पतिर्दिवः) (Rv. 8-98-2 and 4).

The constant struggle between the Devas and the Asuras referred to in the later portions of the Rigveda and the Brâhmanas can hardly have anything to do with the dualistic doctrine. I agree with Dr. Haug that the fight between the Devas and the Asuras is a matter of history rather than that of philosophy. Says Dr. Haug: "One of the topics contained in the Brâhmanas is called *Purâkalpa*, *i. e.* performance of sacrificial rites in former times. Under this head comes the numerous stories of the fights of the Devas and the Asuras, to which the origin of many rites is attributed...... This very interesting part forms the historical (or rather legendary) back-ground of the whole sacrificial art....... We can derive one important historical fact from the legends on the fight between the Devas and the Asuras, *viz.*, the religious contest between the ancient Indians (represented by the Devas) and the Iranians (represented by the Asuras, contained in the name Ahuramazda), took place long before the time of the composition of the Brâhmanas that is, before the 12th century B.C. This is another proof corroborative of the high antiquity ascribed by Grecian writers to Zarathushtra, the prophet of the Asura nation—Iranians—who did manfully battle against idolatry and the worship of the Devas, branded by him as devils." (Haug's Aitarya Brahmana, p. 52).

Yashna Ha 45 § 2.

Pa 45 § 2: "I first declare to you the two spirits of the world, of whom the Bounteous one spoke to him, who was Angra thus: 'not our minds, nor teachings, nor intellects, nor beliefs, nor words, nor actions, nor consciences, nor souls, accord with one another." This passage requires no comment.

Let us now turn to the later Avesta and see what the different writers thought about the subject.

We have already considered the passages in the Sraosha Yashta.

Views of the Writers of Vendidad and Fravardin Yashta.

In Vendidad VII—52, we read about the man, who pulls down the tombs:—*Noit zi ahmi paite nairi dva mainyû rena avstâonghat, frasha fraya vahishtem â ahum, &c.* "Because the two spirits do not stand against this man in fight (*i e.* to make a fight with him) (when he is on his way) to the best world."........."O Zarathushtra, the Stars, the Moon and the Sun bless him and I who am the Creator Ahuramazda bless him."

Here we are told that when a tomb-destroyer dies, he goes to heaven on account of his meritorious act without any opposition from the Spenta Mainyu or the Angra Mainyu. We might naturally ask, why the wicked spirit does not oppose the pious man? The answer is that the wicked spirit is not always wicked, but that at times, he is associated with the Beneficent spirit in pious works.

[It should be said that the above author has propounded a theory, which is a little bit different from that of the writer of Ha 45 § 2, according to which Angra Mainyu was always opposed to Spenta Mainyu in thoughts, words and deeds.]

We have been told that the two spirits do not oppose the pious man, while on his way to heaven, and that Ahuramazda blesses him. Evidently, therefore, Ahuramazda is a separate entity from Spenta Mainyu.

In Fravardin Yt. 12-13 we read "If the strong Fravashis of the pious had not given me (= Ahuramazda) help, then my men and animals, who are of the best type here would not have existed;......... the evil one of the two spirits would have been powerful between the earth and the sky, the evil one of the two spirits would have been victorious between the earth and the sky and he would not have yielded to the victorious and dear Spenta Mainyu."

Also in §§ 76 to 78 we read: "When the two spirits Spenta and Angra created the creation, they (the Fravashis) had stood erect. When Angra Mainyu rushed into the creation of holiness, Vohuman and Atar interposed, so that he could not stop the waters from flowing and the trees from growing."

Here, we have been told that but for the Fravashis, Ahuramazda would have been helpless. This, it must be admitted, gives but a poor opinion of the omnipotence of Ahuramazda. We also find that Angra Mainyu is represented as a weak and impotent spirit, baffled and defeated even by the lieutenants of Spenta Mainyu.

Conclusion.

We thus conclude that Zarathushtra did not preach the doctrine of dualism in the sense, that the world is governed by two independent deities. The two spitits were merely the agents or instruments, whereby the laws of Asha were enforced by Ahuramazda in the world. In course of time, however, Ahuramazda was confounded with the Beneficent spirit, Spenta Mainyu. Also as the true nature of evil was not properly understood, it was believed that Ahriman must be the arch mischief-maker and the creator of all evil; the result was that Ahuramazda was depicted as an antagonist of Ahriman. It must be admitted that this doctrine permeates almost the whole of the later Avesta and the traditional literature,* but in our

* Dr. West has set up the following defence:—

"If it be necessary for a dualism that the evil spirit be omnipresent, omniscient, almighty or eternal, then is the Parsi religion no dualism. The Bundahis distinctly asserts that the evil spirit is not omniscient or almighty (I-16), that his understanding is backward (I-3,9), that he is unobservant and ignorant of the future (I-19), that his creatures perish at resurrection (I-7, 21) and he himself becomes impotent (I-21, III-1) and will not be (I-3, XXX-32). Nowhere is he supposed to be in two places at once or to know what is occurring elsewhere than in his presence. So far, his powers are considerably less than those generally assigned by Christians to the devil, who is certainly represented as being a more intelligent and ubiquitous personage. On the other hand, Ahriman is able to produce fiends and demons (I-10, 24) and the noxious creatures are said to be his (III-15, &c.), in which respects he has probably more power than the devil. The resemblance between the two ideas of Ahriman and the devil is remarkably close, in fact almost too close to admit of the possibility of their being ideas of different origin...............If therefore a belief in Ahriman as the author of evil makes the Parsi religion a dualism, it is difficult to understand why a belief in the devil as the author of evil does not make Christianity also a dualism" (S. B. E. Vol. 5, Intro., pp. 69-70).

I am, however, inclined to admit the accuracy of Dr. L. C. Casartelli's criticism, so far as Bundehishn is concerned. He says:—"Dr. West blames the Parsis themselves for having admitted it (accusation of dualism), at least as regards their doctrines in the Middle Ages......We cannot admit the definition (of dualism as given by Dr. West) that an omnipresent, omniscient, omnipotent or eternal evil spirit is necessary for a real dualism ......The foundation of dualism......appears to us to be precisely in this that *there exists a Being, evil by his own nature and the author of evil, who does not owe his origin to the Creator of good and who exists independently of him*......The fundamental idea of the Devil in the Christian doctrine is that of a creature of God, good in his origin but fallen by his own will...Such a conception does not agree in any way with the description of Ahriman ...... Ahriman is capable of producing spirits and demons (I—10, 24), and evil doing creatures are said to be his (III-15, &c.) He therefore shares with Ahuramazda the power of creation. It is therefore impossible to agree with Dr. West" (Philosophy of the Mazdayasnian Religion under the Sassanids by L. C. Casartelli translated by Firoz Jamaspji Dastur, pp. 50-51).

dispair there is this relieving feature that some of the Avesta writers, such as those of the Sraosha Yashta and the Vendidad Chapter VII, tried to expound the correct doctrine, which our Prophet taught in the Gathas. Swami Vivekanand in his Speeches and Writings (p. 534) says :—

"The Smritis, Puranas and Tantras—all these are acceptable only so far as they agree with the Vedas, and whenever they are contradictory, they are to be rejected as unreliable." Similarly we may say, that when the later Avesta or Pahlvi literature contradicts the Gathas, it should be regarded as unreliable.

I quote here the remarks of Prof. Max-Muller with regard to this doctrine *in extenso* :—"Dr. Haug seems quite right in stating that Zarathushtra, having arrived at the idea of the unity and indivisibility of the Supreme Being, had afterwards to solve the great problem... namely, how to reconcile the imperfections discernible in the world, the various kinds of evil wickedness and baseness, with the goodness and justice of one God. He solved this question philosophically, by the admission of two primeval causes, which though different were united and produced the world of material things as well as that of the spirit... ...The one who produced all reality (*gayâ*) and goodness is called there the good mind (*vohu mano*), and the other, through whom the unreality (*agyâiti*) originated, bears the name of the evil mind (*akem mano*)...These are the two moving causes in the universe, united from the beginning and therefore called twins. They are present everywhere, in Ahuramazda as well as in men. These two primeval principles, if supposed to be united in Ahuramazda himself, are called Spenta Mainyu, his beneficent spirit, and Angra Mainyu, his hurtful spirit. That Angra Mainyu was not coceived then as a separate being, opposed to Ahuramazda, Dr. Haug has proved from Yasna XIX-9,* where Ahuramazda is mentioning these two spirits as inherent in his own nature, though he distinctly called them the *two masters* (*pâyu*) and the *two creators*. But while at first these two creative spirits were conceived as only two parts or ingredients of the Divine Being, this doctrine of Zarathushtra's became corrupted in course of time by misunderstandings and false interpretations. Spenta Mainyu, the beneficent spirit, was taken as a name of Ahuramazda himself, and the Angra Mainyu, by becoming entirely separated from Ahuramazda, was then regarded as a constant adversary of Ahuramazda. ......The origin of good and evil would thus have been transferred unto the Deity itself, though there, the possible evil was always overcome by the real good. Zoroaster had evidently perceived that without possible evil there can be no real good, just as without temptation there can be no virtue. The same contest which is supposed to be carried on within the deity is also carried on by each individual believer." (Theosophy or Psychological Religion, pp. 184-185.)

* "The Beneficent spirit spoke to me (Ahuramazda) about the whole of the creation, which is, which was and which was to be." The reference here is wrongly given.

NOTES.

Devas and Dasyus.

PAGE **2**.—My opinion that there was a time, when there were only two religious sections among the ancient Indo-Iranians is supported by the following remarks of Prof. Bhagvat:—"There seems to have been a time or age, when the known mankind was divided into two great divisions of the Devas and a-Devas or non-Devas. In this age the non-Devas and the Dasyus were the same." (Meher Yt., p. 29). Further up the same scholar identifies the Dasyus with the Dakhyus of the Avestan literature—one of the divisions of the Ahura worshippers.

Lassen attempted to connect the contrast *Daqyu* : *Dasyu* with that of *Daeva* : *Deva* and to see in it a result of the religious difference which separated the Iranians and the Indians (Vedic Index of Names and Subjects, by Macdonell and Keith, Vol. I, p. 349).

Dasa.

PAGE **5**.—We have seen that the Dâsas (= Dâhis) were a tribe of the Iranians. Even to-day, the word Dâsa (or Dâh) survives in the word *Dâha-Mobed* in Persia. The priest who takes an important part in the marriage ceremony of the Iranians is called a Dâha-Mobed. (See the Accounts of the Travels in Iran by Maneckji Limji Hateria, p. 23).

Grehma.

PAGE **16**.—I have identified Grehma (or Gerehma) of the Gathas with Kehram of the Shahnâme. He was the Guhram of the Shatroihâ-i-Airân. In § 9 we are told that Spendadâd, the son of Vishtâspa, sent a message to Guhram, Turchâv, Arjaspa and others to render submission to him. (See Ervad Modi's Shatroihâ-i-Airân, p. 59).

Jamshed Dynasty.

PAGE **45**.—I have shown that Jamshed was the name of a dynasty of kings bearing that name. In S. B. E. Vol. V, p. 131, Dr. West says:—"Dahâk was a name applied to a foreign dynasty (probably Semitic, personified as a single king,) which conquered the dominions of Yim."

Deluge.

PAGE **45**.—According to the Bible Chronology, the date of the Deluge was 2348 B. C. It is worthy of note that the Chinese deluge took place in the time of Yaou and Shun, B. C. 2348. The curious agreement of both the Chinese and the Hebrew records in assigning the year B. C. 2348 to the great flood is strong evidence of something in the nature of a vast, if not an universal catastrophe. (See the Shu King of the Chinese Historical Classic by Walter Gorn Old, p. 28).

Date of Veda.

PAGE **44**.—The following summary is given from the Vedic Index of Names and Subjects by Macdonell and Keith, Vol. I:—

(1) Bentley, by the gratuitous assumption, that Shrâvana always marked the summer solstice, concluded, that the names of the months did not date before B. C. 1181.........Whitney and Thibaut thought it impossible to fix a date by this means.

(2) All the lists of the Nakshatras begin with the Krittikas...... The later list begins with Ashvini; and it was unquestionably rearranged, because at the time of its adoption, the vernal equinox coincided with the star Zeta Piscium on the border of Revati and Ashvini, about the 6th century A. D. Weber

has therefore accepted the view that, the Krittikas were chosen for a similar reason and the date at which that Nakshatra coincided with the vernal equinox has been estimated at some period in the third milleníum B. C. A very grave objection to this view is its assumption that the sun, and not the moon, was then regarded as connected with the Nakshatras. Both Thibaut and Oldenberg have pronounced decidedly against the idea of connecting the equinox with the Krittikas.

(3) The winter solstice in Mâgha is assured by a Brahmana text; for, the Kausitaki Br. XIX—3 expressly places it in the new moon of Mâgha (माघस्य अमावास्यायां). It is not very important, whether we take this with the commentators, as the new moon in the middle of a month commencing with the day after the full moon in Taisha or which is much more likely, as the new moon beginning the month and preceding the full moon in Mâgha.......If the end of Revati marked the vernal equinox at one period, then the precession of the equinoxes would enable us to calculate at what point of time the vernal equinox was in a position corresponding to the winter solstice in Mâgha, when the solstitial colure cut the ecliptic at the beginning of Shravishthas. This would be, on the strict theory, in the third quarter of Bharani, 6¾ asterisms removed from Shravisthas and the difference between that and the beginning of Ashvini—1¾ asterisms—23⅓ degrees; (27 asterisms being — 360 degrees). Taking the starting point at 499 A. D., the assured period of Varâha Mihira, Jones arrived at the date B.C. 1181 for the vernal equinox, corresponding to the winter solstice in Mâgha —that is on the basis of 1 degree— 72 years as the precession. Pratt arrived at precisely the same date, taking the same rate of precession and adopting as his basis the ascertained position in the Siddhantas of the junction star of Mâgha, Alpha Leonis or Regulus. Davis and Colebrooke arrived at a different date, B. C. 1391 by taking as the basis of their calculation the junction star of Chitrâ.

Whitney says, that it is impossible, that the earlier asterisms were of 13⅓ degrees extent each. They were not chosen as equal divisions but as groops of stars which stood in conjunction with the moon...... Nor can we say that the star Zeta Piscium early formed the eastern boundary of Revati. Added to all this and to the uncertainty of the starting point—582 A. D., 560 A.D., or 491 A. D. being variants—is a fact, that the place of the equinox is not a matter accurately determined by mere observation and that the Hindu astronomers of the Vedic period cannot be deemed to have been very accurate observers.

(4). Another chronological argument has been derived from the fact, that there is a considerable amount of evidénce for Phâlguna having been regarded as the beginning of the year, since the full moon in Phâlguni is often described as the "mouth of the year" (Tait. Sam, VII-4-8-1 & 2, Panchavimsha Br. V-9-9. Tai. Br. I-1-2-8, Shata. Br. VI-2-2-18)...... Oldenberg and Thibaut maintain that the choice of Phâlguna as the mouth of the year was due to its being the month of spring. This view is favoured by the fact of the correspondence of Phâlguna and the beginning of spring (Cf. Shata. Br. I-6-3-36, Kau. Br. V-I, &c.). As seen above, in the Kaushitaki Brahman, the new moon in Mâgha is placed at the winter solstice, which puts the full moon in Phâlguna at a month and a half after the winter solstice or in the first week of February, a date not in itself improbable for about 800 B. C.

Krittikas.

PAGE 51.—We have seen that the Krittikas or the Pleiades consisted of seven stars. They have been named as under :—अंबा, दूला, नितत्नी, अभ्रयन्ती (forming cloud), वर्षयन्ती (causing rain), मेघयन्ती (making cloudy) and चुपुणिका (Cf. Tai. Sam. IV-4-5-1. and Kâṭhaka Sam. 40-4.)

Scorpion.

PAGE **65**.—Scorpion is one of the most ancient constellations, originally much extended in the direction of Virgo,—the claws of the Scorpion occupying the region of the sky, where we now see the constellation Libra. (Star Lore of All Ages, p. 326).

On p. 56 we have seen what significance is to be attached to the legend in Shâyast la Shâyast about the Scorpion seizing the testes of the Bull. The passage in the said book runs as under :—" When a sheep is slaughtered and divided into meat-offering (*gâus-dâk*), it is to be thus presented : The tongue, jaw and left eye are for the angel Homa's own, the neck is Ashavahishta's own,......the right shoulder is Ardvisur's, the left is Dravâspa's, the right thigh is for the guardian spirit of Vishtâspa, and the left for the guardian spirit of Jâmaspa, the back is for Ratpok (Rathvo) Berezad, the testicles are for the Star Vanand, the kidneys are Haptoiring's, ...the tail bone is for the guardian spirit of Zarathushtra, the Spitama,... the right eye is in the share of the moon." (Shâyast la Shâyast XI—4. S. B. E. Vol. V, pp. 335-337).

The different portions of the offering are connected with the different luminaries in the sky. Why is it that only Vishtâspa, Jâmâspa and Zarathushtra are specifically mentioned ? Could it be that they belonged to the Taurus (*gâo*) age ?

Ardvisura.

PAGE **71**.—I have tried to show that the Ardvisura was the constellation Eridanus. On page 72 (footnote) I have also put forward the *common* view regarding the Ardvisura being the planet Nâhid (Venus). It might be easily imagined that when a planet comes into conjunction with any constellation, it merges into that constellation, and as it were, assumes its form. If the Ardvisura is the planet Venus, the maiden, in whose form it appears, would be the constellation Cassiopeia, (the wife of Cephens, king of Æthiopia. She was a queen of matchless beauty).

There seems to be a decided resemblance between Cassiopeia and the constella tion Virgo, which was nothing more than a mere coincidence. Virgo was called the lady of the harvest and was represented as holding a sheaf of wheat or an ear of corn in her hand, while Cassiopeia, as seen on the Assyrian tablets, was called the lady of the corn. Cassiopeia is represented on some old maps as holding a palm in her hand. (See Star Lore of All Ages, p. 127).

Cassiopeia is a companion-constellation of Aries. If then the sun was in conjunction with Aries at the spring equinox, Zarathushtra would belong to the Aries age. I, however, do not think, that the Ardvisura was a planet.

ZARATHUSTRIAN CALENDAR.

A Date deduced from Numismatic evidence.

In the history of the Sassanians we come across two dates which have been determined with great accuracy. They are as follow: (1) Dr. A. D. Mordtmann has proved in his book named the "Chronology of the Sassanians" that the Emperor Kobad I died on 12th September 531 A. C.* (2) From the same book we find that the Emperor Khushru II (Parviz) was taken prisoner on 24th Feberuary 628 A. C., that on the next day his son Kobad II (Shirui) came to the throne and that on the 28th Febuary 628 A. C., Khushru II was killed.† We have however nothing to do with the latter date.

Different writers have given different periods for which the Sassanian emperors ruled. As their calculations differ very widely, the evidence of the number of the coins showing how long each emperor ruled, is of great use in fixing the exact period of his sovereignty.

In some instances it is found that although some emperors ruled for a certain number of years and a few months still their coins have exceeded the years of their rules as given in his history by *two*. For example, according to history, Hormazd IV ruled a little more than 11 years and still, strange to say, his coins have been 13.

To explain away this difficulty two scholars have put forward two different theories. The first theory is that of Dr. Mordtmann which is as under:—"The first year of a new emperor was counted from the day that he came to the throne up to the spring equinox or Jamshedi Nowroz (= 21st March). His second year ended on the next Jamshedi Nowroz and so on. His last year was counted from the day following the Jamshedi Nowroz up to the day of his death or dethronement."

We shall illustrate this theory by the date of Kobad II (Shirui) who come to the throne on 25th February 628 A. C., and ruled for 8 months according to Dr. Mordtmann.* Therefore the first year of Kobad commenced on 25th February 628 and ended on 21st March 628; and after the latter date his second year commenced. For this reason we should expect 2 coins (that is, coins for 2 years' rule) of Shirui and that was so.

The second theory is that of Professor Noeldeke who differed from Dr. Mordtmann in this that he counted the years not up to 21st March but up to Nowroz (= the day Ahuramazda of the month Fravardin). It has been proved that Noeldeke's theory is correct. (*See Shudha Ros Mah Report p. 13*).

We have seen that Kobad I died on 12th September 531 and his son Khushru (Anushehravân) came to the throne. We have also seen that Khushru II (Parviz) was dethroned on 24th February 628 and his son Kobad II (Shirui) became the ruler. Now the interval between these two dates is 96 years and 165 days, and as there were 23 leap years during this period, the interval between the said two dates was 96 non-intercalary years and 165 + 23 (= 188) days.

The famous Arab writer Albiruni has in his book named

* See K. R. Cama's translation pp. 21-22.

† See idem pp. 28-29.

* This is not correct. He ruled for more than a year. See Seventh Ori. Mon. p. 689.

"Athâr Ul-Bâkiya" given 4 tables of the rules of the Sassanian emperors. Hamza Isphahani is the author of two of these tables and one is ascribed to Abu Al Faraz Al Zanjani. Now according to one of the tables of Hamza, Khushru Anusheravân ruled for 47 years and 7 months, Hormazd IV for 11 years and 7 months and Parviz for 38 years. Thus the duration of the sovereignties of these emperors would be 96 years and 420 days. But this does not tally with the period abovementioned, namely 96 years and 188 days.

According to the second table of Hamza, the said three sovereigns ruled for 48, 12 and 38 years respectively. The total of these years is 98 which does not help us.

According to Abu Al Faraz the following periods have been assiged to the three emperors.

years,	Months and	Days.	
47	7	„ 5	to Khushru
11	7	„ 15	to Hormazd
38	0	„ 0	to Parviz.

Thus the total is 96 years and 440 days, which also is not useful to us. Prof. George Rawlinson in his seventh Oriental Monarchy (p. 590) says that though Parviz is commonly represented as having ruled for 38 years, still as a matter of fact he ruled only for 37 years and 5 months. Now if we make this emandation in (say) Al Zanjani's table,* the duration of the rules of the three emperors would be 95 years and 590 days or in other words 96 (non-intercalary) years and 225 days. This exceeds the period we have arrived at by (225—188=) 37 days. Therefore according to the above calculation Parviz came to the throne years 47-7-5 plus 11-7-15 (—59 years and 75 days) after 12th September 531. Now taking into consideration the fact that during this period there were 15 leap years we conclude that Parviz came to the throne on 11th November 590. It may be that for the reason stated above Parviz came to the throne 37 days after this latter date. Be that as it may, it is certain that he ruled up to 24th February 628.

Now with regard to the coins of Parviz Dr. Mordtmann says "His coins do not extend any further than 38. It is true, Hr. General V. Bartholomew possesses a coin of the year 39 but which probably was struck at a remote part of the empire soon after the 21st March 628, where by reason of great distance, people were not yet aware of the occurence, which had taken place in the capital in the end of February. The place of the mint is "men," which I interpret as Meibud."

Dr. Mordtmann has made his calculations thus: The first year of Parviz extended from 590 A.C. to 21st March 591 A.C.; his eleventh year was completed on 21st March 601, his 37th year was completed on 21st March 627 and his 38th year lasted from 22nd March 627 to 24th February 628. This is the reason why Dr. Mordtmann thought that the coins of this emperor did not extend further than 38. But he has himself informed us that a coin of the said emperor was also found for the 39th year. We however cannot accept the explanation given by him, the fact being that his theory itself was wrong.

The theory of Dr. Mordtmann is proved to be incorrect by his own writing; for at p. 38 of his book, he says "I accepted ...... that in old Persia *also* there existed an intercalation of one kind or another and on this assumption, all my calculations have nicely harmonized, which certainly would not have happened, if no intercalation had been made during the long reigns of Chusruv I for 48, and of Chusruv II for 38 years." Dr. Mordtmann evidently thinks that the Iranians did their intercalation at the end of every fourth year which, was not the case.

* This table seems to be more reliable. According Hamzas' first table the number of days would be less by 20.

Now if according to Professor Noeldeke's theory we suppose that the day Ahuramazda of the month Fravardin fell before 24th February 628, it is clear that the coins of Parviz must have been for 39 years and as a matter of fact that was so; or to put the matter in other words, the day Ahuramazda of the month Fravardin* must have fallen before 24th February 628, though after 11th November‡ 627, it being a fact that the coins of Parviz extended up to 39.

In the ancient Iran, there were two main systems of reckoning—one followed by the Persians and the other by the Sughdians and others. We shall try to determine to which of these classes the abovementioned Roj Mah belonged. For this purpose we shall turn our attention to Albiruni's book.

Albiruni on intercalation in Iran.

In his book named "Athâr Ul Bâkiya" p. 55†, Albiruni says "when Zoroaster arose and intercalated the years with the months which up to that time had summed up from the day quarters, time returned to its orginal condition. Then he ordered people in all future times to do with the day quarters the same as he had done and they obeyed his command. They did not call the intercalary month by a special name, nor did they repeat the name of another month, but they kept it simply in memory from one turn to another. Being however afraid that there might arise uncertainty as to the place where the intercalary month would have again to be inserted, *they transferred the five Epagomenæ and put them at the end of that month to which the turn of intercalation had proceeded on the last occasion of intercalating.* And as this subject was of great importance and of general use to high and low, to the king and to the subjects, and as it is required to be treated with knowledge and to be carried out in conformity with nature (*i.e.* with real time), they used to postpone intercalation, when its time happened to occur at a period, when the condition of the empire was disturbed by calamities; then they neglected intercalation so long, until the day quarters summed up to two months. Or on the other hand they anticipated intercalating the year at once by two months, when they expected that at the time of the next coming intercalation, circumstances would distract their attention therefrom, as it has been done in the time of Yazdgird ben Sâbur for no other motive but that of precaution. That was the last intercalation which they carried out......In that intercalation the turn had come to Abân Mâh; therefore the Epagomenæ were added at its end, and there they have remained ever since, on account of their neglecting intercalation."

Again on p. 121 Albiruni says: "Further we are informed by traditions, the correctness of which is proved by their mutual agreement that the last intercalation was carried out at the time of Yazdagird Shapur and that the Epagomenæ were put at the end of that month to which the turn of intercalation had come *viz.*, the eighth month (Abân Mâh). If now we count the interval between Alexander and Ardashir as 537 years, we find the interval between Zoroaster* and Yazdagird ben Shapur

* See Sudha Roz Mah Report p. 18 footnote. We shall see hereafter that when Jamshed came to the throne Ahuramazda Roz of Fravardin Mah coincided with the vernal equinox. Also when in 407 Beheram Yezdgird was born, the same Roz Mah fell near the spring equinox. When Yezdgird Sheheriar came to the throne in 682 the same Roz Mah fell on 19th June N. S. This last however was due to the fact the order of the months changed as we shall see.

‡ 11th November was, as we have seen the date when Parviz came to the throne.

† The page refers to the translation of Albiruni's book by Dr. C. E. Sachau. Albiruni wrote this book in 1000 A. C.

* It need hardly be pointed out that this Zoroaster was not our Prophet. In the Pahlvi Ardâvirafnâme we are told that when Alexander invaded Persia (881 B.C.), 800

to be nearly 970 years, in which eight leap months are due, since it was their custom to intercalate one month in 120 years."

We thus gather from Albiruni that when Yazdagird Shapur came to the throne the turn had come for the 8th intercalation and that 10 years had passed by. Now as as Yazdagird came to the throne in 399 A. C., the time for the eighth intercalation had fallen due in 389 A. C. Further (on p. 56) Albiruni informs us that Yazdagird did the intercalation during his sovereingnty (*i. e.* between 399 to 420 A. C.) and also did another month's intercalation in anticipation; but at the same time and almost in the same breath Albiruni says that the Gatha days remained after the Aban Mah (—the 8th month from Fravardin). This leads us to suppose that the abovementioned ninth intercalation (done in anticipation) was not done by changing the position of the Gatha days but by adding an unnamed intercalary month. Thus we see that the effect of the intercation extended as far as 389 +120 =509 A.C., and that the Gatha days were after the month Abân. After 509 A.C. up to the time of Albiruni the Epagomenæ remained in the same position namely after the Aban Mah.

According to the Bundehishn and the Dinkart the month which commenced with the spring was the first month.

---

years had expired since the advent of the Zarathushtrian religion. Thus according to this writer, the religion was established in 681 B.C.; but the writer is under some misapprehension. The Median emperor Cyaxares (682 to 698 B.C.) invaded Nineve, routed the Assyrians and established Magism as the state religion. This revival of the ancient Zarathushtrian religion which was decaying for centuries under foreign rule seems to have been confounded with the advent of the religion by several writers. It was also very common among the ancient Iranians to attribute every important event to Zarathushtra. For these reasons I think, the reform in our calendar was attributed to our Prophet.

Now as the effect of the intercalation extended up till 509 A.C. when the Gatha days were at the end of Aban Mah, it follows that in 509 A. C. Adar was the first month, that is to say, the month which commenced with the commencement of spring; in other words the day Ahuramazda of the month Adar fell on 21st March 509 A.C. (N.S.). We must remember that all we have stated above applied to the Persians only.

It is an established fact that when Yazdagird Shehriar came to the throne, the day was Ahuramazda of the month Fravardin and coincided with 19th June 632 A.C. (N.S.). Now if we suppose that no intercalation had been made between 509 and 932 A.C. by the Persians, it would follow that on 21st March 509 A.C. there was the day Ahuramazda of the month Adar—which is exactly the result we have arrived at above.

Another proof that Ahuramazda Roj of Adar Mah fell on 21-3-509 is this: When Jalalludin Malekshah Saljuki commenced his new era in 1079 A.C. the day Ahuramazda of the Fravardin Mah concided with 3rd March (N.S.). Thus we find that this Roj Mah fell on 21st March in 1007 A. C.

Abul Hassan Kuschiar says that in the reign of Anushehravan the Gatha days followed the Aban Mah and that they remained there up to the year 375 of Yazdagird (1006 A. C.) when they were placed after the month Asfandar.

Now Khushru Anusheravan was the ruler between 531 and 579 A. C. It thus appears that the Persians did not make any intercalation for a long time after the reign of this emperor and that the last intercalation was made either during his reign or before it. The ancient Iranians commenced their year from the beginning of spring and intercalated one month at the intervals of 120 years. Thus before 1007 A. C. the Roj Ahuramazda of the month Adar fell at the vernal equinox in

879, 759, 635 and 511 A.C.* Therefore in 509 A. C. the day Ahuramazda of the Mah Adar fell on the 21st March.

The conclusion we have arrived at is borne out by the followingremarks of Albiruni (p. 211) "Bahâr Cashn,† the 1st of Adar Mah......was the begining of spring at the time of the Kisrâs."

The first month of the Sughdians.

With reference to the Sughdians Albiruni says: "Other people maintain that originally both the Persian and the Sughdian years had the *same beginning* until the time when Zoroaster appeared. But when after Zoroaster the Persians began to transfer the five epagomenæ to each of the leap months, as we have before mentioned, the Sughdians left them in their original place and did not transfer them. So they kept them at the end of the months of their year, whilst the Persians, after they began to neglect intercalation, retained them at the end of Aban Mah." (pp.220—221). We also find on p. 56 that "the Sughdians commence the year with the 6th day of the Persian month Fravardin, Khurdadroz. So the beginning of the months is different until Adar Mah; afterwards they have the same beginnings." This evidently refers to Albiruni's time.

It appears from the above statement that at the commencement of the reformed calendar both the Persians and the Sughdians had the same beginning. Then after 120 years the Persians did an intercalation of 30 days or one month by putting the Gatha days at the end of the month Fravardin. The Sughdians on the other hand simply added one intercalary month.

Albiruni further states that the Sughdians commenced their year with the 6th day of the Persian month Fravardin; therefore the beginnings of the months of the Persians and the Sughdians were differrent until Adar Mah; afterwards they had the same beginnings. This was the state of things in the time of Albiruni and was due to fact that nine intercalations had been made. It must be remembered that the 9th intercalation was done in anticipation by adding an *adhika* month. But when only 7 intercalations had taken place, the beginnings of the Persian and the Sughdian months were diffirent up to Aban Mah and when only 6 intercalations had taken place the beginnings differed up to Meher Mah and so on.

We have seen that the day Ahuramamzda of the month Adar of the Persians fell on 21st March 509; therefore on the same date the Sughdians had their day Ahuramazda of the month Fravardin.

The first month of the Khwarizmians.

Albiruni says on p. 223: "The Khwarizmians agree with the Sughdians regarding the beginnings of the year and the months and they disagree with the Persians on the same subjects. The cause of this is the same, which we have described when speaking of the Sughdians."

It may be stated here that from what Albiruni has stated elsewhere, it appears that in *later* times the Khwarizmians were one month in advance.*

We thus conclude that in 509 A.C. the Sughdian month Fravardin coin-

---

* The years 1000, 900, 700 and 600 were not leap years.

† "The most lucky hours of this day are those during which *Aries* is the horoscope. People consider the hour of the morning as of good omen......On the morning of the *fox-day* the Persians thought it to be a good omen to look at the clouds." (See Albiruni p. 211). This is similar to what we find in Ashi Yashta § 56 which we have already considered. In olden times the lucky hours of this day must have been those in which *Taurus* was the horoscope. Cf. Ashi Yt. §55, Yasna 60 § 2 and 82 § 10.

* This point will be referred to hereafter.

cided with the Persian month Adar, that both these months commenced at the commencement of spring (and were therefore the first months,) and that the Persian month Adar was the first owing to a mere fortuitous circumstance.

Albiruni has himself given us the order of the months of the Sughdians and the Khwarizmians—wherein Fravardin has been mentioned as the first month; and as these people did not change the order of their months even when intercalations were made, it must follow that their first month was Fravardin.

First Roz of Khwarizmian Khurdad Mah.

With reference to the first day of the month Khurdad, Albiruni says (p. 223): "The third month is HarudÂdh......... In *anti-Mahomedan times* this day was the time of extreme heat......In our times this day coincides with the time of the sowing of sesame and what is sown together with it."

The rule of the Mohamedans commenced in 632 A.C. or to be more accute in 652 A.C. We have seen that Yazdagird Shapur did an intercalation of two months although an intercalation of only one month had become due 10 years prior to the commencement of his reign. Therefore about the year 400 A.C. (on the supposition that Yazdagird's intercalation was made at that date) the first day of the month Khurdad would fall on (or about) the 19th June. Now if we suppose that the Khwarizmians were one month in advance of the Sughdians we see that the above Roz Mah would fall on the 19th July, which is very near the day of extreme heat.

Jashne Ajghar among the Khwarizmians.

Two Jashns belonging to the Khwarizmians have been described by Albiruni. These descriptions have led some to believe that the first month of the Khwarizmians was Dae.

On p. 224 Albiruni says: "The 15th (of Ciri) is called AjgÂr......In bygone times it was the beginning of that season when people felt the need of warming themselves at the fire, because the air was changing in autumn. In our time it coincides with the middle of summer."

If the 15th day of the month Tir of the Khwarizmians coincided with the commencement of autumn (or say the 22nd September), the first day of their Fravardin month fell about 15th June. Therfore it might be argued that their month Dae fell near the spring equinox and was therefore the first month. This however is not true. The right explanation is as follows:—

In the Chapter No. 12 "on the Khwarizm Shah's reform on the Khwarizmian festal calendar Albiruni says (pp. 229-230)":—

"Abusaid Ahmad *b.* Muhmad *b* IrÂk followed the example of Almutadid—BillÂh regarding the intercalation of the Chorasmian months. For on being freed from his fetters at Bukhara and having returned to his residence, he asked the mathematicians at his court, regarding the feast Ajghar......He called scholars (such as Al-KharÂji and Al-Hamdaki and others) before him and these scholars gave him a minute explanation and told him how the Parsis and Chorasmians had managed their year. Thereupon he said 'this is a system which has become confused and forgotten. The people rely upon these days (*i.e.*, certain feast days AjghÂr, NimkhÂb, &c.) and thereby they find the cardinal points of the four seasons, since they believe that they never change their places in the year: that Ajghar is always the middle of summer, Nimkhab the middle of winter. Certain distances from these days they use as the proper times for sowing and ploughing. Something like this (*i.e.*, the deviation of the Chorasmian year from proper time) is not perceived except in the course of many years. And this is one of the reasons why they disagree among each other regarding the fixing of those distances, so that some maintain that 60 days after Ajghar is the proper time for sowing wheat, whilst others put this time earlier or later. The proper thing would be that we should find some means to fix things uniformly, so that the proper time for those things should never differ.' The scholars told him that the best way would be to fix the beginning of the Chorasmian months on certain days as the Greeks and Syrians do. This plan they carried out A. Alex. 1270 and they arranged that the 1st of Nawsarji shall fall on the third of the Syrian Nisan, so that Ajghar would always fall in the middle of Tammuz. And accordingly they regulated the times of agricultural works, *i.e.*, the time of gathering grapes for the purpose of making raisins is 40–50 days after Ajghar......In the same way they fixed all the times of sowing."

From Sachau pp. 406 and 70 we see that the Syrian year commenced with Tishrin I. which coincided with 1st October. Now as the Syrian months Tishrin I., Tishrin II., Kanun I., Kanun II. Shebat and Adhar consisted of 31, 30, 31, 31, 28 and 31 days respectively, we find that the 3rd day the Syrian month Nisan fell on 3rd April. (See also Albiruni pp. 60 and 69.)

The above said Khwarizmian Shah reformed the calendar in such a manner that the 1st day of the month Nowsarji (= first month) of the Khwarizmians coincided with the 3rd of the Syrian Nisan. Therefore this Roz Mah fell on 3rd April in the year of Alexander 1270 = 959 A.C. (See Sachau p. 427). Thus the Khwarizmian 15th day of the Tir Mah (= Jashne Ajghâr) fell 104 days after 3rd April, that is on 16th July. We thus see that about the year 1000 A.C., when Albiruni* wrote his book, the said Jashn fell about 6th July—a date which is very near the Maidyoshem (midsummer) gahânbar.

Further up Albiruni says that the Jashn of Ajghar fell in autumn in former times. On pp. 37-38 he says that Khalif Mutadid had also made an effort to reform the calendar. The said Khalif came to the conclusion that no intercalation had been made after the death of Yazdagird Sheheriar up to his time, that is to say for a period of 243 years. During this period the Nowroz fell earlier by 60 days; therefore he fixed the Nowroz (= the day Ahuramazda of the month Fravardin) to coincide with the day Ahuramazda of the month Khurdad, on Wednesday the 11th day of the month Haziran. But still the Nowroz did not fall at the proper time; in other words the said reformed calendar was not based on correct calculations. Thus we see that in the time of Mutadid the Roz Ahurmazda of the Mah Fravardin coincided with 11th Haziran Yazagardi year 264 or 16th June 896 A. C. (N. S.).

The said reform of Mutadid was based on wrong calculations as Albiruni has himself suggested. It was therefore due to this wrong reform that the 15th day of the month Tir (= Jashne Ajghâr) had fallen about 28th September between the years 896 and 959 A.C.; and we can easily understand why Albiruni says that the Jashn fell in autumn in former times.

Jashne-Nimkhab of the Khwarizmians.

This Jashn happened on the 11th day of the 10th month of the Khwarimians. With reference to this Jashn Albiruni says on p. 224 "People say that it (Nimkhab) was originally

* Albiruni was born in 972 and died in 1048 A.C.

† See p. 90 Shudha Roz Mah Report hereafter shortly written S. R. M. Report.

called Minac Akhib. It means the night of Mina. Some of them maintain that Mina was one of their queens or chieftains, that she left her castle intoxicated, dressed in a silk dress at spring time. She fell down outside the castle and lost all self-control; she fell asleep and was smitten by the cold of the night and died. Now people were astonished that the cold had killed a human being about this time in spring...... Nowadays people consider it (this day) as the middle of winter."

We have seen above that the Khwarizmian first day of the first month fell on 3rd April in 959 A.C. Two hundred and eighty days after this (that is on 11th day of the 10th month = Jashne Nimkhab), we have 8th January; and in the time of Albiruni the said Jashne Nimkhab would happen a few days before that date, which can very well be taken as the middle of winter.

We have also seen that in 896 A. C. the first day of the first month of the Khwarizmians fell on 16th June. Therefore in 897 A. C. the 11th day of the 10th month coincided with 23rd March. Thus when Albiruni says that this Jashn fell at spring time in his days, the explanation is that due to the wrong reform of Mutadid, the said Jashn happened near the vernal equinox between the years 896 and 959 A. C. (the latter being the year in which, as we have seen, Abu Sayad made the reform).

We have thus far tried to prove that in 509 A.C. the month Adar of the Persians coincided with the month Fravardin of the Sughdians.

Fravardin the first month according to Shahname.

Firdusi Tusi the well known poet of the Shahnâme says that when the King Jamshed came to the throne, the day of the month was Ahuramazda of Mah Fravardin and it was the first day of spring (see S. R. M. Report p. 28). This shows that Fravardin was the first month in those days.

The same poet says in another place "On the day Ahuramazda of the month Fravardin in the 8th year of his (Yazdagird Shapur's) reign, when the Sun was in conjunction with Aries, a son was born to him. He named the child Beheram" (see Sussanian Shâhnâmu by Pallonji B. Desai p. 48). Now Yazdagird came to the throne in 399 A.C. Therefore Beheram was born in 407 A. C.

The sun was in conjunction with the first point of Aries at the vernal equinox at the time that the Council of Nice was held, that is, in 325 A.C. Therefore in 407 A.C. the Sun entered

Aries $\frac{407-325}{72}$ = 1 day later than 21st March, that is on 22nd March, on which day the Roz Ahuramazda of Fravardin Mah fell. It may be that the difference of a few days may have been overlooked by the Iranians of the time. We should note here that in 407 the month Fravardin commenced with the vernal equinox.

The above said inference almost corroborates the statement of Albiruni that Yazdagird Shapur made an intercalation during his reign, (399 to 420 A.C.). This intercalation he must have done before 407 A.C. or in other words before his son was born. This is also indirectly proved from another piece of evidence which is recorded in history. The Roman emperor Archadius appointed Yazdagird by his will to be the guardian of his minor son. Archadius died in 408 A.C. (see Mordtmann p. 17). Afterwards Yazdagird came into close contact with the bishops. Two of the bishops influenced him to such an extent that he caused the great Atash Beheram (Fire Temple) of Madâin to be burnt by the Christians. Yazdagird must have done the intercalations before he inclined towards Christianity.

Kuschiar on intercalation.

The Arab writer Abul Hassan Kuschiar who lived in about 1060

A. C. says: "The sun* entered the constellation Aries in the days of Khushru Bin Kobad Anushehravan and the Epagomenæ were after the month Aban. When after the expiration of 120 years, the supremacy of the Iranians came to an end and the Arabs came to rule, nobody acted according to the fixed regulation."

The Iranian power ended in 651 A. C., 120 years before which (that is in 531 A. C.) Khushru came to the throne. In 531 A. C. the sun entered Aries on 23rd March. Thus according to the above writer the Epagomenæ at the end of Aban Mah fell near 23rd March† 531 A.C. This practically corrborates the result we have arrived at, namely that the Persian day Ahuramazda of the month Fravardin coincided with 21st March 509 A. C.

Further up the same writer says: "The Epagomenæ which remained after the month Aban were placed at the end of Asfandar on the first day of the month Fravardin in 375 Yazdagirdi year when the sun entered Aries."‡ From this it appears that on 21st March 375 Yazdagirdi (= 1006 A.C.) there was Ahuramazda Roz of Fravardin Mah and that the Gathas were placed after the month Asfandar by the Persians. In short the writer suggests that the Persians made an intercalation of 4 months or 120 days. Now taking into consideration the fact that the year 800 A.C. was a leap year, we find that up till (1006—120×4—4×4=) 510 A.C. (also 509 A. C.) the effect of Yazdgird's intercalation was in force.

Jashne Mehergan at spring time.

Dr. Rapp. (translation by K. R. Cama p. 111) says: "Porphyry informs us 'that a particular position in the Zodiac has been assigned to Mithra, that of the Equinox and in this position he has the north to his right and the south to his left. Mithra is hence celebrated not merely as the light which daily vanquishes the night but even as the one which at each spring time, triumphs over the long winter nights and restores the rejoicing beneficent summer brightness'...... On this account the Mithra festival, which without doubt was celebrated in that age, became a public festival." On p. 264 Dr. Rapp says "This festival was a public jubilee and since Mithra is situated between night and light and is placed at the time of the night and day being equal, we deduce therefrom that this festival was celebrated on the vernal equinox as a festival of rejoicing for light which has vanquished the winter nights and now has received the sovereignty."

In the Ancient Calendars and Constellations, Plunket says (p. 61):— "The worship of Mithras in spite of much opposition gained many followers in Rome. The birth-day of the sun-god was kept at the winter solstice, but the *great festivities in his honour were as a rule celebrated at the season of the spring equinox* and were famous even among Roman festivals."

---

* The passage is quoted from Ideler by Dr. M. E. Davar in his book *re* Zarathosti Calendar pp. 11-12 and 35.

† In 325 A.C. the sun entered Aries at the vernal equinox or 21st March. Therefore in 509 A.C. the sun entered Aries on $21+\frac{509-325}{72}=$ 23rd March. The sun's entering the sign of Aries probably meant the beginning of spring. Albiruni says at p. 201 "In our time Nowroz coincides with the sun's entering the sign of Aries, which is the beginning of spring."

‡ The statement that the sun entered Aries refers to the Vernal Equinox. Because in 1079 A.C. when Jallalludin Malekshah established his new era the Roz Ahuramazda of the Mah Fravardin fell on 3rd March (N.S.) (See S. R. M. Report p. 28). Therefore in (1079—18×4=) 1007 A.C., the same day of the month coincided with March 21st.

Note.—In 1006 A.C. the sun entered Aries $\left(\frac{1006-325}{72}=\right)$9 days after 21st March.

Porphyry was born in 233 and died in 304 A.C. Therefore according to Dr. Rapp the Jashne Mehergan fell near 21st March. Hormazda bin Shapur came to the throne in 273 A.C. Albiruni informs us that during the time of this emperor the festivals of Mehergan were commenced for the first time to be celebrated from Meher Roz to Ram Roz (see Sachau p. 209.)

Now let us test the correctness of the above statements. The day Ahuramazda of the month Fravardin of the Persians coincided with 21st March 509 A.C. We have also seen that two intercalary months were added after Aban. Therefore 240 years before 509 A. C. (= 269 A. C.) the Roz Ahuramazda of the month Aban coincided with 22nd March,* and the Epagomenæ happened before this date. Thus in 273 A.C. (when Porphyry was most probably 40 years of age) Meher Roz of Meher Mah fell on 2nd March and Ram Roz on 7th March.

Also on 23rd March 149 A.C. there was the day Ahuramazda of the month Meher of the Persians. Therefore the Roz Meher of the Meher Mah fell on 7th April 149 A. C. and Ram Roz on 12th April of the same year. Thus on account of the want of intercalation in every fourth year Meher Roz of Meher Mah (= Jashne Mehergan) fell on 21st March in about 220 A.C.† and Ram Roz of Meher Mah about 240 A.C.

* In 509 and 889 the Persian day Ahuramazda of the month Adar fell on 21st March. In 269 the same day of the month Aban fell on 22nd March. In 149 the same day of the month Meher fell on 23rd March. In 29 the same day of the month Sheherevar fell on 24th March and so on.

† It is argued by some that "the worship of Mithra was introduced among the Romans from Iran before the 1st century B. C. The Roman emperor Aurelianus, however, introduced a new element in this worship in the year 273 A. C. and it was this that he fixed the 25th December as the day of Mithra's worship. Thus in the time of the Persian emperor Hormazda bin Shapur, the month Meher was near the winter solstice.' As we have seen above, this argument is not correct. Even among the Romans the great festivities in honour of Mithra were held at the spring equinox, as Plunket has informed us.

First month according to Avesta.

In Fravardin Yashta § 49 we have been told that "the Farohars come into this world at the time of Hamaspathmaedaya."

*Hamaspathmaedaya** literally means "that in which there is sacri-fice at the flying away (= end) of the year."

It appears from the Yasna that as Maidyozaremaya (Midspring) is the first Gahâmbâr, Hamaspathmaedaya is the last gahambar, and is the last day† of the year. Now if the month during which the Farohars come into this world is named after the Farohars, it is easy to see that its place must be near the end of the year. The time of the coming of the Farohars lies on the border line between the end of the old year and the commence-

* *Hama*=Sk. समा f., सम n. meaning "year." Cf. the words पापषम ("bad year") पुण्यपम or सुपम ("good year"). The exact equivalent of *Hamas* is समस् which is not found alone in Sanskrit but is seen in ऐपमस् ("in this year"), ऐपमस्तन ("happening this year"); see Panini 5-3-22; 4-2-105.

Path is equivalent to m. f. n. or पत m. *lit* "flying away, end." *Hamaspath* bears the same meaning as समान्त "end of the year."

Maedaya = मेध्य "sacrificial (thing)."

Hamaspathmaedaya is a Bahuvrihi compound, qualifying ratu ("time")="that in which there is sacrifice at the end of the year."

The Avesta equivalent for *Hamaspathmaedaya* is *aretho-kerethana* which is equivalant to Sk. ऋतकर्तनं "cutting of sacrifice" and which is rendered in Pahlvi as "*pavan Ijashne Kerdâri*" (= for performing Ijashne); see Avijeh Din p. 507 and Khureh Vabijak p 118.

†It should be noted that the passage commencing with "*dat athra vicharenti*" &c., is a later interpotation.

ment of the new year*. Hence misgivings arise into one's mind as to whether the last month of the year could be named after the Farohars or the first month. Fravardin Yashta para. 98 seems to solve the difficulty. Therein it is stated that "the waters and the trees rejoiced at the birth of Zarathushtra, and began to grow." This evidently suggests that Zarathushtra was born in the commencement of spring.†

In Zadsperm's Zarathushtraname 23§ 9 we are told that "Zarathushtra died at the age of 77 years and 40 days on the day Khurshed of the month Ardibehesht." From this we conclude that Zarathushtra was born in the commencement of Fravardinmah.

We thus arrive at the conclusion that during the time of our Prophet, the commencement of the month Fravardin coincided with the beginning of spring.

In Fravardin Yt. § 57 it is said that "The Farohars showed proper paths to the stars, the moon, the sun and countless lights (of the sky) which before that (= before the Farohars rendered help) stood motionless &c." In this passage we find the popular belief of the Avestan people that it was the Farohars who set the world revolving in its beginning. It therefore seems quite appropriate that the very first month in which the world was set in motion should be named after the Farohars.*

In Vendidad 19§ 14 Ahuramazda asks Zarathushtra to praise His own Farohar†. It might well be asked why Ahuramazda did not ask Zarathushtra to praise Himself. I agree with the opinion of the late Mr. Ardeshir Kamdin that the Farohar faculty (= progressive faculty) of Ahuramazda is far greater than his *Dâtare*—faculty (=creative faculty); for the reason that the second faculty is a part and parcel of the first. No wonder therefore that the Egyptians and the Babylonians primarily worshipped the *Ka* and the *Zi* of their gods rather than the gods themselves. This is therefore an additional reason why the first month should be named after the Farohar of Ahuramazda.

---

* As Dr. F. Justi wrote to me on 6-2-1905: "The original idea seems to be that the Farohars appear on earth in the five days, when the course of time is suspended after the end of the 12 × 30 days of the year and a gap reigns between that moment and the first day of the Farvardin month; for, the blessed souls living in eternity do not know time and course of years."

† Similarly in Exod. 12-4 we read "Ye shall not eat leavened bread on this day in that month *when the trees blossom*." As Albiruni says on p. 68, "this day is the 14th Nisan, the beginning of spring when the leaves of the trees and the blossoms of the fruit trees come forth."

*Bundehishm Ch. III also lends us support: "Ganâmino rushed into the world exactly at noontime on the day Ahuramazda of the month Frarvardin.....When Gayomard came out of the sweat, he found that in his world where darkness reigned supreme, the sky was moving and the sun and the moon were in motion." According to this writer, therefore, the first day in the world was the day Ahuramazda of the month Fravardin. See also p. 55 of Albiruni's book which repeats the same story.

In the Spiegel Memorial Vol. Ervad Maneckji Unvala has given the following description of Nowroze Khâs (Khurdad Roz of Fravardin Mah) from a Persian book: "It is said that God created the world on this day and ordered the plants, stars, the sun and the moon to move in their path beginning their journey from Aries and caused the heavens to revolve."

In Cama Memorial Volume p. 122 Dastur Kaikhoshroo Jamaspji shows from a Pahlvi book that on the day Khurdad of the month Fravardin "Ahuramazd created the soul of the worldly creatures." Also see Albiruni p. 201.

† Dr. A. H. Sayce in his "Religion of Ancient Egypt and Babylonia" (p. 57) says "In the older period of Egyptian history the Ka of the god and not the god himself who was primarily the object of worship." On p. 58 Dr. Sayce says "As in Egypt the (Babylonian) gods had each his Zi and as in Egypt it was the Zi of the god rather than the god himself who was primarily worshipped." According to Prof Max Muller Fravashi is "the genius of anything." Dr. Haug identifies the Fravashis with the *ideas* of Plato."

Zadsperm's Zarathushtra-name.

ZÂdsperm in his Zarathushtra-nâme. (Ch. 29 §§ 1-4) says :—

" About his (Zarathushtra's) coming to 30 years of age, it is thus declared that on the lapse of 30 years onwards from his appearance, on the day Aneran of the month Spendarmad, he had proceeded in that direction, in which there occurred the so called festival of spring (Jashne-i-vahâr), 45 days beyond new year's day at a place become specially noted, where people went from many quarters, out to the place of festival (Jashne kâr)...And about his coming out to the conference on the lapse of those 45 days, at the place of festival at dawn on the day Dadvo pavan Mitro of the month Ardivahishta" (S. B. E. Vol. 47 pp. 154-155). From this it appears that in the time of Zarathushtra the Jashna of Bahâr (spring)* fell on the 45th day after Nowroz, that is, on the day Depmeher of the month Ardi beheshta. Thus also we see that the month Farvardin coincided with the spring time.†

In ZÂdsperm Ch. 23 § 9 we read : " Zarathushtra died in the 47th year of the religion at the age of 77 years and 40 days on the day Khurshed of the month Ardibehesht which, *on account of 8 intercalary months*, has been shifted to the day Khurshed of the month Dae ; because his ceremony takes place also in Ardibeheshta Mah." Here also we find that the Iranians made their intercalation by adding one month after 120 years. It should be noted that the reason why the month Ardibehesht had been shifted to the month Dae was not that there were two different systems of years, civil and ecclesiastical but that eight intercalary months had been added.

Pahlvi Vendidad.

In the Pahlvi Vendidad Ch. I-4 we are told :—*Oknu binâ Vohuman binâ Shatvin ait Zamestân labmaman.* " At present the month Bahman is (coincident with) Sheherevar (which) is the heart of winter." Our year commenced with the spring equinox. Therefore, if we assign 4 seasons to the year, the month of extreme cold would be Bahman. Now if the Persian month Bahman coincided with the Sughdian month Sheherevar, then the Persian (11+7 — 18 —6) month Sheherevar must have coincided with the Sughdian (6+7 —18=1) month Fravardin. The Persian day Ahuramazda of the month Meher fell on 23rd March 149* A. C. and the same day of the month Sheherever on 24th March 29 A.C. Corresponding with these dates the Sughdians had their day Ahuramazda of the month Fravardin. Thus it may be that the writer lived between 41 and 157 A.C.

If on the other hand the Sughdian month Bahman coincided with the Persian month Sheherevar, then the Sughdian (11+2 — 18 — 1) month Fravardin must have coincided with the Persian (6+2=8) month Aban. The Persian day Ahuramazda of the month Aban, coinciding with the same day of the Sughdian month Fravardin, fell on 22nd March 269 A.C.; also the Persian month Aban remained coincident with the Sugh-

* Maidyo-Zaremaya Gahanbâr.

† The above statement derives further support from the Zarathushtranâme of Dastur Zarthost Beheram who says : " when in the middle of the month Ardibeheshta, the world had become beautiful like heaven owing to the spring time, the holy Zarathushtra started from Iran at sun rise on the day Depmeher (see Dastur Peshotanji Sanjana's translation p. 68)."

* Ahuramazda Roz of Adar Mah fell on 21st March 509 A.C. and 889 A.C., the first Roz of Aban Mah on 22-3-269, that of Meher Mah on 23-3-149 and that of Sheherevar Mah on 24-3-29.

As we have seen the Sughdians commenced their year on the 6th day of Persian month Fravardin so that the beginnings of Sughdian and Persian months were different until Adar Mah ; afterwards they had the same beginnings. But when only 7 intercalations had been made, the beginnings were different until Aban Mah and so on.

dian month Fravardin up to the time when Yazdagird Shapur made the intercalation.

It thus appears probable that the writer of the Pahlvi Vendidad wrote his book after 41 A.C. but before 509 A.C. Dr. West assigns 550 A.C. as the date to this book; but it was probably written in the commencement of the 5th century A.C., —about the year in which Yazdagird added two intercalary months.*

Passages from Bundehishn re: Intercalation.

In the Iranian Bundehisn of Ervad Tehemurasp D. Anklesheria we have the following Pahlvi passage:

Pavan bindâ i Shatrovar i ait bindâ Tir i vahijkik âigh Medioshehm mâhikân apus yahvund. Pavan bindâ i Fravartin ait bindâ i Spendomat i vahijkik ait âigh Hamaspatmaedem bindâ sarhund.

"In the month Sheherevar, which is (equivalent to) the intercalary month Tir, that is to say, in Maidyoshem, the fishes become pregnant. In the month Fravardin, which is (equivalent to) the intercalary month Spendârmad, that is to say, in Hamaspathmaedem, they give delivery."†

The Vahijkik month was the month of those Iranians who changed the order of the months by placing the Gatha days after Fravardin, Ardibehest and so on.

According to the first passage the Sughdian month Sheherevar coincided with the Persian month Tir. Therefore the Sughdian month (6 + 7 = 13) Fravardin coincided with the Persian month (4 + 7 = 11) Bahman—the epagomenæ being after the Sughdian month Safandâr and the Persian month Dae.

According to the second passage the Sughdian Fravardin coincided with the Persian Safandârmad—the epagominæ being after the Sughdian month Safandâr and the Persian month Bahman.

It appears that the fishes became pregnant at a certain time of the year and after a few months gave delivery.

It also appears from the above quotation that in the time of the author, the Persians or rather some sect of the Persians made an intercalation of one month, so that their month Bahman which was the first month became last, and Safandârmad became the first month.

The Arab writer Hamza Isfahâni (961 A.C.) has given certain dates in his book—which are as follow*:—

Rabiul aval 3 Hijri 323 Tuesday= Bahman month, Aban Roz (10th February 935, O. S.)
Rabiul âkher 1 Hijri 323 Monday =Safandâr month Amerdad Roz (10th March 935, O. S.)
Rabiul âkher 19 Hijri 329 Thursday—Dae month Govâd Roz— (21st January 941, O. S.)

From all these dates we see that in 941 A. C. the Gatha days were not after Dae, Bahman or Safandârmad. Further Albiruni states that among the Persians the Gathas remained after the month Aban up to his time. We have however seen that there was some sect of the Persians which had Safandâr as the first month.†

---

*It is argued by some Scholars out here that the Iranians had two kinds of years, one vague or civil, and the other fixed or ecclesiastical. I cannot agree to this theory, in the absence of any written authority about it. The Gatha days were added at the end of Amerdat, Meher, Aban Dae and even Bahman as we shall see hereafter; consequently the intervals between the so called civil and ecclesiastical years varied considerably at different times. As we have already seen Zadsperm clearly says that the month Ardibehesht had been shifted to Dae because of the 8 intercalations that had been made; he does not say a word about the difference being due to the two systems of years, one civil and the other ecclesiastical. This subject is again referred to at the end of this subject.

† See also Dr. M. B. Daver's book p. 30.

* See Dr. Davar's Book pp. 9—10.

† This probably happened after the Abu Sayad's reform of 959 A. C.

That the Gatha days at some time stood after the month Bahman is found also in Burhâne Kâte, where we are told: "*Va mabâdi in ayâm bar takdiri ast, ke Khumsah mustarkeh dar âkher Bahman Mah afzâyand; va Bahman Mah râ si o panj girand.*" (See Burhâne Kâte Vol. II, p. 373 under *Gâhânbârhâ*).*

"The commencement of these five days is such that they are added at the end of the month Bahman; and they take Bahman as consisting of 35 days."

Medieval Greek references to the Avestan Calendar.

In Dastur Peshotan Memorial Volume (p. 171-3) Dr. Louis H. Gray has quoted references to the Iranian Calendar which are found in the books of certain Greek authors.

Georgios Chrysokokkes (1346 A. C.) says:—"You must know that in the year 378 of the Persians, their year began when the sun entered Aries......The first of the Persian year is the month Pharvardin."

Isaakos Argyos, a Byzantine monk (about 1371 A. C.) gives the order of the Persian months as under:—Pharouartes, Artipeest, Chorlat, Tyrma, Mertat, Sachriour, Mecherma, Apanma, Aderma, Dema, Pechma, Asphandarmat; and the Masiarcha (Persian *mostarkeh*) which the Greek call epagomenal.

The above extract corroborates the statement of Abul Hassan Kuschiar that after 1007 A. C. or thereabouts all or most of the Iranians had Fravardin as their first month.

* Ervad Maneckji Unwalla found out the reference for me. See Hamaspathmaedem under Gâhânbârhâ. See also Dastur Peshotanji Sanjana's Tafsire Gâhe Gâsâni p. 84.

Ceremonies in connection with the dead referred to in the Pahlvi Vendidad.

In the Chapter No. VIII—22 of the Pahlvi Vendidad, the following ceremonies in connection with the dead are referred to:—

Pahlvi:—*Amatash zak panj yum bain barâ yâtunet, mâhikân chigun amat dinâ yehvunt; afash shantikân va yumak pavan gâse nefshman.* "If those 5 (Gatha) days fall before the Mâhikan (*Mâsiso*), the Mahikân shall be made according to the religious law; and his Sâligân (anniversary) and (other) monthly ceremonies at their proper time."

N. B.—Here and in the subsequent passage *dinâ* has been falsely read *dadvâ* and the passage *Mâhikân chigun amat dadvâ yehvunt* is thus rendered: "his Mahigân shall be done as if the month were Dae," that is to say "as if the Gathas after the 12th Month Adar did not exist." This rendering cannot be seriously considered.

The above passage means in plain words that if a man dies so that the Gathâs fall within the first 30 days, his first monthly ceremony should be performed after 30 days from his death, and the ceremonies for the other months of the year should be performed on the day having the same name as the day on which he died and his anniversary after 365 days.

Pahlvi:—*Amat bain zak panj yum barâ yamitunet ash Mâhikân chigun dinâ yehvunt, afash yum Fravartin yum, afash Shantik pavan gâse nafshman.* "If a man dies on (one of) those 5 (Gatha) days, his Mâhigân shall be made according to the religious law, his (other) monthly ceremonies on the day Fravardin and his anniversary at its proper time."

This means that if a man dies on a Gatha day his first monthly and annual ceremonies are to be performed exactly as stated in the first passage, but his ceremonies for the 2nd, 3rd, &c., up to 11th month are to be performed on the day Fravardin. The reason seems to me to be this. The Gathas do not belong to any particular month; therefore, if a man dies on a Gatha day, it must be supposed that the day on which the man died is unknown; and it has been enjoined as will be seen hereafter that when the day is unknown, Fravardin the day of Farohars shall be the day for the performance of the ceremony.

Pahlvi: *Amatash lak yumak lâ khavitunet ash lakyumak pavan Fravartin Yum.* "If his 30th day is not known his 30th day shall be on the day Fravardin."

Pahlvi: *Amat sâlik lâ khavitunet ash shantik Ataro mâh Fravartin Yum.* "If his anniversary is not known the anniversary is the day Fravardin of the Mah Adar."

As seen above if the day is not known, it shall be the day of the Farohars; and similarly we might expect that if the month is not known, it should be the month of the Farohars (= Fravardin). But our author gives us the month Adar.

The explanation is as under:—Dr. West has shown that the Pahlvi Vendidad was written in about 550 A. C. (See Cama Memorial Vol. p. 103). Dr. Haug arrives at almost the same date. (See his Essays p. 35). We have however already seen that it was written about the time of Yazdagird's double intercalation. Thus during the writer's time the Persian month Adar coincided with the Sughdian month Fravardin,* and thereafter intercalation was neglected for a long time. We thus see that the Persian day Fravardin of the Adar Mah coincided with the same day of the month Fravardin among the Sughdians. We can easily see that the Fravardin month was connected with Farohars, but we cannot see any such connection with the month Adar. It was a mere coincidence that the month Adar of the Persians corresponded with the month Fravardin of the Sughdians. Our author therefore mentions Adar as the month of the Farohars for the simple reason that in his time it coincided with the month of Farohars rightly termed Fravardin among the Sughdians.

Dadestane Dini goes a step further, when it says "*Amat aevar khavitunet âigh lâ Ataro binâ, lâ Fravartin Yum yamitunet, ash binâ Dadu, yum Varahrâm âvâyat dâshtan.* "If it is known without any doubt that he did not die on the day Fravardin in the month Adar, his month shall be Dae and day Beheram."

We have seen that in 509 A. C. the Persian month Adar coincided with the Sughdian month Fravardin; and this was so for a long time. It also appears that there was a Zoroastrian sect which was one month in advance of others.* Consequently in the days of Dadestan,†

*Here we see that the Persian month Adar coincided with the Sughdian month Fravardin. While examining the passage "Bahman equal to Sheherevar," we saw that the Persian Aban coincided with the Sughdian Fravardin, Therefore either the two passages may have been written by different persons, or by one man who lived at the time of Yazdagird's intercalation,—the first passage being written before the intercalation, the second after it. It is very probable that the passages were written by different persons at different times.

* Dr. Mordtmann says on P. 88-89 of his book "In the year 1075 A.C. corresponding with the year 444 of the Era of Yazdagird, it was found that the commencement of the year, in consequence of the neglect of intercalations had advanced 112 days and consequently the commencement of the year took place on 1st December 1074 instead of 21st March 1075. Jallaludin Malikshah the then ruler of Persia ordered a correction of the Calendar and ordered the intercalation from the time of Yazdagird to be re-introduced."

† The date of Dadestan is 865 A. C. It may be noted that Moatedid's reform took place in 896 and Khwarizmian Shah's reform in 942 A. C.

this sect had its month Dae corresponding with the Sughdian month Fravardin.

Thus if it is not known in which month a man died, his month shall be taken to be the month of the Farohars (— Fravardin) which in the days of our author coincided with month Dae. It is stated that Adar was the month of the Farohars (See S. R. M. Report p. 83). Even if we admit that that was so, still one thing is certain that Dae cannot be the month of the Farohars.

But what is the explanation that the author mentions Beheram as the Roz for the performance of the ceremony of the Farohars ? I think the explanation is as follows :—

As we have already seen, there were two methods of measuring the length of the day among the Avestan people, *vis*, from morning to morning (— *ayare*) and from evening to evening (— *khshapara*).* Thus if according to one method the day is Fravardin, according to the other method it would be Beheram. Fravardin Roz is connected with the Farohars, but Beheram Roz has nothing to do with the Farohars and is connected with the Fravardin Roz in this way that it is *partially* coincident with the Fravardin Roz.

Hebrew Months.

It is argued that "the Hebrews had come into contact with the Babylonians during the Babylonian Captivity,† when the former adopted the names of their months from the latter. The names of the Hebrew months closely resemble those of our months ; and the resemblance is the closest with regard the third month Sivan, the seventh month Tishri and the twelfth month Adar of the Hebrews. The names of our months have been appearing among the Babylonians since 2800 B. C. Therefore our month Dae was the first month so far back as 2800 B. C." (See S. R. M. Report pp. 14-16).

It is needless to say that it is very hazardous to draw inferences from mere linguistic coincidences.

In the Suddha Roz Mah Committee's Report, (p. 15), we are further told that " the Hebrew third month Sivan resembles the Zoroastrian month Spendarmad and is derived from the latter word." This is not correct. Prof. Rawlinson says that Siv was the god of the month Sivan of happy name and his name was a mere contraction of Sivan. Sivan or Hurki was the moon deity of the Chaldeans (see First Oriental Monarchy, p. 156),

As to Adar Prof. A. H. Sayce says "Oringinally like Merodach, Adar had been a solar deity. We are distinctly told that he was the Meridian sun, whose scorching heats represented the fiercer side of Baael—worship....His name is explained to mean *the lord of the oracle*" (see Religion of the ancient Babylonians pp. 152-3)............"Adar or Ninip or Uras—for, his name has been read in these various fashions and the true reading still remains unknown—played a conspicuous part in Babylonian and Assyrian theology. He was regarded as emphatically the warrior and champion of the gods and as such was naturally a favourite object of worship. *Foot note*.—The reading Adar is derived from the Biblical Adrammelech, but it is quite certain that it is false," (idem, pp. 151-2).

In the S. R. M. Report it is also stated that "the 8th Hebrew month Marcheshwan resembled our month Ameretat and was derived from it." This is quite wrong. Marcheshwan is a contraction of the Hebrew word *Arakh-Shamnu* which means the 8th month, whereas the Av. word Ameretta conveys the idea of *immortality*.

*The Eastern Iranians looked upon the night as preceding the day. They reckoned therefore by nights and not by days (Civilization of Eastern Iranians Vol I. p. 143).

† The seventy years that the Jews were captives in Babylon. They were made captives by Nebuchadnezzar and released by Cyrus (588 B. C.)

In reply to my letter Dr. Louis H. Gray, in his letter dated 7-8-1911, writes to me as under :—

"It is true that the Babylonian year might begin either with Nisan or Tishri (*i. e*, either in spring or in autumn), and there are traces of a similar system among the Hebrews (Cf. Exodus xxiii-16, xxxiv-22, with Exodus xii-18, Liviticus xxiii-5). My own conclusions will be clear from my Hasting's article; but I may remark from what you say in your letter that it is inconceivable that the Babylonian Calendar was borrowed from the Zoroastrians."

Zoroastrian and Babylonian Calendar.

In the Encyclopædia of Religion and Ethics, Vol. iii, we read :—

"The problem of the origin of the names of the Avesta months is a difficult one. Kuka* (Cama Memorial, Vol. pp. 54-73) and Gray (A. J. S. L. xx, 194-201), have sought explanations from different points of view, the former maintaining that the Avesta year originally began with Dae which was primarily the month of spring (falling gradually behind because of the lack of a system of intercalation until by the time of Bundehishn, Fravardin had become the commencement of spring); the latter holding to the Bundehishn and endeavouring to trace a borrowing from the Babylonian system on the part of the Iranians. The entire evidence at our disposal makes Fravartin (March-April) the first month of the year and the parallels with the Babylonian Calendar, which Kuka practically overlooks are too striking to be ignored. For the full elaboration of the position here taken, reference may be made to the study of Gray noted above, in which the name of the month Fravartin is interpreted as referring to the ghosts of the righteous dead, Ardavahisht as the re-vivification of the earth after its death in winter (Cf. Dinkart 7-30-14, 8-37-14, 9-30-14); Horvatat as the vernal rains preparing for the coming harvest; Tir as the month of the rising of the dog-star; Amerdat as the vegetation of the harvest time; Satvairo as the month either of the new ploughing or probably building; Mitro as the sun month (Cf. Shamash as the guardian of Tishtri, the seventh Babylonian month); Avan as the rains of autumn; Ataro as the fire which protects against the cold winter; Dae possibly in defiance of Ahriman who created winter; Vohuman as the first-born of Dae—Hormazda; and Spendarmat as a fertility deity of early spring."

*My friend Mr. Meherjibhoy Nasserwanji Kuka, M. A.

Babylonian and Avestan months.

Dr. Louis H. Gray has written a monograph entitled "The Origin of the names of the Avesta month," a few extracts from which are given here.

"The first Babylonian month is Nisan. The Lords of Nisan are Anu and Bel of whom the former was the head of the Assyro-Babylonian pantheon (Jastrow, p. 677), primarily the sky-god, and the father of the gods, while the latter was the god of the earth, the lord of the countries and also the father of the gods, but likewise a god of death, punishment and vengeance.... The first Iranian month, March-April is under the regency of the Fravashis the guardian spirits of the righteous......They originally represented the ghost cult, which must have been prominent before the Zoroastrian reform. To them, then, as to the beneficent ghosts of the righteous dead, the first month of the year is appropriately dedicated."

I am of opinion that as the Accadian first month Bar-gig-gar was the month of the *sacrifice* of righteousness, so also was our month Fravardin. In the Suddha Roz Mah Committee's Report (p. 14) it is stated that the word *Nisan* is derived from the Av. words *Nava+asan* (=new day, Nowroz). Nothing would be more absurd; it is much to be regretted that learned men out here should have fallen into such ridiculous errors due to linguistic coincidences. The word Nisan is derived from the Arabic *nasaa* (=to intercalate). This derivation suggests that at an early period the year began with Airu the coronation month of the Assyrian Kings; and in point of fact the inscriptions bear witness to a second Nisan, *i.e.*, intercalary Nisan. Albiruni also uses the word *nasi* for intercalation (see p. 14 Sachau).

(2) "The month Aru was under the dominion of Ea, a benignant god and the sovereign of the waters, a fitting deity, therefore, for the rainy spring of April-May......The second month April-May is sacred to Asha Vahishta, who represents meteorologically the fire, although it must be noted that he is specially the healer of sickness (Dinkart 8-37-14), who gives to drink of the fountain of life (ibid 9-30-14), having sovereignty in heaven (Saddar xi-5). The underlying idea of the dedication of this month to Asha Vahishta may be, therefore, the revivification of the earth after the death of winter."

(3) "Over the third month presided the moon-god Sin. If the name of the month Siwan or Simanu really signifies 'signal, sign, trophy,' it would seem to suggest the appearance of the crops, giving token of the coming harvest......Over the third month May-June presides the Angel Haurvatat, who represents in the material world the water, evidently in allusion to the vernal rains which prepare the way for the coming harvest."

(4) "The deity of the month of Tammuz himself a sun-god, who at midsummer (June-July) gains his greatest vigour was Ninib, the morning sun. . . . . The regent of the fourth month June-July is the Dog-star Tishtrya whose heliacal rising occurs in that hottest part of the year."

(5) "The month Abu which was a month for laying the foundation of cities and houses, was under the auspices of Nin-gish-zida, originally a solar deity, later identified with Ningirsu and finally with Nin-ib, who was at first the sun-god in his destructive aspect, then the storm god and at last, losing his meteorological character, the god of war, while appropriate to the advancing summer, he presided over the growth of trees (Jastrow, pp. 99, 217, 547). The fifth month July-August was ruled by Ameretat who represents in her physical aspect vegetation, thus typifying the harvest time."

(6) "Over the month of Ululu ruled Ishtar, a goddess of fertility, representing the culmination of the harvest. * . . . The sixth month had as a presiding genius the arch-angel, Khshathra Vairya who is meteorologically the god of metals. He is furthermore in this aspect the instrument by which channels are drawn (Vend. 9-10, 16-6, 17-6, Yt. 10-125). This may then have referred either to the plough, in allusion to the new tillage after the gathering of the summer crop or more probably to the tools used in building. If the latter hypothesis be possible, an analogue might be found in the Babylonian Abu (the fifth month) which distinctly implies that this month was especially devoted to building. The Iranian building period would then be separated from the Babylonian only by a month."

(7) "Samash, the sun-god, *par excellence* is lord of Tishritum, probably from the fair weather prevailing in the autumn. † . . . The

---

* One of the common titles of Ishtar is "the mistress of countries." With the Assyrians Ishtar became a goddess of *war and battle* (see Jastrorw, p 83).

†Shamash was hailed as the god that gives *light* and life to all things upon whose favour the prosperity of the fields and the well-being of man depend. He creates the light and secures its blessings to mankind......He

seventh month September-October, the last of summer, is under the lordship of Mithra, the deity of the sun so that we have here an exact parallel with the seventh month of the Babylonians, which was under the governance of Shamash in allusion to the fair autumn weather."

(8) "Marduk, * the herald of the gods and a solar deity is lord of Marcheshwan......The regents of the eighth Iranian month, October-November, were Apo or the waters, pointing evidently to the rainy season beginning in the autumn."

(9) "Nergel,† the god of war rules over Kislimu......Over the ninth month November-December rules Ataro, the fire, obvioulу the deity who gives protection against the cold of winter."

(10) "Tebetum ‡ is under the regency of Pap-sukkal, the messenger of Anu and Ishtar as well as of Shamash and other gods; and if as is possible, he is identical with Nabu, who is called 'the lofty messenger, lengthening the days of his life,' he may have this place as announcing the return of the spring and summer by the lengthening of the days after the winter......The ruler of the tenth month Dae, December-January was the supreme Lord, Ormazd himself. This has given rise to a conjecture, which has hardly proved tenable that the Iranian year originally began with the month of Dae, instead of Fravartin, especially as the first day of every month is under the auspices of Ahura Mazda......All the sources thus far known are unanimous in making Fravartin the first month..... Why Ormazd should preside over this month is an extremely doubtful problem. It can hardly be on account of the reminiscence of his original functions as a sky-god; for, Anu his Babylonian analogue, is one of the deities who presides over the first month Nisan (March-April). The only explanation which I can suggest is an extremely fanciful one, on which I myself lay little stress, presenting it in lieu of none at all. It will be noted that in conformity to Zoroastrian custom in general, no month is dedicated to an evil spirit. This would be giving recognition to Ahriman, a thing blasphemous to the Iranian mind, although the Babylonians could consecrate a month (Adar), to the seven evil spirits. Now the only season of the year which was, according to the Avesta, created by Ahriman, was winter......This season created by the demon (*daevo-dâta* Vd. 1-3, Bd. xxviii—1) is mentioned as a curse equal to the serpent, the special object of hatred to the Iranians as early as the times of Herodotus (I-140). The heart of this period is the month which received the name of Dae. May it be then, that in conscious defiance of the power of Ahriman, the centre of the time of his power was made sacred to his great opponent and conqueror Ahuramazda?"

N. B.—I quite agree with Dr. Gray that *all the sources are unanimous in making Fravartin the first month*. As I have already stated, the month sacred to the Progressive * Faculty of Ahuramazda was Fravardin, and that sacred to the Creative Faculty of Ahuramazda was Dae (Dathusho); and because the former includes the latter, it is quite right

---

was represented as seated on the throne in the chamber of *judgment*......He puts an end to wickedness and destroys enemies (Jastrow p. 71.)

* Marduk was the child *par excellence* of Ea, the *great god of the deep*......Marduk seems to have become a solar deity in later times, *viz.*, in those of Hummurabi (Jastrow, p. 119.)

†Nergel is essentially a destroyer and has various epithets......He is at times the "*god of fire*," again the "raging king," "the violent one," "the one who burns" and finally identified with the great glowing heat of flame (Jastrow, p. 67).

‡The tenth month is sacred to Papsukkal, Anu and Ishtar......Anu was the *supreme god of heaven* (Jastrow pp. 468 and 154).

* *Fravashi* —from *fra* and *vaksh* to increase, progress. *Dathusho*—from *dâ* to create.

that Fravardin should be the first month.

(11) "Ramman 'the thunderer', the god of the storms, is the fitting ruler of the month Shabatu, so called from the heavy and destructive rains and floods which prevail throughout it. * . . . The reason for the succession of Vohuman after Ormazd is not meteorological but theological. This is made clear by the Pahlvi texts which call Vohuman the first creation of Ormazd (Bd. I-23, Dadestan XL-1, Dinkart 9-38-6 &c.), while the Gathas term Ahuramazda 'the father of the good mind' (Ys. 31-8, 45-4, &c.)."

(12) "During the month Addaru† the rains continue so that evil spirits are appropriately its lords...... Spendarmat is the daughter of Ormazd (Ys 45-4). Meteorologically she represents the earth and this is essentially a deity of fertility... She therefore appropriately presides over the opening spring."

It may be noted here that on the day Spendarmat of the month Spendarmat (=the day of the Jashne Rukke Kazdum) it was a custom among the Iranians to paste an amulet on the door to stop the mischief of scorpions.

*In the religious productions the relationship between Anu and Ramman is expressed by making Ramman, the *son of Anu*, the supreme god of heaven. (See Jastrow, p. 154).

† The last month Adar falling within the rainy season is presided over by the seven evil spirits......In an incantation text we read "Hostile to Ea are they (*i. e.* evil spirits)... To work mischief in the street, they settle themselves in the high-way. Evil are they." ......The number seven is not to be taken literally......It signifies a large number...... In the old testament seven is similarly used to designate a large number. A group of seven spirits accordingly meant a miscellaneous mass of spirits......Elsewhere we are told that they dwell in the hollow of the earth......They slip through bolts, door-posts and sockets like snakes. (Jastrow, pp. 468, 264, 265).

Accadian Calendar. *

Epping and Strassmaier in their book Astronomisches aus Babylon have translated three small documents originally inscribed on clay tablets in the second century B. C. The year according to these tablets began with *Nisan, hence in spring*. This is therefore a sketch of the Babylonian Calendar in the 2nd century B. C. In the British museum a great number of trade documents corver a period of over 2,000 years. There are tablets of Rim-sin (2300 B. C.), Hammurabi (2200 B. C.,) Samsuiluna (2100 B. C.) and others. These documents are all dated in such and such a year of some King.

In 1814 Pro. Sayce, in his paper Astronomy and Astrology says "The Accadian months derived their names from the signs of the Zodiac." The following months are those in which the resemblance is very striking:—

First month—Bar-zig-gar ("the sacrifice of righteousness") Aries.

Second month—Khar-sidi ("the propitious bull") Taurus.

Third month–Kas ("the twins") Gemini.

Sixth month—Ki Gingir-na ('the errand of Istar") Virgo.

From Epping's tablets we know that the months and the constellations did in the 2nd century B. C. correspond with each other in the above order. Thus the Accadian Nisan always corresponded to the time during which the sun traversed Aries and so on.

That the Accadian year began at the winter solstice is proved as under. The 12th month is named Si-ki-sil "sowing of seed." Seed is sown in many latitudes in spring and also in winter. "Sowing of seed" might therefore describe a month at the ending of an equinoctial or of a solstitial year, but the

* See Ancient Calendars and Constellations by E. M. Plunket, pp. 1-23.

13th month (that is the occasionally intercalated month) is named that of the "dark sowing." The epithet *dark* added to the sowing of the 12th month very plainly points to the solstitial or midwinter ending of the year.

As centuries rolled by, Aries receded from the winter solstice. Bar-zig-gar was no longer the first month in the sense of being the first winter month, still the originators of the Calendar held sway. It was still looked upon as the first month of the year. Between 6000 B. C. and 200 B. C. the winter solstice moved on steadily through almost a quarter of the circle of the ecliptic.

In the Encyclopædia of Religion and Ethics Vol. iii, pp. 73-75, Prof. Hommel has given a number of tables of the Accadian and Babylonian months. The first table contains the names of months before the time of Sargon, the second after the time of Sargon, the third during the time of the Kings of Ur and the fourth after the time of Hammurabi. On an examination of these tables we see that the month Se-kin-kud ("corn reaping") was at first the 10th month, subsequently it became 11th, and then 12th. Similarly Se-illa was at first the 11th month, then it become 12th, and then (in the list of Ur) it became the 1st month. In the days of Hammurabi, this month was given the name Bar-zig-gar or Bar, and also the Semitic name Nisan. From the period of Hammurabi onwards we note the important fact that besides the Sumerian names, their Semitic renderings are often met with. Thus we have Arakh Rabuti (month of the gods Anu and Enlil) for Bar-zig-gar, subsequently Nisan and so on.

We have seen that Nisan was the first month between the years 2300 to 200 B. C. It was therefore the 12th month* before 2200 B. C.

*This is also indirectly proved from the the fact that in the inscriptions we come across a second Nisan, i.e., intercalary Nisan (which is derived from *Nisaa* to intercalate a month).

Prof. Sayce in his Religion of Ancient Babylonia (p. 232) says "In Babylonia Tammuz was the *sun god of spring*. His foe was the summer heat; his death was mourned in the month of June......The anniversary of his death was shifted to the fall of the year. *He ceased to be the sun god of spring* and became the sun god of summer." From this it appears that if Tammuz was the month of spring, Nisan was the month of the winter solstice. As seen above Nisan was the first month from the commencement of spring between 200 to 2300 B. C. It was the 12th month between 2300 to 4400 B. C., and 11th month between 4400 and 6500 B. C.; and before 6500 B. C it was the 10th month from the beginning of spring and 1st month from the winter solstice.

If we suppose that the Accadian month Se-illa (the Nisan of former times) was before 6500 B. C. coincident with our month Dae, then Dae would be the first month of the winter solstice, and Fravardin the first month of spring. The Accadian Calendar was however sidereal whereas the Iranian Calendar was tropical. We can thus see that Fravardin would remain fixed with the spring, whereas the month Nisan would, between 6500 B. C. and 2300 B. C., change its position from the winter solstice to the spring equinox. Could it be that about 2300 or 2200 B. C. (during the time of Hammurabi) the Babylonians, being inflenced by the Iranian ideas, appointed guardian deities over their months? Jastrow (p. 462) says: "The early epithets of the months among the Babylonians are connected with agriculture and the life of the agriculturist......The part of the Calendar which touches upon the religion of the Babylonians is the sacred character given to the months by making each one devoted to some god or gods......The assigning of the months to the gods appears to partake more or less of an arbitrary character. Absolute unanimity did not prevail throughout Babylonia until *a comparatively late period*."

Nowroz on the first Jamshedi Nowroz.

In his Shahnamé, Firdusi says about the King Jamshed:—*Ba Jamshid bar gohar afshândand, mar ân rugrâ rus no khwândand. Sar sâl nu Hurmaz Fravardin, bar âsudah az ranj tan dil za kin......Chanin rus farrukh azân rusgár, ba mândah az ân khusravan yâdgâr.*

"They gave Jamshed joy, with presents, and called that day Nowroz. It was the day Hormazda of the month Fravardin—the first day of the year. All gave rest to their bodies from work and to their minds from animosity......From that day this auspicious Jashn has been known after the name of this King."

Elsewhere Firdusi gives a beautiful description of the Jamshedi Nowroz which was the first day of spring.

We thus see from Shahname that Fravardin was the month of spring.

Cappadocian Months.

The names of the months among the Cappadocians are as under: Artaioten, Araicta, Araiotata, Teirei, Amartot, Santheri, Mithri, Apomena, Athra, Dathousa, Osman, Sondara. Dr. Gray observes: "The influence of the Zoroastrian calendar was far-reaching, extending not only to the Transoxian regions of Chorasmia and Sogdiana but to Armenia and Cappadocia.......This is indeed no new discovery—it has been known at least since 1836 when Benfey and Stern......themselves following Reland's suggestions of exactly two centuries ago—demonstrated that the Cappodocian month-names were borrowed one and all, from the Zoroastrian Calendar."*

*See Encyclopædia of Religion and Ethics Vol. iii-180.

It appears from Prof. Rawlinson's Herodotus, Vol. i, p. 537, that the Medes occupied Cappadocia long before 650* B. C. Thus the Cappadocians borrowed their calendar from the Zoroastrians at about this date.

Armenian months and days.

In the Encyclopædia of Religion and Ethics, iii-p. 70, † the Armenian months are given as follows:—

(1) Nawasard, (2) Hori ‡ (="second month"), (3) Sahmi ¶ (="third month"), (4) Tir (=Tir), (5) Khaloch (="month of harvest"), (6) Arach, (7) Mehekan (=month sacred to Meher), (8) Areg (="sun-month"), (9) Ahekan (Pahlv. Adargân), (10) Mereri, (probably from Maidya-yâirya), (11) Margach (Armenian form of Markzan, or month of medows), (12) Hrotich (Armenian form of Fravartakân). The following Armenian day-names are similar to those in the Avesta:—Mihr the 8th day (Cf. Meher); Aramazd the 15th day (Cf. Ahuramazda); Anâhit the 19th day (Cf. Av. Anâhita); Npat the 26th day (Cf. Av. Apâm Napât); Vahagn the 27th day (Cf. Beheram).

Sughdian months.

The names of the Sughdian months were as under:—

Nusard, Jirjin, Nisan, Bisâk, Ashnâkhandâ, Mazikhandâ, Faghâj, Abânaj, Fugh, Masâfugh, Zimdâ and Khshum.

The third month Nisan (=May-June) is clearly the Assyrian Nisânnu (=April-May). It is easy to see that on account of the retrogression of the calendar, the third month would after a period of about 120 years retrograde from May-June to

*Benfey gives 750 B. C. as the date.

† See also pp. 831-834, Journal of the American Oriental Society, article by L. H. Gray.

‡ Hori is derived from the Gregorian *ori*=two.,

¶ From *Sami*=three.

April-May. Could it be that at a very early period the Sughdians adopted the name from the Assyrians?

The fourth month Bisâk seems to me to be identical with the Hindu month Baishâkh.

The eighth month Abânaj is the same as Abân.

The ninth month Fugh is supposed to be a dialectic from corresponding to Av. *Bagha*=god, old Persian *Baga*, new Persian *Fugh*.

The tenth month Masâfugh comes from mas=great and Bagha=god (see also L. Gray's paper, pp. 336-340).

It may be noted here that the first day of Faghakân (7th month of the Sughdians) was called *Nim-sard*, i.e., "the half year," which proves that Nausard (corresponding with Fravardin) must have been the first month.

Khwarizmian months.

The names of the Khwarizmian months closely resembled those of the Persians. They were as under:—

Nâusârji, Ardiwisht, Harudâdh, Ciri, Hamdâdh, Ikhsharewari, Umri, Yânâkhun, Adu, Rimazhd, Akhamman, Ispandârmaji.

The seventh month Umri is clearly Meher. *

The names of the Khwarizmian Gâhâmbars closely resemble those of the Persian Gahambars but their order and the respective distances of time from each other vary from those of the Persians. The 4th Gahambar, *Mithzarmi-red* (=Av *Maidyozaremahe-rathvo*) attracts our special notice. It fell on the 15th day of Umri (=Meher). It would thus appear at the time when this festival came into vogue among the Khwarizmians the month Meher (probably due to want of intercalation), fell near the commencement of spring. Here we have a further proof of the fact that at one time the angel Mithra was the presiding divinity of the spring equinox.

* The seventh month of the inhabitants of Kuba was also Meher (see Albiruni, p. 82).

Months of the Calendar of Almutadid.

We have already seen that in 896 A. C. Almutadid reformed the Calendar. As to the months in this calendar Albiruni says (p.81): "The months of Almutadid are the Persian months *with the same names and the same order*. But the Persian days are not used in these months because to the Epagomenæ in every fourth year one day is added by way of intercalation." On p. 52 Albiruni names the Persian months commencing with Fravardin. No doubt Almutadid placed the first day of the month Fravardin on 16th June; but it must be remembered that "he had made the basis of his computation that year in which the Persian empire perished by the death of Yazdajird" (see Albiruni, p. 37); in other words, the said Khalif continued up the system of the Persians whose Fravardin month fell in June at the close of the Sassanian empire.

Months in the Cuniform inscriptions.

In the Cuniform inscriptions of Darius we come across the names of some of the months. Scholars are not agreed about the order of these months. In the Shudha Roz Mah Report (p. 17) the months have been given in the following order: Baghayâdaish, Thurvâhar, Thâigrachish, Adukanaish, Garmapada, Margazan, Athriyâdiya, Anâmaka, and Vyakhna. In the said Report we are told that Baghayâdaish was the month of the commencement of spring and it coincided with the Babylonian Nisan and our Dae."

We however find the following in the Encyclopædia of Religion and Ethics, Vol. iii. pp. 128-133:—

"The old Persian calendar was divided into 12 months but the names of only nine of these are known and their exact sequence is a *matter of doubt*. The old Persian inscriptions of Darius at Behistan records the names as follows:—

Garmapada (footpath of heat), Thuravâhara (mighty spring), Thaigarci (garlic gathering?) Bâgayâdi (homage to deities), Adukani, (digging of canals), Athriyâdiya (worship of fire), Anâmaka (nameless), Viyakhna (ice-free? assembly month?), to which a new Elamic version (iii-43) adds Markazanash (Old Pers. Margazana "brood of birds"). It is clear from a comparison of the Old Persian and Babylonian versions of Behistan inscriptions that Thuravâhara 30 corresponded to Iyyar (April-May) 30; Thaigarci 9 to Sivan (May-June) 9; Athriyâdiya 26 to Kislev (Nov.-Dec.) 26; Anâmaka 27 to Tebeth (Dec.-Jan.) 27; and Viyakhna 14, 22 to Adar (Feb.-March) 14, 22.

The orders of these months corresponding with Nisan &c. according to different writers are given below :—

According to Rawlinson—1 Bâgayadi, 2 Thuravâhara, 3 Thaigarci, 4 Adukani, 5 Garmapada, 6 None, 7 None, 8 Margazan, 9 Athriyâdiya. 10 Anâmaka, 11 None, 12 Viyakhna,

According to Opport—1 Garmapada, 2 Thuravâhara, 3 Thaigarci, 4 None, 5 None, 6 None, 7 Bâgayâdi, 8 Adukani, 9 Athriyâdiya, 10 Anâmaka 11 Margazan, 12 Viyaknah.

According to Unger—1 Thuravâhara, 2 Thaigarci, 3 Adukani, 4 Margazan, 5 Garmapada, 6 None, 7 Bâgayâdi, 8 None, 9 Athriyâdiya, 10 Anâmaka, 11 None, 12 Viyakhna.

According to Justi—1 Thuravâhara, 2 Thaigarci, 3 Adukani, 4 None, 5 Garmapada, 6 None, 7 Bâgayâdi, 8 None, 9 Athriyâdiya, 10 Anâmaka, 11 Margazan, 12 Viyakhna.

According to Prasek—1 None, 2 Thuravâhara, 3 Thaigarci, 4 Garmapada, 5 None, 6 None, 7 Bâgayâdi, 8 Adukani, 9 Athriyâdiya, 10 Anâmaka, 11 Margazan, 12 Viyakhna.

The writer of the above article (Dr. L. Gray) says—"Of all these series, Opport's seems the most probable to the present writer. The date at which the year began is as uncertain as the order of the months. Opport suggests that it commenced with Bâgayâdi (Sept-Oct.) which is admitted by all to have corresponded with the Babylonian Tishri. This would of course correspond with the beginning of the Hebrew civil year and might receive a certain degree of support from the name of the month 'the homage to the deities.' It seems far more probable that the year actually began with Garmapada (or according to Justi, Thurvâhar) corresponding to Nisan (March-April). This would make the commencement of the old Persian year harmonize both with the Avesta and the Babylonian systems as well as with the Hebrew year."

If we compare the five series of months as given by different writers we find that all of them agree in regarding Athriyâdiya as the ninth month and Anâmaka as the tenth month. There is not slightest doubt that *Athriyâdiya* means "the worship of Atar (=fire)" or is at any rate connected with *Atar* (=fire) As Atar is unanimously regarded as the ninth month and as according to the Babylonian version of the Behistan inscription, it coincided with the month Kislev (Nov.-Dec.), it must follow that Fravardin was the first month from the commencement of spring.

As to *Anâmaka* Paul Horn says that it is the name of a Persian month (not the "nameless" which would be the intercalary month but the "month of the nameless," *i.e.*, of the Highest God—therefore perhaps ânâmaka). We thus see that according to the unanimous authority of the five Scholars, the month of the Highest God is the tenth month.

It will also be seen that according to four Scholars, *Bâgayâdi* is the seventh month. Now we find that the seventh month of the Sughdians was *Faghâz* and also the 16th day of the Chorasmians was *Figh* (see Albiruni, pp. 56-57). *Faghâz* and

Figh are both connected with the Turfan form *Baghakânj** "god-month." We thus see that Bâgayâdi was the month named after the *god*, *i.e.* angel, Meher.

Month named after Ahuramazda.

It is argned that just as the day named after Ahuramazda is the first day, so also we should have the month named after Ahuramzda as the first month. There is little weight in this argument. If this argument were to be carried to its legitimate conclusion, the months named after the Ameshaspents must also appear in their proper order, which is however not the case.

In Bundehishn Ch. V-1 the author has mentioned the seven Planets but Auhormazd (Chorasmian Rimazd=Jupiter) is mentioned as the third Planet. Albiruni (p. 172) mentions it as the second Planet. It cannot be seriously said that Ahuramazda's dignity is lowered by calling the Planet named after him the third or the second.

We have already seen that in Avesta, Ahuramzda is represented as having a Farohar† (progressive faculty) and as the progressive faculty of Ahuramazda necessarily occupies a higher place than His creative faculty, I say that the month named after the Farohar of Ahuramazda is quite appropriately the first month.

Afrine Gahanbar.

In the Afrine Gâhânbâr we find the following Avestan passage: "*Panchâcha chathwaresatemcha maidyozare mayehe ashavahishahe dathusho.*" "The 45th (day) of maidyozarem (=mid-spring) is (the day) Dae (-pa-Meher) of (the month) Ardibehesht." It is clear from this passage that Fravardin must be the month commencing with spring that is, the first month.

First month according to Bundehishn.

In Bundehishn Ch. 25 § 1 we have: Pahlvi: *Pavan Hamaspatmedem gâs—ait panje pavan binâ i Spendomat rovashman—yum lelia râsta lakhwâr yehvunet. Chegun min binâ i Fravartin yum Auhormazda Vehijkik vad binâ i Mitro yum Anerân Vehijkik yehvunet hafta binâ hâmin; va min binâ i Avan yum Auhormazda Vehijkik vad mâh Spendomat—i Vehijkik pange barâ valman sar yehvunet—pani binâ jamestân.*

"On Hamaspathmaedem Gâhânbâr—which consists of the last five days of the month Spendarmat—the day and night become equal again. Because from the auspicious.* day Ahuramazda of the month Fravardin to the auspicious day Aneran of the month Meher, there are seven months of summer; and from the auspicious Ahuramazda Roz of the month Abân up to the month Spendarmat—at the end of which there are the five Epagomenal days—there are the five months of winter."

Also in § 7 we read: *Mâhi Fravartin Vehijkik binâ i Artavahisht va binâ i Khurdat Vahâr.*

"The auspicious month Fravardin, the month Ardibehesht and the month Khurdad (are the months of) spring."

It is clear from these passages that our year commenced with spring, and that the first month was Fravardin.

That our year commenced with spring is also seen from the Zend Pahlvi Glossary (p. 43) where we find the following Avesta fragment: *Dvadasanghâthrem asti aghrem ayare.* "The first day consists of 12 hours." This must refer to the equinox.

* Av. *Bagha* =god. The Sogdian 9th month was also called *Fugh* (=Bagha)=the month of the *god* (Fire). The Sogdian 10th month was appropriately called *Masafugh* (Av. *mas* =great, and *fugh* or *bagha*=god).

† As we have seen, among the Egyptians it was the Ka of the god and not the god himself who was the primary object of worship. Similarly among the Babylonians it was the Zi of the god rather than the god who was primarily worshipped.

* Vehijkik properly means "intercalary." I have adopted Ervad Modi's translation.

Avardadsalgah.

With regard to Avardâdsâl-gâh we find the following remarks in the Shudha Roz Mah Report (p. 42):—"It appears to be the name of the intercalary day or the sixth Gatha which was added every fourth year. *Avardâd* means (બીજો આપેલેા, ઉમેરેલેા, ઉપલગવેા) 'given over and above (something), additional, superadded.' Its jashn is different from (that of) Khurdâdsâl. In the Khshnuman of the Afringân of Avardâdsâl-gâh* the five Gatha days have been specifically mentioned by name; whereas such is not the case in the Khshnuman of Khurdâdsâl. This shows that Avardâdsâlgâh has some connection with the Gatha days. Therefore in very ancient times this day must have followed the Gatha days as the sixth Gatha once in four years...... But subsequently this name was given to the Khurdâd Roz of the Asfandar month. Just as the word *gâh* appears after the Gatha days, so the word *gâh* in Avardâdsâlgâh is the same word."

It has been admitted in the above named Report (p.58) that neither the Persians nor the Sughdians nor the Khwarizmians added an intercalary day every fourth year between the years 505 and 682 A. C. Albiruni, several other Mehomedan writers and Zadsperm have clearly said that the Zoroastrians did an intercalation of one month after the expiration of every 120 years.

The word **Gah** does not necessarily mean "Gatha;" it also means "time." In the expression "*Hamâsor gâhe gâhânbâr,*" *gâh* does not mean *Gâtha* but simply means "*time.*"

In his essays (1869) Mr. K. R. Cama thought that the word *Avardâdsâlgâh* was the Pahlvi form of the Avesta word *Aparadâta saredhagâthâ* (which is not found in the extant Avesta and) which meant "time placed after the year" (વરસની પાછળ મેલેલેા વખત).

I think that a more correct meaning to be assigned to this word would be "additional time of the year." *

In Khureh Vahijak (p. 157) Dastur Edulji Darabji Sanjana states that Avardâdsâlgâh was the jashn for adoring the epagomenal quarter of a day at the end of every year.

Dastur Mulla Feroze has written many pages about the Khshnuman of Avardâdsâlgâh in his Gujrati book Avizeh Din, from which I propose to give a few extracts in the original Gujrati.

"એ દીવસના જશ્નની ક્ષ્નુમન હીંદુસ્તાનના બેહેદીનોએ પોતાની એક મહીનાની ચુકને સમજીને રોજ ૬ ઠો માહા ૧૨ મેા રશમીને દીને શ્રી ઇરાનના કુલ બેહેદીનો એ કદીમ પારસીઓના દહાડા સાથે સામેલ થવાને વાસ્તે જશ્ન કરવું મુકરર કીધું છે...... દારાબ હોરમજદીઆરની રેવાયતમાં લખ્યું છે કે એ બેહેદીનોની રસમ છે અને એ ક્ષ્નુમન નોરોજે જાવલી તથા દરીઆઇ નોરોજની છે." (p. 29).

"એ ખોરદાદ રોજ તે કદીમ વરસનો યાને કદીમ પારસીઓના વરસનો પેહેલો દહાડો છે, તે વખતમાં સામેલ થવા સારૂં હિંદુસ્તાન મધેના દાના દસ્તુર મોબેદોએ નેક અંદેશો કરીને એ દહાડે ક્ષ્નુમન ઉભી કરીને એ દહાડે દરૂન આફ્રીન ગાન કરે છે. પણ એ દહાડાની ક્ષ્નુમનને મથાલે તે વેલાના સાચા લોકોએ પોતેજ લખ્યું છે કે એ ક્ષ્નુમન બેહેદીનોની રસમ છે." (p. 31)

"પણ એ અવરદાદ સાલગાહની ક્ષ્નુમન તો શ્રી ઇરાની લોકોની બાજધરનાંની કેતાબો મધે તથા બીજી શ્રી ઇરાનની આવેલી કેતાબો મધે, તે કોઇ કેતાબોમાં ઇરાનવાળાઓએ લખેલી નથી.†

---

* With this compare the second kind of tropical year mentioned in Dinkard, namely *Zamun vahizakik i min shantân* "that in which the hours (*lit.* small portions of time) out of years are added."

† The Dastur does not seem to be correct here. This Khshnuman is found in Nirangestân also.

અને શ્રી ઇરાન મધે એ અવરદાદ સાલગાહની ક્ષ્નુમન કોઇ દસ્તુર મોબેદ પઢતા બી નથી અને એ ક્ષ્નુમનને ઇરાનવાળા મોબેદો જાણુતા બી નથી" (p. 547)

"રાસ્તીના શોધનારા સાહેબોને સારી તરેહથી વિચારવું જોઇએ જે વરશ એક ફરવરદીન મહિનો ને હોરમજદ રોજે પુરૂં થાય છે, કે વરશના બારમાં મહિના અસફંદારમદમાં પુરૂં થાય છે? અગર એ આપણી તારીખ કબીસાની હોય તોબી પા દહાડાની કસર તો ફરવરદીન મહિનો ને હોરમજદ રોજને દીને આવે કે અસફંદાર મહિનાના ખુરદાદ રોજે પા દહાડો આવે? બારમાં અસફંદાર મહિનામાં તો વરશ હજુર પુરૂં થયું નથી એટલામાં કસર કયાંથી પેદા થઇ જે પા દહાડાનું જશન કરે?" (p. 590)

The reason why the jashn of Avardâd-âlgâh* was performed on the day Khurdad of the month Asfandar is given as under: "Khurdâd Ameshaspent presides over time; therefore the jashn for the new year is made on the sixth day of the first month; and for the same reason the jashn of Avardâdsâlgâh belonging to the finishing intercalary year might have been made on the Roz Khurdâd of the last month." (see S. R. M. Report p. 43) This reason is, to say the least, very fanciful. As Dastur Mulla Feroze says, it is absurd to believe that before the epagomenal quarter of the day came into vague its Jashn could be performed.

Dinkard on intercalation.

An attempt has been made to show from Dinkard that in ancient times, we added one intercalary day every fourth year. In support of this the following passage of the Dinkard is relied upon; *Yum vahij vad bind i bundik yehvunet lâ kardan; min panje bind i fareh lâ spukhtan.* **This passage is thus translated in the Shudha Roz Mah Report p. 54: "Intercalation of a day (— intercalation of one day in four years) should not be done until the month (— the last month of the years) comes to an end; and one should not wait longer than five months (— after the expiry of the five months of winter at the end of the year and the five Gatha days following them)."**

The commentary given within the brackets above clearly shows how the sense has been twisted. It is impossible to believe that in the above passage the writer speaks of the intercalation of one day in four years, in view of what Albiruni, Zadsperm and others have stated: namely that the quarter of a day (beyond the 365 days) they neglected in their computation till these quarters of a day had summed up to the days of our complete month, which happened in 120 years (See Sachau p. 54).

In Khureh Vahijak the above passage is translated as follows (pp. 25—25):—

"અને વેહીજક (ઇઆને કસરના) દહાડાઓ જાહાં લગી મહીનો (૧) એક પુરો એકઠો થાએ તાંહાં લગી (કબીશો) નહિ કરવો; પાંચ દહાડા વીગેરે (ઇઆને પાંચ દહાડા ગાથાના છે તે બી ખોરશેદની ચાલના કશરોના છે, તેહુને એ કબીસાના મહિના સાથે નહી મેળવવા જોઇએ તેહુનો હોકમ જેમકે ઉપર લખેલો છે તે પ્રમાણે)."

Mulla Firoze in his Avijeh Din (p. 105) translates the passage thus:—

"દહાડા કશરના જાંહાંલગી એક મહીનો પુરો થાય, નહી કરવો વગેરે પાંચ દહાડા કશરના, નહિ મેલવા (કશરના દહાડા જ્યાં લગી એક મહિનો પુરો થાએ ત્યાં સુધી નહિ કરવો; કશરના પાંચ દહાડાં વગેરે શાવાય— નહિ મેળવા)."

I translate the passage thus:— "The intercalary days should not be added up till the end of the last month. The intercalary month

* Avardâdsâlgâh was also called "Sudi Nouroz," which I think is a corrupt form of Sugdi Nouroz.

should not be separated from the Panji (—five Gatha days)."*

Two important points have been referred to in this passage, firstly that the Gatha days should come after the *last* month † and secondly that the intercalary month should remain in touch with the Gatha days; that is to say, after the intercalary month is added, the Gatha days should occur.

If the above passage refers to a day's intercalation, as has been suggested, we might well ask how it was that intercalation, was forgotton throughout Persia. It is true that Khalif Almutadid tried to reform the calender and ordered that "in every fourth year one day should be intercalated" (See Albiruni p. 36); but we do not know how long his calendar remained in force. One thing however is certain that if we in our times try to reform the calendar we must intercalate one day every fourth year.

Further we are told in Dinkard: "*Shant hangâm bun vahâr*" "The first season of the year is spring." Consequenly we must commence our year from the vernal equinox, (21st March).

Feast of Purim.

With reference to this feast my friend Mr. M. N. Kuka says: "The Jews have commenced celebrating the feast of Purim since the time of Xerxes. This feast falls in their Adar month, and is a corruption of our feast of Farvardagân." Now as the 12th Jewish month Adar falls near March it is contended that our month Adar was also the 12th month.

In the Encylo. Bri. VIII p. 560 we read "The Book of Esther relates how a Jewish maiden Esther.....was raised to the position of Queen by the Persian King Ahasurus (Xerxes) after he had divorced Vashti; how she and her uncle Mordecai frustrated Haman's resolution to extirpate the Jews out of the Persian empire, how Haman fell...and lastly how a festival was instituted to commemorate their deliverance."

The origin of the feast of Purim which falls on the 14th and 15th day of the Jewish month Adar is described at great length by Albiruni (pp. 273-274).*

In the Encyclo. Bri. XX p. 115 we read: "Purim was a feast of the later Jews celebrated in honour of the deliverance of the nation from the schemes of Haman recorded in the book of Esther. The historical value of this record is made of the now very prevalent opinion, that the feast is an adaptation of a Persian festival. The derivation of the name Purim from the Persian Furdigân (Pordigân, Por-

* In Bundehishn Ch. 25 § 1 *Panli* is used in the same sense. Albiruni says that the five additional days were called *Pangi* (*Panji*). See p. 68.

† This also shows that the month after the Gatha days is the first month. Dr. West in the introduction to his "Marvels of Zoroastrianism" says "The position of the 5 extra days always indicated the end of the rectified year."

* Haman, a man of no importance had become a very rich man by unlawfully demanding from people a few dirhams for every dead body that was carried. He went on demanding money until the daughter of the King Ahasurus died. When people came with her corpse he demanded something from the bearers, and on being refused, he did not allow them to pass, until they yielded. He was afterwards carried before the King who when he heard about his immense wealth said in astonishment "a man who gathered so much money from the rule of the dead, is worthy to be made a Wazir." Accordingly he was made a Wazir. Haman was an enemy of the Jews. He fixed the 14th and 15th of Adar for killing all the Jews in the empire. He hated the Jewish wife of the King named Esther and her brother (Mordekhai). He wanted to kill them both. When the King heard about the plans of Haman, he ordered him to be killed. So Haman and his partizans were killed on the 14th of Adar, the same day on which Haman intended to kill the Jews. This was therefore a day of great joy to the Jews, (Albiruni pp. 273-274).

diyân) has been raised above the level of a mere guess by Lagarde, who has shown that the readings....in one of the Greek recensions of Esther point with great probability to a form...exactly corresponding with the Persian word. The feast falls on the 14th and 15th Adar and is in accordance with Esther IX-22 of a joyous character, but quite secular in tone with a great deal of hard drinking, the only quasi-religious features being the reading in the synagogue of the book of Esther and the section about Amabk Exod. XVII 8-9. This celebration appears to have made its way among the Jews gradually. According to Josephus (A.D. 87-93) however, it was generally observed in his day in all the parts of the Jewish world."

The King Xerxes ruled between the years 486 and 465 B. C. We have seen that on the 21st March 509 A. D. there was the day Ahuramazda of the month Fravardin of the Persians, and that 9 intercalary months had been added since the reform of the calendar. We thus conclude that the reformed calendar was introduced in (120×9 —509=) 571 B. C. Therefore between the years 571 and 451 B.C. the Persian month Fravardin (and similarly the month Fravardin of the Sughdians, Khwarizinians &c.,) commenced *near* the spring equinox, and the Farvardagân days almost coincided with the commencement of spring. If therefore the Jews borrowed their feast of Purim * from the Persian Farvardagân festivals on about 465 B. C. it would not be wrong to say that the feast of Purim corresponds with the Farvardagân.

From what is stated above, it follows that in the time of Xerxes also Farvardin was the first month falling near the spring equinox.

What was the first month according to Albiruni ?

In the Shuddha Roz Mah Report pp.72-74, several passages have been quoted from Albiruni to show that Dae was the first month of spring. The following passages have been referred to:

(1) "So Nouroz comes again to be there, where it used to be in the time of the Kisrâs, when it used to coincide with the summer solstice" (p. 185).

(2) "This day (Mihrjân) used in former times to coincide with the beginning of winter. Afterwards it advanced when people began to neglect intercalation" (p. 209).

(3) "This (the day Adar of the month Adar) is the end of the winter months when the cold at the end of the season is most biting" (p. 211).

(4) "The beginning of their (Khwarizmians') summer was the first of Nausarji" (p. 223).

(5) "The first day of the Sughdian month Nausard was the first day of Summer" (p. 220).*

It is an undoubted fact that during the time of the Sassanians and specially at the time of their

* Prof. Morris Jastrow in his "Religion of Babylonia and Assyria p. 686 says :— "The 15th of Adar is an old solar festival, that modified and connected with the historical reminiscences, became popular during the Persian supremacy in the Semitic orient and survives to this day under the name of Purim festival. *Foot Note:*— The non-Jewish origin of the Purim festival is generally accepted by critical scholars. Lagarde endeavours to trace it back to a Persian festival. Zimmern connects it with the Babylonian Zagmerku....The origin of the Jewish feast and fast is still obscure. The fact that there is both a fast (14th Adar) and a festival (15th Adar) is a safe indication of antiquity. Zimmers view is... untenable but that there is a connection between Purim and some Babylonian feast, follows from the fact that the two chief personages in the book of Esther namely Mordecai and Esther bear names identical with the Babylonian names Marduk and Ishtar."

* The passages about Ajghâr and Nimkhab given in S. R. M. Report have been already considered.

overthrow at the hands of the Arabs, the month Fravardin of the Persians fell near the Summer solstice, as we have already seen; and that therefore in those days the month Dae was the month of spring or the first month. But as we have already fully discussed that was not the actual position of Dae. If three more intercalations had been made, the month Dae would have returned to its original situation *i. e.*, the winter solstice. Thus the first three passages above quoted do not require to be dealt with any further.

From the last two passages we find that the first day of the first month among the Sughdians and the Khwarizmians was the beginning of *Summer*. We have been told that these people did not change the order of their months when the intercalations were made. We have also been told by Albiruni (p. 220). that "there was no difference between them and the Persians regarding the beginning of the year." It would thus appear that the Nouroz of these people fell at the commencement of Summer. But I do not think that, that is what Albiruni means to say. For, about the last month of the Sughdians he says: "On the last day of this month, the Sughdians cry over those who died in the past times....They lay out for them dishes and drinks, as the Persians do in Farwardagân. For, the five days...they fix at the end of this month, as we have mentioned before" (p. 222).

If then the Farwardagân days of the Sughdians were placed at the end of their 12th month Khshum and if the 1st day of their first month Nausard coincided with the commencement of summer, it would follow that their Farwardagân days fell near the beginning of summer. This result would be in direct contravention of the 49th paragraph of Fravardin Yt, according to which the Farohars come into this world at the time of Hamaspath maedaya (spring equinox). It seems to me therefore that Albiruni uses the word *summer* in its wider sense much in the same way as Bundehishn uses the word *Hâmin* (summer) for "the seven months from Fravardin to Meher—the winter being the period between Abân and Safandâr with the five Gatha days (which have the Hamaspathmaedem Gahânbâr having the day and night equal)" (see Chap. 25 1).

The above argument also applies in the case of the Khwarizmians who "in the last five days of Ispandârmaji and the following five *epagomenæ*, did the same which the Persians did in Farwardagân *i.e.* they lay out food in the temples for the spirits of the dead" (p. 226).

As regards the 1st day of the Sughdian seventh month Faghakân Albiruni says "The 1st is called *Nim-sarda i. e.* half year. Some people put *Nim-sarda* five days earlier, *i. e.* on the 1st of Mihr-Mah, to make it agree with the Persian calendar," (p. 221).

This evidently refers to the time of Albiruni. Now in another place (p. 201) Albiruni says about the Nouroz of the Persians that "it coincided with the sun's entering the sign of Aries, which is the beginning of spring." We thus see that in the time of Albiruni the Sughdian month Faghakân *almost* coincided with the Persian month Mihr. Now as the Sughdians did not change the order of their months, it follows that their month Faghakân was seventh month from the commencement of spring.

When did the Persians begin to neglect intercalation?

On page 88 Albiruni says: "The Persians had already begun to neglect their intercalation *nearly* * 70 years before the death of Yazdajird."

---

* On the same page Albiruni uses the expression "nearly—*but not exactly*—70 years."

As Yazdajird died in 651 A.C., it would appear that the Persians began to neglect intercalation since 581 A.C. We have however seen that intercalation was neglected from 509 A.C. We have therefore to seek the correct explanation.

On pages 12–13 Albiruni says: "The Persians reckoned their year as 365 days and neglected the following fractions until the day-quarters had summed up in the course of 120 years to the number of days of one complete month and until the fifth parts of an hour, which according to their opinion, follow the fourth parts of a day (*i. e.* they give the solar year the length of 365 1/4 days and 1/5 hour) had summed up to one day; then they added the complete month to the year in each 116th year."

On p. 220 Albiruni says that "The ancient Persians used a solar year of 365 days 6 hours and 1 minute."

The above two year-lengths * given by Albiruni might be compared with the year mentioned by Dinkard, having 365 days, 6 hours and portions of an hour.

There was however a third year-length among the Persians which consisted of 365¼ days which is referred to by the Iranian Bundehishn and also by Albiruni. On p. 121 of his book Albiruni says: "It was their custom to intercalate one month in every 120 years." Also on p. 54 we read: "The quarter of a day (beyond the 365 days) they neglected in their computation till these quarters of a day had summed up to the days of one complete month, which happened in 120 years." (see also pp. 38 and 185). A fourth year-length is also referred to by Albiruni on p. 18: "The Peshdadian kings reckoned the year as 360 days and each month as 30 days; they intercalated one month in every sixth year...and two months in every 120 years." This shows that the average year-length was 365¼ days.

In Bundehishn Ch. 34 we have a description of the millenniums—the last of which began with the advent of the Zarathushtrian religion and ended with the overthrow of the Sassanians. According to Justi's text of the Bundehishn, this last millennium is made up as follows:—90 years of Gushtâspa after the advent of the religion, 112 years of of Aspandiar, 30 years of Homâi, 12 years of Dara, 14 years of Darae Dara, Ashkanians 284 years, Sassanians 460 years—total (excluding 14 years of Alexander) 1002 years.

In the D H and T D texts of the Bundehishn, the durations of the Ashkanian and Sassanian dynasties are stated to be 290 and 447 years respectively. According to these texts, therefore, the last millennium consisted of 995 years.

If we take the average of 1002 and 995 years we get 998½ years.

Now Zadsperm and other Iranians thought that 8 intercalary months had been added. Let us suppose that these intercalations were made at the intervals of 116 years. As Zarathushtra is said to have introduced the reformed calendar, we find that the Persians neglected intercalation (998½—116×8) 870½ years before the death of Yazdagird Sheheriar.

We thus see that when Albiruni says that intercalation was neglected nearly (but not exactly) 70 years before the death of Yazdajird, the explanation is that owing to wrong notions, some Iranians believed that a month's intercalation was made every 116th year and that 8 such intercalations had been made during the millennium which commenced with the so-called advent of the Zarathushtrian religion and ended with the fall of the Sassanian dynasty.

* These two year-lengths indicate that in ancient times our ancestors knew the lengths of a sidereal year. There is however no positive proof whether such a year was ever used in practice.

On the same page on which Albiruni makes the above statement he says: "At the time of Yazdajird ben Shâpur they had intercalated into their year two months, one of them as the necessary compensation for that space of time, by which the year had moved backward...The second month they intercalated with regard to the future." "If you subtract from the sum of years between Yazdajird ben Shâpur and Yazdajird ben Shehryâr 120 years, you get a remainder of nearly—but not exactly 70 years, there is much uncertainty and confusion in the Persian Chronology."

It would appear from the above passage that the period between the deaths of the two Yazdajirds is supposed to be 190 years, while from history we find that it was (651 A. C. *minus* 420 A. C. —) 281 years, and in the five Tables *re* the Chronology of the Sassanians given at pp. 128-8 by Albiruni, we see that the period is variously given as consisting of 233 year, 237 years, 220 years, 239 years and 300 years.

It is clear that when Albiruni says that the interval between the two Yazdajirds was 190 years, he merely states what he heard; for he declares that "there is much uncertainty and confusion in the Persian Chronology."

If we want to find out when the Persians began to neglect intercalation we must rely upon the most difinite statements of Albiruni on page 121 of his book, namely that "the interval between Zarathushtra and Yazdajird ben Shâpur was nearly 970 years in which 8 leap months had become due" and also on page 55 that "at the time of Yazdajird ben Shâpur they intercalated into their year two months." Yozdajird ruled from 399 to 420 A. C. The turn for making intercalation had come 10 years before the reign of Yazdajird, that is in 389; and as one month's intercalation was made in anticipation, we see that the effect of the intercalation existed as far as 389+120—509 A.C.

Was intercalation neglected after 584 A.C.?

In the Shuddha Roz Mah Report (pp. 37, 38, 55), we read: "The Romans adopted the cult of Mithra in the first century after Christ.... This cult obtained great vigour, when the Roman emperor Trajan (98 A. C.) came to the throne. "The winter solstice which according to the calculations of the Romans fell on 25th December (O. S.) was observed by them as the birth day of Mithra and was called Dies Natalis Solis Invictis (see Symbobsin of the East and West by Mrs. Murray Ainsley p. 19)....In the first century A. C. the vernal equinox fell on 25th March (O. S.).

"*If we suppose that our day Ahuramazda of the month Dae coincided with this date*....then our day Ahuramazda of the month Meher would fall exactly on 25th December.

"Now in 632 A. C. the same Roz Mah fell on 13th December that is 12 days earlier, which shows that intercalatian was neglected about 48-51 years before 632 A. C. that is after 584-581 A. C."

The above argument is based upon the conjecture that the day Ahuramazda of the month Meher coincided with the "Dies Natalis Solis" of the Romans. Let us suppose for a moment that the Roz Ahuramazda of the Mah Meher fell on 25th December 98 A. C. Now if we assume that the Iranians did intercalations of one day every fourth year, then 175 years after 98 A. O. (that is in 273 A. C. which was the date when Porphyry lived), the said Roz Mah would fall on the said date. If however we take it that an intercalary month was added every 120 years, or that intercalation was not done at all, we see that the said Roz Mah would fall in December or November in 273 A. C. But we have already seen that according to Porphyry (273 A. C.) the Mehergân feast fell near the spring equinox during his time. It will thus be seen that the argument advanced above is worthless.

The epoch of the Zoroastrian chronology is the "coming of the religion." In Dinkard VII-8-51 we are told that the first century of the religion is that from the time when Zarathushtra * came forth to his "conference with the sacred beings," which event happened when he was 30 years old. Also Bundehishn 34 § 7 states that Vishtaspa reigned 30 years before the advent of the religion.

Now in Zadsperm 23 § 12 we have the statement that the religion was disturbed and the monarchy destroyed by Alexander 300 years after the coming of the religion. Also it is stated in the Ardavirâfnâme I. § § 2 to 6 that the religion remained in purity for 300 years and then Alexander came to Iran and destroyed the monarchy.

We know that Alexander invaded Persia in 331 B. C. We also know from Zadsperm that Zarathushtra lived for 77 years. We thus conclude that Zarathushtra lived between the years (331+300+30=) 661 B. C. and (661-77=) 584 B. C.

Albiruni has told us that nine intercalary months had been added since the reform of the Calendar by Zarathushtra. Therefore supposing that the said reform was made in the last year of Zarathushtra (584 B. C.), we find that intercalation was neglected after (120×9—584—) 496 A. C. at the latest.

On the other hand, Bundehishn (Ch. 34) places the death of Alexander 272 years after the coming of the religion. Alexander died in 323 B. C. Thus Zarathushtra lived between (323+272+30=) 625 B. C. and (625-77)=548 B. C. According to this mode of reckoning we see that intercalation was neglected after (120×9—548 —) 532 A. C. at the latest.

It will thus be seen that in neither case do we reach the date 584 A. C.

If, as we have seen intercalation was neglected after 509 A. C. the reformed calendar must have been introduced in (120×9—509—) 571 B. C. The calculations of the Bundehishn thus appear to be more reliable.

Dr. West's calculations.

The discussion on the above subject would be incomplete, if we did not take notice of the arguments advanced by Dr. West in S. B. E. Vol. 47, introduction. The learned Doctor says: "In the first place we want to know at what season, the Parsi year *originally* began and we learn from Bundehishn XXV 7-20 that the winter of the rectified year ends with the extra 5 days and the spring begins with the next month which means that the rectified year begins with the vernal equinox....The exact length of the tropical year is 365-2422 days. We may calculate back from any vernal equinox, which occurs not too far from noon, say that of March 22nd 1865, when the beginning of the Parsi year had retreated to 24th August 1864 or 210 days, in addition to a previous retreat of a whole year of 365 days, or altogether 575 days since the establishment of the Calendar....Dividing 575 days by -2422 we get a quotient of 2374 years and this carries us back to 510 B.C. as an approximate date of the establishment of the Parsi calendar with the first day of the year coinciding with the vernal equinox.... The old observers not being aware of the effect of refraction would antedate the vernal equinox by rather more than a day. The most probable date of the establishment of the Parsi Calendar was therefore B.C. 505."

* Not our Prophet.

Dr. West has forgotten to take into account the 11 days whereby the English Calendar was brought into conformity with the Gregorian reform in 1752. This would add about 11×4—44 years. We thus arrive at the date 554 B.C. It must also be remembered that the average length of our year consisted of 365¼ days, whereas the tropical year consists of 365·2422 days. Dr. West relying upon the statement that our year began with the vernal equinox thinks that one month's intercalation was done at the interval of $\frac{30}{\cdot 2422}$ = 124 years; but we have the most positive statement of Albiruni and other writers that intercalation was done after the expiration of 120 years. The statement of Bundehishn that our year commenced with the vernal equinox must be taken to be good for all *practical* purposes only.

In his "Zoroaster," Prof. Jackson says "Interesting is the fact noticed by Anquetil du Perron that a certain religious sect that immigrated into China A.D. 600 is evidently of Zoroastrian origin and that these believers have an era *which dates approximately from B.C. 559*" (p. 165). This corroborates the conclusion we have arrived at.

Jashne Sadeh.

We are told that "This Jashn was performed on the Roz Aban of the Mah Bahman. It had come into vogue even before the time of Zarathushtra. This Jashn was one of spring." *

There is no authority for the above proposition. Dr. Sachau in his notes (p. 424) suggests that "according to some there is an interval of 100 days between this day and Nouroz, if you count days and nights separately, and therefore the day was called *Hundred-day* in the same way as Nuwad Roz."* If this explanation is accepted, Fravardin must be the first month.

Jashne Rukke Kazdoom.

This Jashn which is observed on the day Asfandar of the month Asfandar, is the day on which the Iranians write a Nirang † (or charm) and paste it on the front door of the house with a view to abate the nuisance of scorpions, noxious insects and reptiles. My friend, Mr. M. N. Kuka, thinks that this Jashn did not exist before the Sassanian times. He opines that the sting (in the tail?) of the constellation Scorpion was called *Mula* by the Hindus and *Shaule* by the Arabs, that during the Sassanian times this constellation stood the longest in the skies in June and that as the month Asfandar fell in June at that time, the custom of inscribing charms was introduced in that month.

It is not correct to say that the above custom was first introduced during the Sassanian times. Dr. Rapp (Tr. by Cama, p. 264) says "The Persians celebrate a festival which is greater than all the rest, 'the destruction of the evil,' on which they kill Ahriminian animals and produce them before the Magi in evidence of their purity. This too was a jubilee festival serving the realm of light. Since Herodotus already knows of the obligation to kill Ahriminian creatures, we may safely assume that the festival was not got up first in the Sassanian times only."

Avesta Calendar.

Ervad Sheheriarji D. Bharucha published a pamphlet in 1905 with a view to prove from Avesta that

* See Mr. Kuka's Paper, p. 6.

* "The first day of Dae Mah is also called Nuwad Roz (90 days) and is celebrated as a feast, because there are 90 days between this day and Nouroz" (See Albiruni, p. 212).

† For the Pahlvi Nirang, See Ervad Modi's Anthropological Papers, p. 125.

Dae was the first month in ancient times. I give below a short summary of his arguments.

In the first 10 paras of Yasna Ha I, thirty-three Ratus (or time-periods) are mentioned. In the 10th para we read : "*Nivaedhayemi hankâryemi vispaeibyo ratubyo yoi henti ashahe ratavo thryascha thrisânscha nazdishta pairish-hâvanayo.*" "(I invoke and honour) all these time-periods which are 33 and which are time-periods for holiness (=holy deeds) belonging to the year named Parish-hâvana (*i. e.*, almost-complete-year) appertaining to the first (age)."

These 33 time-periods have been divided into 5 classes—Ayara, Asnya, Mâhya, Yâirya and Saredha.

Ayara is "probably" equivalent to Sk. वार and is the Jashn of the day when the day and the month are of the same name. These Ayaras are 9. They are :—(1) Dathusho, (2) Bahman, (3) Ardibehesht, (4) Sheherevar, (5) Safandarmad, (6) Khurdad, (7) Amardad, (8) Geush Urvan, Geush Tashna, and (9) Adar.

Asnya or the time-periods of day are the 5 Gahs.

Mâhya or the time-periods of month are (1) *Antaremâongha*=(new-moon day), (2) *Perenomâongha*—(full-moon day) and (3) *Vishaptatha* from *vi+shap*, क्षप (=क्षिप)=Pahl. *vishepa* falsely read *vahijkik*=(addition, intercalation); plus *tatha*=(तिथि) day.

Yairya or the time-periods of year are 6. They are the well-known six Gahânbars.

Saredha is equivalent to Sk. श्राद्ध These are the days at the end of the शरद् season. They are the 10 Farvardegan days mentioned in the Fr. Yashta.

In this manner Ervad Sheheriarji arrives at the 33 Ratus. He says that at first the 9 Ayars were the names of the 9 months, and as Dae is mentioned first in the Yasna Ha I. and Adar last, Dae must be the first month and Adar the last month.

Then Ervad Sheheriarji proceeds to explain some of the difficulties. If the months were 9, the days of a month must be 40 and he says that the 40 days are referred to in Yasna Ha 16. It is seen that among the 9 Ayaras, the first seven are the names of Ameshaspents in their usual order. How is it then that two more Ameshaspents are found here and also in Ha 70 § § 1-2. Ervad Sheheriarji explains that in the Avesta later than the Gathas, Khurdad and Adar have been looked upon both as Ameshaspents and Yazads (see Khurshed Yt. § 1, Yasna Ha 1 § 2). Khurshed has been called Amesh (=Ameshaspent). Geush Tashna and Geush Urvan are Meher and Aban of the later Avesta and were in the Avestan times the name of a certain *sky* between the terrestrial and celestial world. In a later age the months became 12 and each month consisted of 30 days. During this age "most probably" the months Fravardin, Meher and Tir were added. Also it was arranged that in each one of the four seasons (each of 3 months) of the year a female Ameshaspent or Yazad was to preside; for example, the female Safandarmad in the first season, the female Khurdad in the second season, the female Ameretat in the third season and the female Aban in the fourth season. I may point out once again that the above is a bare summary of Ervad Sheheriarji's book; for details the book itself should be referred to.

The theory of Ervad Sheheriarji is incorrect in several respects. I agree with the Ervad in the translation he has given of Ha I § 10 with the exception of the meaning he has assigned to *Pairish-hâvana* (almost-complete-year). I say that the word means "complete year" (cf. परिषावण); [*pari* means complete, as in *pairi-kkshafno*, परिवत्सर, परिसंवत्सर, &c.]

There is a good deal of difference among the scholars as regards the

33 Ratus (see Kanga's Yazashne bâ Mâini, p. 18).

In the Arctic Home in the Vedas (p. 284) Mr. Tilak has shown that in ancient inscriptions in cave-temples, we come across many instances where dates of events are recorded by reference to seasons, fortnights and days. For example, we read "In the 24th year of the King Vasithiputra, the illustrious Pulimavi, in the 3rd fortnight of winter months on the 2nd day, &c.;" "On the 10th day in the 6th fortnight of Grishma in the 8th year of King Madhariputra, &c." Dr. Bhandarkar has shown in his "Early History of the Deccan" that Pulumavi reigned in Maharashtra from 130 to 154 A.C. and Madhariputra from 190 to 197 A.C. We thus see that so far back as the 2nd century after Christ there was the custom of recording events by giving the seasons and fortnights.

It also appears that in much earlier times the same was the custom among some Vedic tribes; for example, in Rv. 4-12-11 (already quoted) we read "On the 40th day of Autumn, &c., &c." See also Vedic Index of Names &c. Vol. I, p. 50.

Similar statements are found in our Afringane Gâhânbâr also; thus, "On the 45th day of Maidyozaremaya, *i.e.*, on the day Dae of the month Ardibehesht, &c." "On the 60th day of Maidyoshma on the day Dae of the month Tir, &c." Here we find both the systems put together but as Ervad Jamshedji Dadabhoy Nadirsha has shown in the Cama Memorial Vol. (pp. 251-254), the months and days in the above Afringan are later interpolations. It is clear that among the ancient Zoroastrians also (or at any rate among some of them) the method of recording dates with reference to seasons and days was very common.

In the Civilisation of the Eastern Iranians Dr. Geiger says (Vol. I, p. 152) "I am convinced that the Gahânbar numbers are based on the synodical half-month of fifteen days; this half-month must be regarded as the basis of the whole chronology in general."

Asnyas.—(Portions of the day) were 5 Gâhs, Hâvani, &c.

Ayaras.—(Day) were 15. They constituted a fortnight. They have been mentioned in several places in the Yasna but most clearly in Ha II § § 3 to 7. They are: (1) Meher, (2) Râma, (3) Ashavahisht, (4) Atarsh, (5) Apâm Napât, (6) Ap, (7) Fravashayo, (8) Ghenâo, * (9) Yâirya Hushiti, (10) Ama, (11) Verethraghna, (12) Vananti Upartât, † (13) Sraosha, (14) Rashnu, and (15) Arshtât.

It will be noted that in Ha II § § 3 to 7 the Gâhs and their Hâmkârs have also been mentioned, but we have nothing to do with them, as they are not Ayaras. It will also be seen that the Yazads and other Divinities which bear close relationship with certain Gâhs are mentioned along with those Gâhs; *e.g.* Mithra (—sunlight or sun) has been mentioned along with Hâvana Gâh, because the sunlight and Hâvana are both connected with the morning. Similarly Rapithvan and Atash are both connected with heat. Sraosha and Rashnu are rightly connected with the Ushahin Gâh in which the actions of the dead are adjudicated upon.

The Gâh with which the Farohars were connected was Aivisruthrem; and as in ancient times one of the day-lengths was reckoned from

* Most of our months were named after constellations. In the starry host we come across many male and female figures. Could it be that the Ghenâo were Gemini "the Young Women" as the South African Bushmen called them (See Star Lore of All Ages, p. 206)? Or were they Pleiades (idem p. 426)?

† Could this have any connection with the Star Vanant?

evening to evening, * it seems that the Farohars were connected with the *commencement* of this day-length* it is therefore probable that the Ayara named Fravashyo was first day of the fortnight according to the system in which the day commenced with one evening and ended with the next. In other system where the day-length extended from morning to morning the Ayara named Meher was probably the first day of the fortnight.†

I also think that due to a similar reason when the system of reckoning by months and days was introduced, the Farohars were accorded the first place in the first half year and Meher the first place in the second half year.

It may also be noted that Ahuramazda is not one of the Ayaras. Could it be that the system of reckoning by seasons and fortnights preceded the time of Zarathushtra who was the first to bring into prominence the monotheistic idea of Ahuramazda.

Mâhyas—(fortnight) are two. They are *Antaremâongha* (fortnight after the new moon) and *Perenomâongha* (fortnight after the full moon, the latter being *vishaptatha* (=that during which the darkness of night is destroyed.)

Yâiryas—(portions of the year) are six. They are the six Gâhânbârs commencing with Maidyozaremaya.

Sharedhas ‡—are the 5 Epagomenæ or Gatha days. They have been called *Khumsah Mustarkah* by the Persian writers, as they do not belong to any particular month or season but the whole year. (See Albiruni, p. 58). According to Dinkard they are the 5 days at the end of the year (*pavan shant royashman*). I am of opinion that the Sharedhas are the *sâl*-days or year-days, that is to say, days which do not belong to any particular fortnight or season of the year, but which really belong to the whole of the year.

On a reference to the 1st Chapter of the Vispard we find that in § 2 the Yâiryas are praised and then each one is named. Similarly in § § 4 to 7 the Saredhas have been adored and then each one is mentioned separately. We thus see that the Saredhas are the 5 Gatha days.

Ervad Sheheriarji connects *Saredha* with the Hindu श्राद्ध days and supposes that they were the ten Farvardegan days. In the ancient past, at any rate, the Farvardegan days were never more than 5 as we see from Minokherd Ch. 56 § 18 : *Va vinârishn i Alburz pirâmun gehân, va paetâkinitan i hafta keshvar zamik, va âsmân, va azapar koh i Alburz, robishn i Khurshed va mâh va dvâsdah akhtarân, va shah gâs i Gâsânbâr, va panj gâs i Farvartikân.* "And the arrangement of Alburz around the world, the manifestation of the earth of seven regions and the sky above the mountain Alburz, the motion of the Sun, Moon and the 12 constellations, the six times of the season festivals and the five times devoted to the guardian spirits.....are produced and allotted through the power of Wisdom" (S.B.E., Vol. 24, p. 100).

We have also other authorities which prove that originally the Favardegan days were five. Albiruni says on p. 210 "regarding the position of these (5 days) of Farvardegan there was a controversy.... But with a view to avoid all disputes the Persians adopted all the 10 days to put the matter on a firm basis."*

The ten days of the Farvardegan referred to in Fr. Yt. § 49 is as

* Cf *Pairi-khshafno* in Fr. Yt.; also "*jighaesha tâo Khshapano yâo jvahi*" (Atash Nyaesh, § 10.)

† Similarly among Hindus according one system the month begins with Sudi 1st and according to another system with Vadi 1st.

‡ In the word Khurdad-sâl, *sâl* (=Saredha,) is a "day of the year."

* For further proofs about the subject see my pamphlet *re* Farvardegan.

several scholars have proved, a later interpolation.

We thus see that the 38 Ratus (time-periods) which make up the *Pairish-hâvana* (complete year) are the 5 Asnyas, 15 Ayaras, 2 Mâhyas, 6 Yâiryas and 5 Saredhas.

Ervad Sheheriarji thinks that in Ha I § § 1-2 we have a reference to the 9 Ameshaspents, namely Ahuramazda, Bahman, Ardibehesht, Sheherevar, Aspandad, Khordad, Amardat, Geush-Jashn, Geush-Urvan and Adar.

If we turn to Ha IV § 2 we find that after Ahuramazda, Sraosha is mentioned, then the Ameshaspents, then the Farohars, then Urvan and lastly Atash. It is evident that here at any rate Adar is not an Ameshaspent. We also see that Geush Tashn Geush Urvan are not mentioned at all in that passage.

Ervad Sheheriarji regards Geush Tashn Geush Urvan as one entity but in Yasna Ha 29 we find that Geush Tashn is entirely different from Geush Urvan. In Ha 16 where the days have been mentioned, the name for Gosh is Geush Urvan only.

As regards the year of 9 months Ervad Sheheriarji says: "We know that in or about the 7th or 8th century B.C. the Cappadocians borrowed the names of their months from the Zoroastrians. From the order of the months it is clear that Fravardin was their first month. (See Shuddha Roz Mah Report, p. 17). Therefore the arrangement of 12 months (each month of 30 days) plus the 5 Epagomenæ in a year [instead of the arrangement of 9 months (each of 40 days) plus the 5 Epagomenæ] must have been introduced before the above date."

Ervad Sheheriarji's above statement carries with it its own condemnation. Even according to him for the last 2,600 years, at any rate, the year is known to contain 12 months.

From the Vendidad Ch. I. we find that in the Avestan times the months were 12; for, we read "(In Iravej) there are 10 months of winter and 2 of summer; but here there are 7 months of summer and 5 of winter." Are we then to believe that the Vandidad was written after the 7th century B. C.?

Also in the Mâh Nyâesh we read. "The moon waxes for 15 days and wanes for 15 days. This passage gives 30 days to a month.

In several places in the Rigveda, the year-length of 12 months is referred to, for example, in Rv. I-25 8 we read वेद मासो धृतवतो द्वादश प्रजावतः । वेदा य उपजायते "True to his holy law, he knows the 12 moons with their progeny; * he knows the moon of later birth." Cf. also Rv. I-164-11, I-164-48.

In Atharva Veda IV-7-35-4 we have यस्माद् मासाः निर्मिताः त्रिंशदराः । संवत्सरः यस्माद् निर्मितः द्वादशारः ॥ "From which the months of 30 days were made; from which the year of 12 months was made."

The years of the Egyptians, Babylonians and all other ancient nations consisted of 12 months. Even the Peshdâdiyans reckoned their year of 360 days and each month of 30 days (See Albiruni, p. 18). We therefore cannot place any reliance upon Ervad Sheheriarji's theory that at one time our year consisted of 9 months. The whole fabric of his theory rests on sands.

Diagram showing the order of the months.

In one of the meetings of the Zarathoshti Dinni Kholkarnâri Mandli (Society for the Promotion of Researches into the Zoroastrian Religion) Mr. M. N. Kuka produced a diagram, showing how the order of our months was derived from the names of the planets, the "houses" of which are the twelve well-known Zodiacal constellations. I give diagram on the next page.

---

* The 12 months with the days. The moon of later birth is the intercalary month.

Mr. Kuka's diagram.

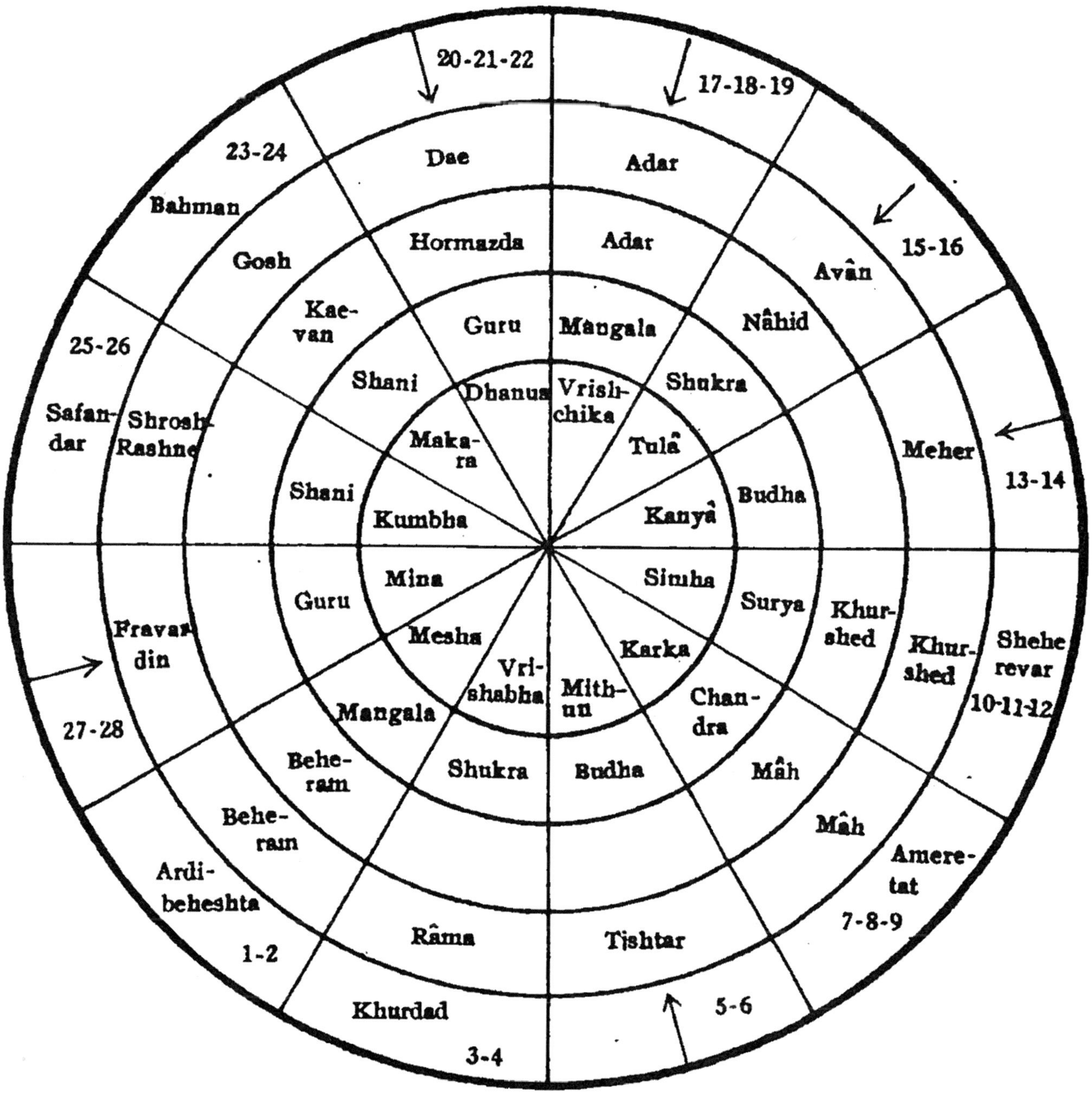

It may be explained that the innermost circle gives the twelve Zodiacal constellations. The next circle gives the names of the Hindu planets—each planet being given in front of the constellation which is the "house" of that planet. In the third circle the names of the corresponding Pahlvi planets are given. In the fourth circle the names of our days corresponding to the names of the planets are given—the blanks being filled up by the names of other days, in respect whereof Mr. Kuka gives long explanations. Then in the fifth circle the names of the months corresponding to the names of the days are given. Some of these months are the Hamkârs or coadjutants of the corresponding days; as for example, Bahman, Ardibehesht and Sheherevar are the Hamkârs of Gosh, Beheram and Khurdad respectively. For other months Mr. Kuka gives certain explanations; for instance, as to Ameretat he says that it comes to be in the place of the Karka Râshi in the order of the months, and that one of the Nakshatras of the month is Punarvasu, whose deity is Aditi, *i.e.* Immortality (=Ameretat). This is undoubtedly far-fetched, but we must give Mr. Kuka the credit of being the first to put forward an ingenious theory about the order of our months.

Mr. Kuka has also given a sixth circle, giving the asterisms of the constellations. I have not given the same but with a view to save space I have given the figures 1—2 &c., indicating the asterisms Ashvini, Bharani &c. A seventh circle is also given containing the names of eight out of the twelve divinities according to the Hindu system. Three of these divinities may be noted here, namely Prajâpati (=year) placed in front of Vrishabha Râshi, Aditi in front of Karka and Brahma in front of Dhanus.

Mr. Kuka urges that our calendar was at first lunar and that the diagram shows that Dae was the first month at the time when the calendar was introduced.

Our year, however, was so far as we know tropical, and I shall show from the same diagram that Fravardin was the first month.

I give my diagram on the next page.

I shall explain the diagram. The innermost circle contains the Zodiacal constellations—not necessarily the Hindu ones. The Babylonians, the Egyptians and other nations had perfect knowledge of these constellations.

In the second circle I have given the planets in front of the constellations which are the astrogical "houses" of those planets. These houses were well known in the ancient Astrology of all the nations.*

The third circle gives the name of the corresponding Pahlvi planets. I have also filled in all the blanks.

In the fourth circle, I give the names of the months. The names of our months are connected with the planets as under:

Hormazda is seen in two places, in one of which he is Dae (-pavan Adar)—the *creative* faculty of Ahuramazda; and in the other He is the Fravashi (of Ahuramazda)—the *progressive* faculty of Ahuramazda. Beheram is equated in one place with his Hamkâra Adar; and in another with his other Hamkâra Ardibehesht.

The name of the month Aban from that of the planet Aban is clear enough; Ap. (waters) are presided over by Haurvatat (Khurdad), and hence we read in the Patet "*Khurdâd av av tokhmagân jasta.*" Our months seem to have been named after a certain

*See Star Lore of All Ages, pp. 58, 840, 207, 91, 285, 886, 253, 828, 820, 119, 84, 811.

scheme whereby preference is given to the names of the Ameshaspents over other names.

Khurshed, Meher and Tishtar are found together closely connected as in Meher Nyâishn.

As to Ameretat Mr. Kuka's explanation is elaborate and based upon Hindu conceptions. I think that the Moon is connected with Ameretat as under: In the Mah Nyaishn §6 it is stated that when the Moon shines, the trees grow. * Now Ameretat is an Ameshaspenta presiding over trees; cf. Patet "*Amardâd urvar urvar sardagân jasta.*" Thus the Moon and Ameretat which are related with the trees, interchange places.

The planet or rather the star Kaevân is Geush Urvan. The Gao, cow or the animal kingdom is connected with the Bahman Ameshaspenta, as we see in Patet "*Behman gâo gospand gospand sardagân jasta.*" Also Gao means the Earth with which Safandarmad is connected; cf. Patet "*Safandarmad zamin zamin sardagân jasta.*"

It will thus be seen that it is quite appropriate that the month named after the Farohar of Ahuramazda should be the first month.

But it might be said that if Fravardin was the first month, the calendar must have been introduced at a time when the constellation Pisces ushered in the spring equinox (or say about the 4th century B.C.). We, however, see from Bundehishn Ch. VII that at the time of the Great Deluge the month Tishtar belonged to Karka (Cancer). We have seen that our year was tropical and consisted of 365 days, and the quarter of a day was neglected until the error amounted to one month. Our ancestors knew about the lunar calendar but whether they ever put it into practice is a question. One thing is certain that according to Albiruni the calendar was tropical even in the Peshdadian times.

It appears therefore that if our theory is correct the calendar must have been introduced at a time when the months had receded almost 80 days; and at that time Tir would be the month of Karka Râshi, and Fravardin the month of Aries.

Concluding Remarks.

The students who have discussed the subject of the Zoroastrian calendar out here have tacitly assumed that there were two systems of calendar among our ancestors, one *civil and the other ecclesiastical.* I have repeatedly requested my friends to point out any written authority for the above statement. I say that there is no such authority to be found anywhere.

No doubt there had been in existence at one time in Iran two or even more distinct systems namely those followed by the Persians, Sughdians and Khwarizmians, but these systems (as we have already stated) were due to the arrangement whereby the Persians added an intercalary month every 120 years "by transferring the five Gatha days and putting them at the end of that month to which the turn of intercalation had proceeded on the last occasion of intercalating." The Sughdians however simply added an additional month. Thus the result was that both among the Persians and the Sughdians the Gatha days remained bound with the season; but they always came at the end of the month Spendarmat among the Sughdians and followed the Persian months Fravardin, Ardibehesht, Khurdad, &c., after each period of 120 years.

We have seen that at one time, the Gathas were placed after Aban

* This is quite correct; see Humfrey's Botany, p. 606.

My diagram.

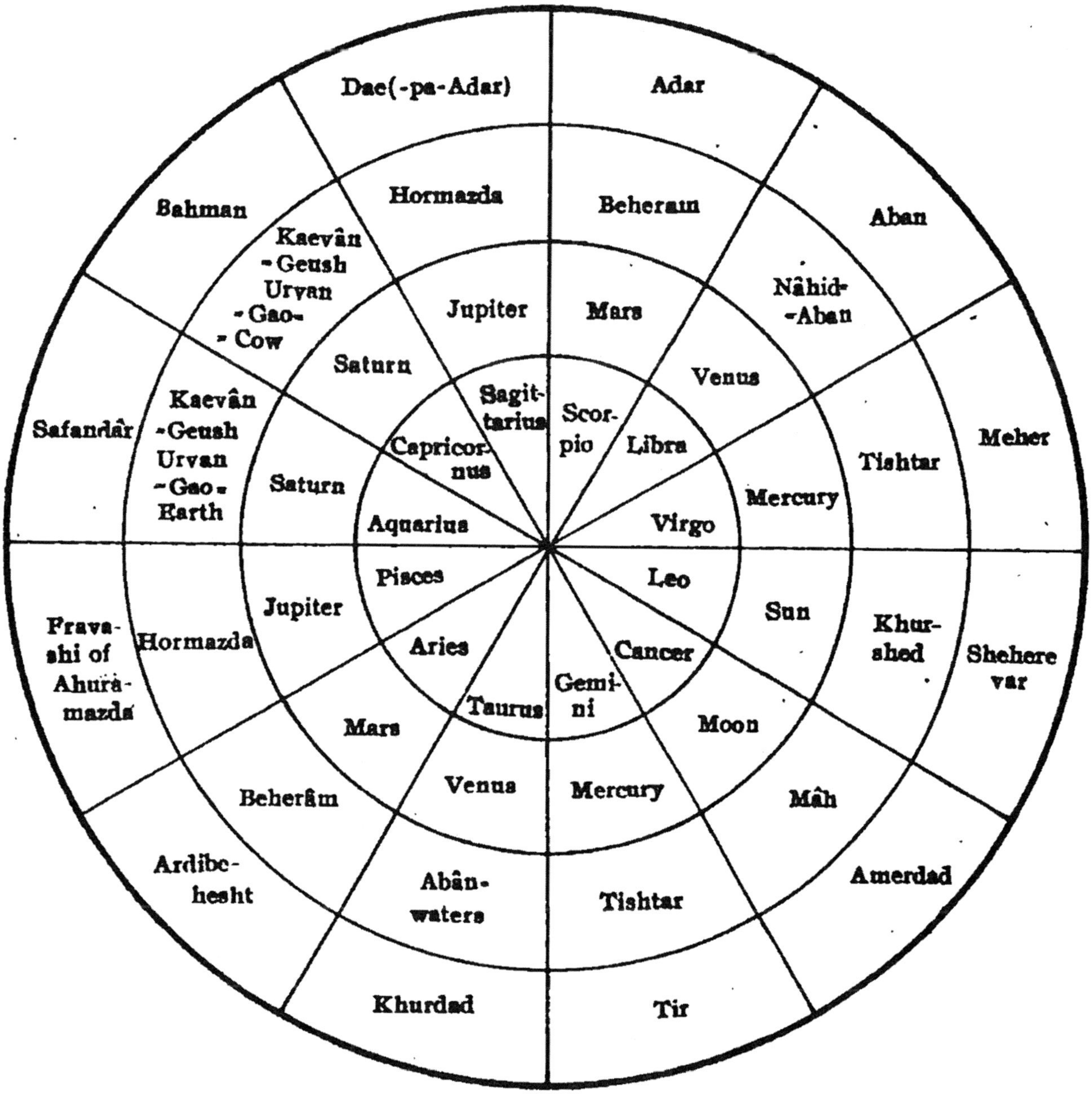

Dae(-pa-Adar)
Adar
Bahman
Hormazda
Beheram
Aban
Kaevân
-Geush
Urvan
-Gao-
-Cow
Nâhid-
-Aban
Jupiter
Mars
Saturn
Venus
Sagit-
tarius
Scor-
pio
Libra
Capricor-
nus
Safandâr
Kaevân
-Geush
Urvan
-Gao-
Earth
Saturn
Tishtar
Meher
Mercury
Aquarius
Virgo
Pisces
Leo
Jupiter
Sun
Frava-
shi of
Ahura-
mazda
Hormazda
Aries
Cancer
Khur-
shed
Shehere
var
Gemi-
ni
Taurus
Mars
Moon
Venus
Mercury
Beherâm
Mâh
Ardibe-
hesht
Abân-
waters
Tishtar
Amerdad
Khurdad
Tir

Mah* (see Albiruni), at another time after the month Ameretat or Meher, Dae and Bahman (see Pahlvi Vendidad), at a third time after Bahman Mah (see Burhane-kâte), and at a fourth time after Spendar Mah (see Kuschiar). Thus the interval between the two kinds of years civil and ecclesiastical must have varied at different times and if so we should have to assume that intercalation was done regularly in the ecclesiastical year but was neglected in the civil year—an assumption which on the face of it is absurd and devoid of any authority.

But if we admit that the abovementioned two kinds of years did exist in Iran, then all the dates we have come across become absolutely useless for arriving at any decision as regards the first month. All our Jashns, Gâhânbârs and festivals partake of religious as well as secular character. It would thus be very easy to support or contradict any conclusion derived from any given date by one or the other system. We should therefore have to brush aside all the evidence afforded by the dates. Such a result would no doubt be very desirable, as we would be spared a lot of trouble over the dates.

For a similar reason those passages in the Pahlvi literature, which contain two dates placed side by side, would also be of little assistance.

It is quite true that at the close of the Sassanian empire the Persian month Dae did fall near the spring equinox, but as already seen, that was a mere coincidence; in point of fact at that very time the Sughdian month Fravardin coincided with Dae.

Yazdgird Sheheriar came to the throne on 16th June (O. S.)—19th June N. S.—632 A.C. on the day Ahuramazda of the month Fravardin. It is argued that if we make our calculations backwards, say, from the last Kadim New Year's day, we see that the Roz Mah abovementioned exactly coincides with the English date. But this argument loses sight of the historical fact, recorded by Abul Hassan Kuschiar that on or about 1006 A.C. the Epagomenæ were transferred at the end of the month Safandâr.

As to the Babylonian evidence I must say that it is certainly not of the most convincing character; if at all, it decides the question in favour of Fravardin being the first month.

Nor can we place much reliance upon the highly speculative and imaginary statements made in connection with the months and their order in the Shudha Roz Mah Report and elsewhere.

I think that the great influence of our calendar on the Cappadocian and Arminian months is of some importance in deciding the question before us. A very important piece of evidence, however, is afforded by the Fravardin Yashta section 49 wherein the Farohars have been represented as being intimately connected with the Hamaspathmaedaem Gahanbar or the spring time.

The theory that Dae was the first month was started only about 50 years ago. There is not the slighest evidence that our ancestors in the remote past had even the faintest knowledge about this question. This coupled with the fact that all the writings of the Parsi, Mahomedan and other writers are *absolutely*

---

* Cf. also 14-1-615 A.C. = Jamyâdha Roz of Meher Mah.
25-2-628 A.C. = Depâdar Roz of Adar Mah.
27-4-630 A.C. = Abân Roz of Bahman Mah.
8-6-632 A.C = Depdin Roz of Safandâr Mah.
16-6-632 A.C = Ahuramazda Roz of Fravardin Mah.

unanimous in regarding Fravardin as the first month and most of all the fact that at the present day our year commences with Fravardin must decide the question before us.

That our year commenced with the vernal equinox follows from Bundehishn, Dinkard, Shahname and many other sources (See S. R. M. Report, pp. 12-18) as we have seen already.

One thing, however, must be remembered that the old system of adding an intercalary month after every 120 years should have no place with us. In any event we must add an intercalary day every fourth year.* and then the last Gatha day may consist of 48 hours.

It is deeply to be regretted that we, Zoroastrians, whose rituals and ceremonies should remain closely linked together with the seasons, have neglected intercalation altogether for the last many centuries. The sooner we rectify our error, the better. If a few *popular* leaders take up this question and press it before the public, we shall all be on the right path in no time.

* In 1897 Ervad Maneckji R. Unwalla produced a Persian Dictionary named "Beher ul Fazâel, &c.," before the Kholkarnari Mandli, in which the writer says that the Parsis intercalated one day every fourth year. We have seen that Khalif Moatedid had tried to introduce this reform. How long it continued, we do not know.

Spring was the commencement of the year among many nations.

Prof. MaxMuller in his Science of Mythology (pp. 714-719) says :— " The birth of the new year and the death of the old were still celebrated in Germany when I was a boy. They probably continue to be celebrated in outlying villages even now, though those who celebrate them are hardly aware whether these festivities are of Christian or pre-Christian origin.........These customs seem to continue to form the staple of public festivities among many of the Slavonic tribes in the east of Europe. To them the birth of the vernal sun, his fight against the army of winter, his summer sway, his autumnal decline and at last his death are the great events of the year......In many places (in Europe) it is neither Christmas nor the Silvester-night but the Epiphany which is considered as the real beginning of the Christian new year. With the ancient people the fight of the sun against the old year or against the might of winter continued till the first signs of spring, of new light and warmth appeared. The ancient Romans began their year with the month of March, the Slaves with the return of spring. At that time about the vernal equinox, it is still the custom in many parts of Europe '*to carry out the year*,' that is, to bury it. *To carry out* was meant originally for the carrying the dead body out of the village to burn or bury it. In the Voigtland (in Saxony) the children were seen some thirty years ago and possibly may still be seen on the Sunday of Laetaro (March), marching through the streets and singing :

'We all, we all are coming forth,
And carry out Death to-day,
Come, Spring, with us into the village,
Welcome dear Spring.'

Here Death is clearly meant for Winter, the death of nature, and opposed to Spring as the new year and the new life.

These customs and traditions change according as winter or the dying year is conceived as an old man or an old woman. Their time also varies slightly according as the seasons vary and as the real periods of the vernal and autumnal equinox are modified by civil or ecclesiastical holidays. Besides the days already mentioned, the Sunday of Laetare (Mid Lent), Good Friday, the day of St. Gregory, the day of St. Rupertus (27th March) or the Monday after the vernal equinox, the first of April and even the first of May, have all been chosen in different parts of Europe for *carrying out Death or Winter*.' "

The "Holi" is also a festival of spring. " It is a popular Hindu festival called in Sanskrit Holikâ or Fâlgunotsava. It is supposed to relate to the vernal equinox and to be similar to the Persian new year's day. It commences about the full moon at the approach of the vernal equinox. It is one of the greatest festivals among the Hindus and almost all sects seem to partake in its festivities; all ranks from kings downward appear animated by the season which is peculiarly dedicated to Krishna. Images of this deity are then carried in *pâlkies* and on elephants and horses attended by music and singing......During these holidays the Hindus spend the nights in singing and dancing and wandering about the streets besmeared with a red powder......The analogy of the goddess of the spring (Saturnalia) Phâlguni and the Phagesia of the Greeks will be recognised. The Egyptian Phallica is the Holikâ of the Hindus " (Encyclopædia of India).

In Rigveda X-90-6 the poet mentions the three seasons in the following order :—Spring (*Vasanta*), summer (*grishma*) and autumn (*sharad*). A more usual division (not found in the Rigveda but met with in Av. VIII-2-22, XIII 1-18, &c.) is into five seasons *vasanta*, *grishma*, *varsâ*, *sharad* and *hemantashishira*. Sometimes (as in Av. VI-55-2, &c.) six seasons are reckoned, *hemanta* and *shishira* being divided. The last season according to the Shatapatha Brâhmana I-5-8-13 is *hemanta*. Thus we see that *vasanta* was the first season.

It may be observed here that the growth of the division of the seasons from three to five is correctly explained by Zimmer as indicating the advance of the Vedic Aryans towards the east. Traces of an earlier division of the year into two seasons, namely summer and winter, do not appear clearly in the Rigveda. In the first chapter of the Vendidad, however, only two seasons have been mentioned.

Among the Vedic Aryans *Châturmâsya* denoted the festival of the Vedic ritual held at the beginning of the three seasons of four months each, into which the Vedic year was artificially divided. It is clear that the sacrifices commenced with the beginning of each season (Shat. Br. I-6 3 36) and it is certain that the first of them, the Vaishvadeva, coincided with the Phalguni full moon, the second, the Varuna—praghâsas with the Ashâdhi full moon, and the third, Sâka-medha, with the Kârttiki full moon (Shat. Br. II-6 3 13). The Taittiriya Samhitâ (VII-4 8-1-2) and Panchvimsha Brahmana (V-9-8-11) recognize the full moon in the month of Chaitra as an alternative to the full moon in the month of Phâlguna, for the beginning of the year.

Oldenberg and Thibaut hold that the Phâlguni full moon coincided with the beginning of spring. (See Vedic Index of Names and Subjects by Macdonell and Keith, Vol. I, pp. 259-260).

The Chinese new year generally coincides with Mâha Sudi 1st but in intercalary years with Fâgan Sudi 1st (See R. F. Vacha's Panchâng Pothi, p. 310).

Among the Babylonians the list of months which dates from the dynasty of Ur began with the month Se-kin-kud, which was the beginning of spring. "The practice of beginning the year with spring belonged to Babylonia proper" (Encyc. of Religion and Ethics Vol. III, p-p. 73-75).

We have already seen that according to the Bundehishn, the Dinkard and the Fravardin Yashta the new year of the Zarathushtrians commenced with spring.

NOTE.

On p. VIII, Col. 2, I have given a quotation about the birth of Beheram in the eighth year of his father's reign. The passage in the Shâhnâme is slightly different. It runs thus :

Sare sâl hashtum me'e Fravardin.
Ke pedâ kunad dar zehân hure din.
Yaki kudaki amash Hurmazda rus.

"The beginning of the eighth year, in the month Fravardin, produced in the world the sun of religion. One child came on Ahuramazda Roz."

I must admit that there is no reference to Aries here, though it is clear that Fravardin was the first month.

Fravardin the month named after Ahuramazda's Fravashi.

Referring to my diagram on page XL., the reader will see that the planet Ahurumazda appears in two places. Now as the months were named after the planets, we should have two months connected with Ahuramazda. It should be borne in mind that there is no month named after Ahuramazda. *Dae* is a Pazend word, (originally *Dadh*), the Avesta form of which was *Dadhvâo*, which itself was a contraction of *Dadhvâo Ahuro Mazdâo* (=the Creator Ahuramazda). Similarly I say, that *Fravardin* is a short form of *Fravashish Ahurahe Mazdâo* (= Fravashi of Ahuramazda). [See Vendidad 19 § 14, Ys. 26 § 2 and Fr. Yt. § 80]. From the derivation of the word Ahura (*ah* = to be), from the first name of Ahuramazda, namely *Ahmi* "I am", and from His 20th name, namely *Ahmi yat Ahmi* (=" I am that I am"), we gather that the first conception about Ahuramazda was only this, that He was "the Existing One." In the Gathas Ahuramazda is nowhere mentioned as *Dadhvâo Ahuro Mazdâo*. In two places (namely Ha 44 § 7 and 50 § 11). He is referred to as *Dâtar*; but this word simply means the "Giver," as the Pahlavi translator, Nerioshang and Dr. Mills correctly render it. In course of time new conceptions were attributed to Ahuramazda. According to Fr. Yt. §§ 80-81, He is said to have Fravashi and Urvan. His Fravashi is the Fravashi of Fravashis of Holy Existences (=*Ashaunâm Fravashayo*; see §§ 80-82). In Vendidad 19 § 14 Ahuramazda Himself commands Zrathushtra to praise His own Fravashi. As already seen this idea is closely allied to the systems of the Egyptians and the Babylonians, among whom the Ka and the Zi of their gods were primarily the objects of worship and not the gods themselves. In Fr. Yt. § 76 we are told that the Fravashis of the Holy Existences were standing erect, when the two Mainyus created the creation. We are not told who created the Fravashis. At any rate we can see that Ahuramazda could not have created His own Fravashi, which was a part of Himself. The *Dadhusho* (=creative) power could have been attributed to Ahuramazda, only when the creation was created. We can thus infer that the *Fravashi* of Ahuramazda has been justly given a preference over the *Dadhusho* power of Ahuramazda.